California Real Estate

POWER TEST PROGRAM FOR SALESPERSONS

Third Edition

Real Estate License
Exam Preparation

ANTHONY SCHOOLS®

A **Kaplan Professional** Company

Ted Highland
Director of Education

Anthony Schools

A **Kaplan Professional** Company®

2646 Dupont Drive
Irvine, CA 92612

California Real Estate Power Test Program For Salespersons
Real Estate License Exam Preparation
Second Edition

Published by Anthony Schools, A Kaplan Professional Company®
© 2002, 1999, 1998, 1997 Dearborn Financial Publishing, Inc.

ISBN: 1-5799-1184-6
PPN: 6401-0503

Disclaimer
This material is for educational purposes only. In no way should any statements or summaries be used as a substitute for legal or tax advice.

05   15 14

Printed in United States of America

Table of Contents

Instructions For

Power Test Program

The Anthony Schools Power Test Program is specifically designed to supplement your Principles course and help you pass the state exam. You will realize the greatest benefit by correctly using our Power Test Program.

The Power Test Program can be done either in your book or on your computer if you have acquired our software (if you have a windows based computer). The questions are the same in either format but the method of presentation differs.

Ideally you should take one test per day, in the order in which they appear in the textbook. It is okay to miss a day here and there, but try to do one test almost every day. This has proven to be the most effective formula. You should not repeat any test until you have completed all 11 exams. Then, only repeat a test when your score on that test is less than 85% correct. For example, if you score 80% on test number 2, don't come back to that test until you have finished all 11 exams.

When taking these tests from your book, use the answer sheet provided in the back, making extra copies if necessary to begin simulating the State Exam experience. Read each question and only mark on your answer sheet. You may use scratch paper - just like the State Exam, be careful not mark directly on the exam because any stray marks may influence you in the future should you need to repeat a particular test. When you are through with a test, look up the answers and score yourself. Write down your scores on your Scorecard that can be found in the front of the book.

Finally, review the explanations to every question, to insure your full understanding. As mentioned earlier if you receive a score on an exam of 85% or higher, we do recommend that you repeat that test.

Follow these directions and you're on your way to passing your state exam. Good luck!

Ted Highland
Director of Education

Anthony Schools,
A Kaplan Professional Company

Power Test Program

Scorecard

Test Name	Score	Score	Score
Exam 1 – Definitions			
Exam 2 – Preliminary Evaluation			
Exam 3 – Real Property and Laws Relating to Ownership			
Exam 4 – Transfer of Property			
Exam 5 – Financing Real Estate			
Exam 6 – Valuation/Appraisal of Real Property			
Exam 7 – Real Estate Practice			
Exam 8 – Tax Implication of Real Estate Ownership			
Exam 9 – Brokerage: Responsibilities and Functions of Salespersons			
Exam 10 – Screening Exam A			
Exam 11 – Screening Exam B			

Exam 1 - Definitions

The first test in this series of Real Estate Practice Examinations is the test on Definitions.

° Use one of the pullout exam answer sheets at the back of this book.
° Take this test and then grade it by looking up the answers on the answer sheet.
° Look up and study the explanation for each question you missed, guessed or were unsure of.
° Add those terms to your real estate vocabulary.
° You can take this test as many times as necessary to achieve your appropriate score.

1. To alienate title to real property, one:
    (A) Secures an ALTA policy of title insurance
    (B) Clouds a title
    (C) Records a homestead
    (D) Conveys title

2. Liquidation of a financial obligation on an installment basis is which of the following?
    (A) Acceleration
    (B) Conventional
    (C) Amortization
    (D) Conversion

3. A tenant who transfers an entire leasehold interest does so by:
    (A) Assignment
    (B) Sublease
    (C) Transfer
    (D) Alienation

4. Jones signed a listing agreement with broker Brown stating that he would pay 6% commission to Brown upon the sale of his house. Broker Brown promised to use diligence in attempting to find a buyer. This contract is:
    (A) Unilateral executory
    (B) Bilateral executory
    (C) Unilateral executed
    (D) Bilateral executed

5. A licensee put a blind ad in a local newspaper. A blind ad:
    (A) Does not identify the advertiser as an agent
    (B) Does not give the address of the licensee
    (C) Does not give the address of the property
    (D) Does not disclose the selling price

6. The approach in which income is projected to a future date and discounted to today's rates to attract investors relates to a technique known as:
    (A) Income projection
    (B) Equity formulation
    (C) Unearned increment
    (D) Capitalization of income

7.   A commercial acre is best defined as:
    (A)   Any parcel of 43,560 square feet
    (B)   Any acre located outside of "R" zoning
    (C)   An acre after deductions for streets and alleys
    (D)   An acre zoned for commercial purposes

8.   What is the best definition of "company dollar" with regard to a real estate office?
    (A)   Office expenses
    (B)   Gross income minus operating expenses
    (C)   Gross income minus commissions
    (D)   Cost to set-up the business for a specific length of time

9.   The term "default" in most mortgages means that the mortgagor:
    (A)   Is delinquent in monthly payments
    (B)   Is not using the property for its intended purpose
    (C)   Failed to maintain the property
    (D)   Any of the above

10.   Which of the following is not a type of soil or soil condition?
    (A)   Alkaline
    (B)   Expansive
    (C)   Adobe
    (D)   Deciduous

11.   Davidson has an easement on Parkins' property. If Davidson is not a property owner, his easement is:
    (A)   A restrictive easement
    (B)   A non-possessory encroachment
    (C)   An easement in gross
    (D)   An appurtenant easement

12.   Which of the following would be the best and most nearly complete definition of the term encumbrance?
    (A)   Degree, quantity, nature, and extent of interest a person has in property
    (B)   The use of property by a debtor to offer a creditor security for debt
    (C)   Any action taken relative to a property other than an acquisition
    (D)   Anything that affects or limits the fee simple title to property

13.   A listing agreement in which the owner promises to pay a commission under all circumstances of sale, except if the owner sells the property himself, is known as:
    (A)   An exclusive right to sell
    (B)   An exclusive agency
    (C)   A net listing
    (D)   None of above

14.   Which of the following would not be applicable to a will?
    (A)   Executor
    (B)   Devise
    (C)   Administrator
    (D)   Testator

15. A contract between two or more persons where one grants the other the right to sell, offer to sell, or exchange goods or services under a marketing plan designed by the grantor is a:
    (A) Business opportunity
    (B) Securities and exchange agreement
    (C) Franchise agreement
    (D) Financing agreement

16. The length of distance of a parcel abutting a thoroughfare would be considered the:
    (A) Frontage of a lot
    (B) Front foot of a lot
    (C) Width of a lot
    (D) Taxable width

17. Which of the following is a freehold estate?
    (A) Estate in fee
    (B) Estate at will
    (C) Estate for years
    (D) Estate at sufferance

18. Percolation refers to:
    (A) Ability of buyer to qualify for a loan
    (B) Depth of foundation
    (C) Ability of soil to absorb water
    (D) Size of water tank

19. A broker negotiates a hard money loan secured by a deed of trust for which he receives a commission. In this transaction, hard money most nearly means a:
    (A) Tight money loan
    (B) Secondary loan
    (C) Purchase money loan
    (D) Cash loan

20. A person who is an innocent purchaser of a negotiable note for value without knowledge of any defect, is customarily called:
    (A) A holder in due course
    (B) An assignor
    (C) A receiver in trust
    (D) An endorser in blank

21. The customary procedure used to enforce private restrictions on real property is:
    (A) Judgment
    (B) Injunction
    (C) Indictment
    (D) Desist and refrain order

22. An owner of property located near a local airport was constantly bothered by the noise of low-flying aircraft. If the owner were to bring suit to force the city to condemn his property because of the noise, this would be an example of:
    (A) Condemnation
    (B) Inverse condemnation
    (C) Subrogated inversion
    (D) Equitable severance

23. A real property sales contract is defined as an agreement wherein one party agrees to convey title to another party upon the satisfaction of specified conditions set forth in the contract and which:
    (A) Must be acknowledged by both buyer and seller to be eligible for recording
    (B) Does not require conveyance of title within one year from date of formation of the contract
    (C) Must be recorded to be enforceable
    (D) Is not required to be in writing if contract period is for one year or less

24. A specified charge against real property, which is used as security, is defined as:
    (A) An easement
    (B) Subdivision restrictions
    (C) A lien
    (D) Zoning and planning

25. The personal, revocable, and unassignable permission or authority to do one or more acts on the land of another without possessing any interest therein, is the definition of:
    (A) License
    (B) Easement
    (C) Encroachment
    (D) Option

26. Market price is:
    (A) The price that a property might bring on the open market
    (B) The price an informed buyer offers for a property
    (C) The price an informed seller asks for a property
    (D) The price that a property actually does bring in the open market

27. A zoning designation that allowed multiple dwellings was changed. What effect would this have on an existing apartment building in the area?
    (A) It would be in violation of the zoning law
    (B) It would be violation of the zoning law with regard to municipal and local ordinances
    (C) It would be a variance
    (D) It would be a nonconforming use

28. Mr. John Lee owned a ranch and gave Ms. Joan Kimball an option to purchase it at a figure of $92,500 down and the balance payable in annual installments of $14,000 plus interest at 7% per annum. The term of the option was 60 days and Ms. Kimball gave Mr. Lee a personal check for $10. This constitutes:
    (A) A lien on Mr. Lee's ranch
    (B) A contract to keep an offer open
    (C) A fiduciary agreement
    (D) An offer to execute a contract in the future

29. A developer built a home on speculation, selling it for $90,000 with $18,000 cash and a note for $72,000. Later he used the $72,000 note as security to borrow $50,000 to build another house. The note in this instance is:
(A) A chattel mortgage
(B) A purchase money mortgage
(C) A holding agreement
(D) A pledge

30. An increase in value, resulting from improved usability where one or more contiguous lots are joined together under single ownership, would be a definition most appropriately applied to:
(A) Severalty ownership
(B) Plottage
(C) Assemblage
(D) Appurtenance

31. A quiet-title action is defined as a:
(A) Result of a "dummy" transaction
(B) Quitclaim deed
(C) Foreclosure by court
(D) Procedure through court action to remove cloud on title

32. "A" led "C" to believe that he had the authority to act for "B." "B" went along with "A." The agency created was by:
(A) Expressed contract
(B) Ratification
(C) Estoppel
(D) Ostensible

33. An escrow closing statement that refers to "recurring costs" could be describing:
(A) Deed transfer taxes
(B) Title insurance
(C) Impound accounts for taxes and insurance
(D) Escrow charges

34. Rescind most nearly means:
(A) Terminate
(B) Rewrite
(C) Reject
(D) Annul

35. The highest member of the frame in a conventionally constructed home is the:
(A) Rafter
(B) Collar beam
(C) Girder
(D) Ridge board

36. Which of the following would cause an owner of a fee simple estate to convert her interest to a less-than-freehold estate?
(A) By granting oil and mineral rights to third party
(B) By leasing for purpose of agricultural use for a period of 5 years
(C) Both (A) and (B)
(D) By sale-leaseback

37.   Soil pipe is most likely to be used for:
      (A)   Cold water pipe
      (B)   Sewer pipe
      (C)   Irrigation pipe
      (D)   Gas line

38.   A promise by the lender to make a permanent loan on the demand of a borrower is known as:
      (A)   Standby loan commitment
      (B)   Interim loan commitment
      (C)   Backup loan commitment
      (D)   Incremental loan commitment

39.   A landlord and tenant mutually agree to terminate a lease. This is often referred to as:
      (A)   Rescission
      (B)   Surrender
      (C)   Release
      (D)   Abandonment

40.   Of the following types of financing, which two are synonymous?
      (A)   Take-out lease—Secondary financing
      (B)   Construction loan—Take-out loan
      (C)   Interim loan—Construction loan
      (D)   Obligatory advances—Installment loan

41.   In real estate, the word "tenancy" means:
      (A)   Two or more people joined in an enterprise
      (B)   A method or mode of holding ownership by lessees or owners
      (C)   A tenacious person
      (D)   A device

42.   A property that is referred to as "turnkey" is which of the following?
      (A)   Government subsidized low-income housing projects
      (B)   Parcels on which the planning is complete and ready for building
      (C)   A contractor's package is complete and ready for occupancy
      (D)   Illegal ranch subdivision

43.   Three persons hold undivided interests in real property as tenants in common. This most likely means that they:
      (A)   Hold equal shares
      (B)   Hold unequal shares
      (C)   Cannot locate their particular interests in the property
      (D)   Took title at the same time

44.   The process of determining market value, investment value, or insurance value as of a specific date would be:
      (A)   Depreciation
      (B)   Valuation
      (C)   Highest and Best Use
      (D)   Evaluation

45. An order by a court directing an officer to sell real property to satisfy a judgment is:
   (A) Abstract of judgment
   (B) Writ of Execution
   (C) Deficiency judgment
   (D) Injunction

46. A nice yard, beautiful trees, and good neighbors usually increase the value of residential property. These things are known as:
   (A) Amenities
   (B) Bilaterals
   (C) Co-ordinates
   (D) Tangibles

47. The most important factor to a lender who is contemplating a loan to a developer of a shopping center would be the:
   (A) Anchor tenant
   (B) Long-term leases
   (C) Credit of the purchaser
   (D) Number of tenants

48. Which of the following is most like having an annuity? The ownership of a:
   (A) Farm in the path of progress
   (B) Well located parcel next to new apartment buildings
   (C) Lease to an experienced individual running a hardware store
   (D) Well secured long-term ground lease

49. Seizure of property for payment of money before judgment is known as:
   (A) A Writ of Execution
   (B) An attachment
   (C) A condemnation
   (D) A lis pendens

50. Equity financing most nearly means:
   (A) Borrowing against equity
   (B) Buying with borrowed money
   (C) Buying with the purchaser's own cash
   (D) The same as an equity loan

51. What best describes an attorney in fact?
   (A) A lawyer appointed by the court
   (B) A lawyer acting as an attorney for a client
   (C) A legally competent person appointed to represent another person through a power of attorney
   (D) A person with a dual agency

52. What kind of mortgage covers more than one parcel of land?
   (A) Blanket mortgage
   (B) Package mortgage
   (C) Purchase money mortgage
   (D) None of the above

53. The method of appraisal that bases the "present market value of the property on the anticipated future benefits of ownership in dollars and discounting them to a present worth, at a rate which is attracting purchase capital to similar investments" is known as:
    (A) Cost analysis
    (B) Market data
    (C) Capitalization
    (D) None of the above

54. To an investor in real property, cash flow means:
    (A) Gross income less an allowance for vacancies
    (B) Net income used for capitalization purposes
    (C) Income left after deducting taxes from net income
    (D) Monies left after deducting operating expenses, interest and principal payments from gross income

55. An individual that holds a leasehold estate has a:
    (A) Fee simple estate
    (B) Remainder
    (C) Reversion
    (D) Chattel real

56. In the planning and engineering of a tract for subdivision purposes, a "cul-de-sac" is frequently employed. This term is in reference to the installation of:
    (A) Sewage disposal
    (B) Drainage
    (C) Streets
    (D) Recreation areas

57. The term "demise" means:
    (A) Something given to induce entering into a contract
    (B) Testamentary transferability of real property
    (C) Transferring the right to or right in an estate
    (D) Witnessing the signing of a document

58. "Duress" is most closely associated with matters of:
    (A) Easements
    (B) Contracts
    (C) Commissions
    (D) Adverse possession

59. The right to use and enjoyment of another's property short of an estate is an example of:
    (A) Deed
    (B) Leasehold
    (C) Subordination clause
    (D) Easement

60. Which of the following is the best definition of "economic rent"?
    (A) The amounts the owner actually receives in rents
    (B) The amount left after the lessor pays expenses
    (C) Current rents being paid for comparable space
    (D) Payment for use of property designated in a lease

61. "Escheat" is a legal term meaning:
    (A) That a fraud has been committed
    (B) Property has reverted to the State
    (C) An agent's license has been revoked
    (D) Property under a trust deed may be reconveyed

62. A property is deeded to "John Jones, et ux." The Latin phrase "et ux" means:
    (A) And others
    (B) Amount over and above
    (C) And wife
    (D) Without recourse

63. An estate in real property for a definite and specified period of time with an agreement for the payment of rent is known as:
    (A) Periodic tenancy
    (B) Month-to-month tenancy
    (C) Estate for years
    (D) Freehold estate

64. Which of the following represents the greatest interest a person can have in real property?
    (A) Easement
    (B) Fee simple
    (C) Life estate
    (D) Freehold, less-than-freehold, leasehold

65. Metal that is used in a roof to prevent water from seeping through is called:
    (A) Mud sill
    (B) Lath
    (C) Soffit
    (D) Flashing

66. To find the size of footings, size and dimensions of concrete piers, construction measurements and details of the subfloor area, a real estate broker would look at which of the following:
    (A) Plot plan
    (B) Floor plan
    (C) Foundation plan
    (D) Elevation plan

67. A roof that inclines from four sides is:
    (A) A gable roof
    (B) A gambrel roof
    (C) A trussed roof
    (D) A hip roof

68. The words "ingress" and "egress" are related to:
    (A) Streams
    (B) Utilities
    (C) Easements
    (D) Fee title

69. Involuntary alienation of an estate means:
    (A) Estate cannot be transferred without the consent of the owner
    (B) Aliens are forbidden to own estates in fee simple in California
    (C) Ownership of estates may be transferred by operation of law
    (D) No one can be compelled to transfer title without his consent

70. Which of the following forms of ownership consists of an undivided interest with the right of survivorship?
    (A) Joint tenancy
    (B) Life estate
    (C) Severalty
    (D) Tenancy in common

71. Which of the following words placed in a promissory note would commit all the borrowers for payment?
    (A) Jointly
    (B) Individually and severally
    (C) Jointly and severally
    (D) Individually

72. The legal term "laches" is best described as:
    (A) Inexcusable delay in asserting a legal right
    (B) A Writ of Attachment
    (C) A deficiency judgment
    (D) A court with no jurisdiction

73. The person who receives personal property through a will is called:
    (A) A devisee
    (B) A testator
    (C) A legatee
    (D) An administrator

74. An investor purchased an apartment building with a very small downpayment and was able to secure financing for the balance. A year later, he sold the property for profit with no increase in his investment. This is an example of:
    (A) Debt reduction
    (B) Appreciation
    (C) Leverage
    (D) Inflation

75. The quickness with which assets can be converted into cash is known as:
    (A) Yield
    (B) Leverage
    (C) Liquidity
    (D) Risk

76. A document deposited with the county recorder to indicate pending litigation is a:
    (A) Promissory note
    (B) Trust deed
    (C) Lis pendens
    (D) Pending deed

77. "Megalopolis" is a term, which most nearly means the formation of:
    (A) Shopping centers
    (B) Roads
    (C) New subdivisions
    (D) Cities

78. An agreement with a lender, which prohibits early pay off of a loan, is known as:
    (A) Lock-in clause
    (B) Prepayment penalty
    (C) Exculpatory clause
    (D) Open-end mortgage

79. In real estate financing, lenders will sometimes refer to "nominal rate" when granting a loan. This means:
    (A) That the rate of interest in the final granting of the loan will be greater than the commitment
    (B) Points will be required, as the rate required by the lender would exceed the legal rate of interest
    (C) The term used by lenders when the maximum rate of interest allowed by law is obtainable on financing a property
    (D) It is the rate of interest specified in the promissory note

80. In a subdivision, which of the following is considered an "off-site" improvement?
    (A) Barn
    (B) Private well
    (C) Streets and curbs
    (D) Septic tank

81. Which of the following best describes an "open end mortgage"?
    (A) One in which personal property is held for added collateral
    (B) One in which additional financing could be obtained without rewriting the contract
    (C) One in which the mortgage represents a partial payment for the parcel of the land
    (D) One under which several parcels of land are included under one mortgage

82. An offer expressing a contractual intent supported by a collateral contract not to revoke for a specified period of time is properly termed:
    (A) A power coupled with an interest
    (B) A condition precedent
    (C) A consideration
    (D) An option

83. The degree of angle of a roof, or slope, is termed:
    (A) Span
    (B) Hip
    (C) Pitch
    (D) Shingle

84. The term "potable" refers to:
    (A) Earth fill
    (B) Septic tanks
    (C) Water
    (D) Trust deeds

11

85. "Privity" would most likely exist in:
    (A) Torts
    (B) Agency
    (C) Contractual relationship
    (D) Taxation

86. A purchase money mortgage may be defined as one:
    (A) Taken on several parcels
    (B) Taken on all or part of the purchase price
    (C) Which includes chattels, such as household appliances, as additional collateral
    (D) Which provides for additional advances to the mortgagor without the necessity of writing a new mortgage

87. The balancing of a broker's trust account record to the bank balance is known as:
    (A) Posting
    (B) Reconciliation
    (C) Trial balance
    (D) Closing out the books

88. The term associated with urban renewal programs, when existing structures are demolished and new ones built, is:
    (A) Renovation
    (B) Relocation
    (C) Redevelopment
    (D) Reclamation

89. To restore an old home to its original condition without making any changes in the floor plan or style is referred to as:
    (A) Rehabilitation
    (B) Reclamation
    (C) Remodeling
    (D) Modernization

90. In real estate transactions, the term "reversion" most nearly relates to:
    (A) Title to land acquired by action of flow of water
    (B) The right of a mortgagee in event of default
    (C) The right of a lessor under a lease
    (D) The action of the state under law of escheat

91. Which of the following is most closely associated with the term "rider?"
    (A) Accretion
    (B) Amendment
    (C) Person
    (D) Lien

92. Riparian rights differ from littoral rights in which of the following ways?
    (A) Riparian rights are associated with water and littoral rights are associated with land
    (B) Riparian is a possessory right, littoral is a nonpossessory right
    (C) Littoral is a possessory right; riparian is a nonpossessory right
    (D) Riparian rights deal with streams and watercourses, while littoral rights deal with oceans and lakes

93. A lender, speaking of a loan in his portfolio, said it was "seasoned." The lender was referring to the:
    (A) Maturity date of the loan
    (B) Quarter of the fiscal year in which the loan was taken out
    (C) Pattern of payments of the trustor
    (D) Type of market in which the loan could be sold

94. Most lending institutions are limited as to the amount they can lend, the types of loans, and length of loans. Because of certain limitations, some lenders are not interested or are unable to give construction loans, but are willing to issue long-term financing after the construction is completed. Long-term loans, to be issued by one lender upon completion of the interim construction financing by another lender, are known as:
    (A) Discount loans
    (B) Take-out loans
    (C) Redemption loans
    (D) Renewal loans

95. Co-ownership of property with undivided interests without the right of survivorship would be:
    (A) Joint tenancy
    (B) Severalty
    (C) Life estate
    (D) Tenancy in common

96. Jacobs is purchasing a parcel of real property. The provisions of the contract require the seller to convey title to the property when the buyer pays the full amount of the contract to the seller. When the buyer offers to fulfill his or her part of the contract and requests the seller to convey title, the seller refuses to fulfill his contractual obligation. Under these circumstances, the buyer is said to have made a:
    (A) Tender
    (B) Demand
    (C) Covenant
    (D) Condition

97. A "title plant" is:
    (A) The ownership and lien records of property maintained by a title company
    (B) A false document found in title records that is intended to give wrong information
    (C) Collection of instruments affecting real estate ownership that is kept in the county recorder's office
    (D) None of these

98. The term "walk-up" is used in which of the following?
    (A) Drive-in restaurant
    (B) Hotel
    (C) Department store
    (D) Apartment

99. Alienation expresses a meaning most nearly opposite to:
    (A) Acquisition
    (B) Ad valorem
    (C) Acceleration
    (D) Amortization

100. Property is:
    (A) Personal if a fixture
    (B) Personal if not real
    (C) Real if tangible
    (D) All of the above

Exam 2 - Preliminary Evaluation

This second exam is designed to give you an opportunity to test your strengths and weaknesses in the seven major subject areas on which your State real estate license-qualifying exam will be based.

In the *Reference Book*, a real estate guide, published by the Department of Real Estate, the DRE has identified the Test Outline and Content Weighting of licensing examinations for real estate salespersons and brokers.

Department of Real Estate Content Weighting:

Real Property and Laws Relating to Ownership	Salespersons	11%
	Brokers	9%
Tax Implications of Real Estate Ownership	Salespersons	8%
	Brokers	8%
Valuation/Appraisal of Real Property	Salespersons	15%
	Brokers	15%
Financing Real Estate	Salespersons	17%
	Brokers	16%
Transfer of Property	Salespersons	10%
	Brokers	9%
Real Estate Practice	Salespersons	22%
	Brokers	21%
Brokerage: Responsibilities of Salespersons Responsibility for Agency Management	Salespersons	17%
	Brokers	22%

You can give yourself a weighted score on each of the seven subject areas after you complete the entire exam. Calculate your weighted score for each subject area by dividing the number you got right by the number of questions in that subject to get your percentage scores by subject.

Passing Score: Sales	=	70%	Recommended: Sales	=	80%
Brokers	=	75%	Brokers	=	85%

Real Property and Laws Relating to Ownership (11%)

1. Which of the following has the least effect in determining whether an item is personal property?
    (A) Manner of annexation
    (B) Time of annexation
    (C) Relationship between the parties
    (D) Intention of the parties

2. A farm was sold on which a crop of corn was growing. During the entire transaction, neither the buyer nor seller discussed who was going to harvest the corn. The man who purchased the property assumed that the corn was his but the seller had plans to harvest the crop at a later time. Under these circumstances:
   (A) The corn is considered real property; therefore the seller had no right to it
   (B) The seller has the right to harvest the corn because his intention is the controlling factor
   (C) If the buyer wanted the corn, he should have specified this in the sales agreement
   (D) The seller does not have a right to harvest the corn because he left the property even though his intentions were there

3. Which would be the best description of a fee simple absolute estate?
   (A) Estate of inheritance
   (B) Owning property
   (C) Estate for years
   (D) Greatest interest held in land

4. Which of the following is incorrect regarding a fee simple estate?
   (A) Indefinite duration
   (B) Can be transferred with or without consideration
   (C) Generally free of all encumbrances
   (D) Transferable by will or intestacy

5. In administering the Subdivision Map Act, a local planning commission would be responsible for ensuring which of the following?
   (A) Adequacy of sewers, street design, and drainage
   (B) Proper financing for required construction of offsite improvements
   (C) Ascertain and plan for new industries moving into area
   (D) All of the above

6. With respect to easements, which of the following statements is correct?
   (A) The dominant tenement is the land burdened and benefited by the easement
   (B) An easement always gives the rights of ingress and egress
   (C) All encumbrances are liens but all liens are not encumbrances
   (D) If the grantor conveys title to property, the easement passes automatically with the land.

7. Which of the following would be least likely to make the title of real property unmarketable?
   (A) Private restrictions in a deed
   (B) Public restrictions under zoning ordinances and building codes
   (C) Cloud on title through adverse possession of the property
   (D) A lis pendens filed by the wife of the owner

8. Which of the following liens would most likely have had priority?
   (A) A trust deed executed March 27, 1998 and recorded March 29, 1998
   (B) A trust deed executed and recorded March 28, 1998
   (C) A public improvement assessment created April 15, 1998
   (D) A mechanic's lien resulting from work started March 27, 1998

9. Riparian rights refer to:
    (A) Rivers and streams
    (B) Bays and arms of the ocean
    (C) Subterranean cavities
    (D) All of the above

10. A lessor receives quarterly payments on a 3-year lease. The lease expires, but the tenant remains on the premises and makes a payment on the lease. In these circumstances, the tenancy is:
    (A) A renewal not to exceed one year
    (B) For three years
    (C) Month to month
    (D) An estate for years

11. What would be included in local building codes?
    (A) Protecting the health and safety of the city
    (B) The establishment of building materials that may be used and the costs of materials
    (C) Architectural design of buildings as well as size and height
    (D) All of the above

Transfer of Property (10%)

12. If a change of ownership is not recorded, how many days after the change does an owner have to inform the County Tax Assessor about a change of ownership?
    (A) 15 days
    (B) 30 days
    (C) 45 days
    (D) 60 days

13. All of the following are required for acquiring title by adverse possession except:
    (A) Open and notorious use
    (B) Confrontation with the owner
    (C) Hostile to the true owner's title
    (D) It must be under a claim of right or color of title

14. A quitclaim deed releases present claim, rights and title of the:
    (A) Grantor
    (B) Grantee
    (C) Servient tenement
    (D) Property

15. A deed was given by "A" to "B" with oral instructions not to record the deed until "A's" death. The deed was:
    (A) Valid
    (B) Void
    (C) Voidable
    (D) Illegal

16. If a seller received a check from escrow in the amount of $37,187.10 and escrow had deducted a commission of 6% of the selling price and other expenses of $403.50, the gross selling price was:
    (A) $31,609.00
    (B) $38,182.40
    (C) $37,590.60
    (D) $39,990.00

17. Unless otherwise specifically stated, a grant deed presumes to convey:
    (A) An estate for years
    (B) In fee simple
    (C) A life estate
    (D) A fee simple defeasible estate

18. Which of the following is most frequently employed to assure title to real property for a grantee?
    (A) Certificate of title
    (B) Title insurance
    (C) Recordation of deed
    (D) Warranty deed

19. A joint tenancy can be created by deeds conveying undivided interests in which of the following?
    (A) By transfer from a wife deeding her separate property to herself and husband as joint tenants
    (B) By transfer from joint tenants deeding their interests to themselves and others as joint tenants
    (C) By transfer from tenants in common deeding to themselves as joint tenants
    (D) All of the above

20. When transferring fee simple title to real property that has been financed by a first deed of trust, you must first:
    (A) Receive permission from the beneficiary
    (B) Pay the beneficiary in full
    (C) Have the grantor sign the deed
    (D) None of the above

21. Which of the following would appear as a credit to the seller on a closing statement?
    (A) Cash charge for recording buyer's deed
    (B) Proration of prepaid taxes
    (C) Proration of prepaid rents
    (D) Cash charge for a quitclaim deed

Financing Real Estate (17%)

22. A balloon payment would be a characteristic of:
    (A) An amortized loan
    (B) A partially amortized loan
    (C) A self-liquidating loan
    (D) A standing loan

23. A person borrowed $2,500 on a straight note at 9% interest for 3 years, 10 months and 20 days. The interest paid was most nearly:
    (A) $225
    (B) $637
    (C) $862
    (D) $875

24. Which of the following would *not* likely cause a loss to a lender?
    (A) Inflation
    (B) Recession
    (C) Prepayment without a penalty
    (D) Unemployment

25. Which of the following situations, where an extension of credit for more than four (4) installments is made, would be exempt from the federal Truth-in-Lending Act?
    (A) Purchase of agricultural land
    (B) $20,000 personal loan from a commercial institution
    (C) $20,000 household loan from a credit union
    (D) Loan from a consumer finance company

26. Joe wants to purchase property but does not have the cash to pay the $85,000. He contacts Harris who purchases the property and offers it for sale to Joe for $98,000 on a land contract. The contract is:
    (A) Voidable by Joe
    (B) Disguised as a mortgage
    (C) A valid sale and resale
    (D) Voidable by Harris

27. Under which of the following loans would the borrower be required to apply for term life insurance?
    (A) Cal-Vet
    (B) FHA
    (C) Savings and loan company
    (D) VA

28. In a purchase money mortgage, the mortgagor is identified as the party who:
    (A) Lends the money
    (B) Receives the note
    (C) Holds the property in trust
    (D) Signs the note

29. A buyer purchasing real property using a conditional sales contract would acquire:
    (A) A possessory interest
    (B) An estate of inheritance
    (C) A freehold estate
    (D) All of the above

30. A clause in a second trust deed that permits the first trust deed to be refinanced without affecting its priority would be known as:
    (A) Acceleration clause
    (B) Alienation clause
    (C) Submortgage
    (D) None of the above

31. The secondary money market creates a marketplace for the transfer of mortgages between which of the following parties?
    (A) Mortgagees and mortgagees
    (B) Mortgagors and mortgagors
    (C) Mortgagees and mortgagors
    (D) Trustors and mortgagees

32. A conventional lender considering a real estate loan would be most concerned with which of the following?
    (A) Federal and state regulations
    (B) Degree of risk involved
    (C) Amount of mortgage funds available
    (D) Economic and financial conditions of the nation

33. Under the Truth-in-Lending Law, which of the following is not to be included in the finance charge?
    (A) Appraisal fee
    (B) Loan points
    (C) Time price differential
    (D) Finder's fees and similar charges

34. Berg sells to Mann a property by conditional sales contract. The contract is recorded and a $25 deposit is made. Mann continues to live on the property but stops making payments and avoids Berg. He then abandons the property one night. In this situation:
    (A) There is a cloud on title
    (B) Marketability of title is not affected
    (C) The new buyer would not be concerned with Mann
    (D) Sale has no effect on title

35. A salesperson takes a listing that requires that the buyer "assume" the existing loan. From the standpoint of the salesperson, the sale would be easiest if the existing loan is:
    (A) A Cal-Vet loan
    (B) A conventional loan
    (C) An FHA loan
    (D) An insurance company loan

36. Which of the following factors would least directly influence the level and movement of mortgage rates?
    (A) Inflation
    (B) Unemployment
    (C) Tight money
    (D) Demand for funds

37. All but which of the following would directly limit the amount of a GI loan to purchase a home?
    (A) Certificate of Reasonable Value
    (B) Certificate of Eligibility
    (C) Buyer's paying capacity
    (D) Lender's requirement

38. What is the maximum period of time an owner might be able to stay in possession after judicial foreclosure:
    (A) 90 days
    (B) 120 days
    (C) 1 year
    (D) None of the above

Valuation/Appraisal of Real Property (15%)

39. Which of the following is not an element of value?
    (A) Utility
    (B) Scarcity
    (C) Transferability
    (D) Expectation

40. A comprehensive method of estimating a building cost including labor, material, overhead and profit is considered in:
    (A) Quantity survey
    (B) Unit-in-place
    (C) Comparative cubic or square foot measurements
    (D) Considered in all of the above

41. An investment property is appraised at $400,000 based on a net income of $36,000 and a 9% capitalization rate. The value of the property based on a 12% capitalization rate would be:
    (A) $250,000
    (B) $300,000
    (C) $450,000
    (D) $423,000

42. In a city that inflicts a heavy tax burden, an appraiser would view this fact with particular interest because:
    (A) Such a city tends to provide more services and hence attracts more investors
    (B) Such a city may have a lower bonded indebtedness
    (C) New construction may shift away from such a city under these circumstances
    (D) Such a city may have the best location and markets for urban development

43. A two story commercial building measures 46' x 80' at its base. The height of the first story is 16' and the height of the second story is 14'. Replacement cost of the first story is calculated at $1.60 per cubic foot; the second story cost is $1.20 per cubic foot. Based on the above, the replacement cost of the building would be:
    (A) $ 94,208
    (B) $ 61,824
    (C) $156,032
    (D) $184,824

44. All of the following are physical characteristics of land except:
    (A) Scarcity
    (B) Non-homogeneity
    (C) Fixity
    (D) Permanence

45. The expansion and contraction of available space to meet demand is stimulated most by market fluctuations of:
    (A) Prices and rents
    (B) Elasticity of demand
    (C) Permanence of residence
    (D) Financing terms

46. When property tax increases and all other items remain the same, an income property:
    (A) Decreases in value by the amount of the taxes
    (B) Decreases in value by more than the amount of the taxes
    (C) Increases in value by the amount of the taxes
    (D) Increases in value by more than the amount of the taxes

47. Silverman is going to make extensive improvements on an old apartment building. Which of the following is most important for him or her to take into account:
    (A) Cost
    (B) Land value
    (C) Area
    (D) Net income

48. An appraiser is called upon to appraise a property on which there was a building of no value. The appraiser should:
    (A) Ignore the building
    (B) Add the salvage value of the building
    (C) Appraise for highest and best use and deduct the cost demolition
    (D) Appraise for highest and best use and disregard the cost of demolition

49. Functional obsolescence would not be attributable to:
    (A) Items of surplus utility
    (B) Eccentric design
    (C) Lack of air conditioning
    (D) Proximity of nuisances

50. The capitalization rate in the valuation of income property would least likely provide for:
    (A) Return on investment
    (B) Return of investment
    (C) Depreciation
    (D) Taxes

51. In appraisal, the following are recognized methods for the valuation of land except:
    (A) Comparative method
    (B) Economic method
    (C) Abstraction method
    (D) Development method

52. An appraiser determines the accrual for depreciation in using:
    (A) Market data
    (B) Cost
    (C) Income approach
    (D) None of the above

53. Land value is estimated whenever possible on the basis of:
    (A) Size, location and utility
    (B) Original cost plus the expense of making it usable
    (C) Purchase price plus the cost of making on site and off site improvements
    (D) Sale price of comparable sites

Real Estate Practice (22%)

54. With regard to an oral listing agreement on real property, the payment of a commission to a broker is:
    (A) Contrary to public policy
    (B) Prohibited by the Commissioner's Rules and Regulations
    (C) Permissible if the seller elects to do so
    (D) Illegal

55. When a buyer revokes an offer prior to the acceptance by the seller:
    (A) The broker may sue the buyer for specific performance
    (B) The broker is entitled to one half of the earnest money deposit
    (C) The broker must refund to the buyer any earnest money deposit
    (D) The seller may sue the buyer for specific performance

56. In the general field of real estate advertising you may encounter the terms "classified," "display," and "reading notice." These terms apply to which of the following advertising media?
    (A) Newspapers
    (B) Magazines
    (C) TV
    (D) Direct mail

57. Broker Ricker had made an oral agreement to pay Broker Hanson one half of the commission on an open listings he had obtained, if Broker Hanson found a buyer. Broker Hanson did find a buyer but Broker Ricker refused to pay Hanson his or her share of the commission. It is generally agreed that Hanson could:
    (A) Not collect because of the Statute of Frauds
    (B) Not collect because it was an open listing
    (C) Not collect because she had violated the real estate law
    (D) Start a civil action, probably get a judgment, and receive her commission

58. Considering the nature of real estate investments in that they are made over a long period of time, require a considerable amount of money, are harder to care for, and generally have a slower turnover, the return on these investments should be:
    (A) The same as first trust deeds
    (B) Higher than bonds but lower than first trust deeds
    (C) The same as bonds
    (D) More than bonds and first trust deeds

59. Since land is unique in character and often cannot be substituted for another parcel, the courts have made available the right to request specific performance. Which of the following would least likely request such an action?
    (A) The seller of a large tract of land
    (B) The seller of a single-family residence
    (C) A broker acting as an agent of the seller
    (D) The buyer of a single-family residence

60. Franklin offered to perform all of the obligations in a purchase contract. This act is considered as a:
    (A) Covenant
    (B) Condition
    (C) Demand
    (D) Tender

61. Which of the following would be necessary to establish a bilateral listing agreement?
    (A) A promise by owner for monetary consideration to be paid to broker
    (B) A promise to act by owner for a promise to act by broker
    (C) Signatures of the husband and wife if the property is community property
    (D) All of the above

62. An agency agreement may be terminated by all of the following except:
    (A) Destruction by fire of the property that is subject matter of the agency agreement
    (B) Principal's refusal of an offer to purchase presented in the name of a third person
    (C) Renunciation of the agreement by the agent
    (D) Mutual termination by both the principal and agent prior to the original termination period

63. Which type of investment serves best as a hedge against inflation?
    (A) An income property that will maintain its value
    (B) An investment that acts as an annuity
    (C) An investment in municipal bonds
    (D) An investment that has great liquidity

64. A contract between two or more persons where one grants the other the right to sell, offer to sell, or exchange goods or services under a marketing plan designed by the grantor is:
    (A) Business opportunity
    (B) Securities and exchange agreement
    (C) Franchise agreement
    (D) Financing agreement

65. Mr. Borg purchased a new mobilehome two months ago and contacted broker Wilson to take a listing on it. With respect to the above, Wilson:
    (A) Could take a listing anytime but could not sell the mobilehome for one year.
    (B) Could not list the mobilehome if it had not been registered with the Department of Housing and Community Development
    (C) Could not list the mobilehome unless she was also licensed by the Department of Motor Vehicles as a Vehicle Dealer
    (D) Could not take a listing and sell the mobilehome unless it was installed on a foundation and properly registered with the county recorder

66. A 17-year-old divorced woman wants to list her part of what had been community property with a broker. With regard to the listing, the broker:
    (A) Should wait for court approval
    (B) May not take the listing because the divorced woman is a minor
    (C) May take the listing when she becomes 18 years old
    (D) Can proceed with the listing request

67. Some contracts are printed and some contracts are handwritten. Most contracts are a combination of printed and handwritten material. If litigation arose over this kind of contract, which of the following would be true?
    (A) The printed part takes precedence
    (B) The handwritten part takes precedence
    (C) Each is given equal consideration and evaluated on its own merits
    (D) Written material copied from printed material takes precedence over other written portions

68. An offer is terminated by:
    (A) Revocation by the offeree
    (B) Rejection by the offeror
    (C) Revocation by the offeror
    (D) A change in the offer made by the offeror

69. Which of the following is the major advantage of 100% equity in a personal residence?
    (A) Lack of mortgage payments as a form of savings
    (B) Greater flexibility of personal income
    (C) Personal residence is readily resalable if owned free and clear
    (D) Leverage

70. In comparing real estate investments to other types of investments, the turnover is:
    (A) Slightly slower than an average of other investments
    (B) Faster than other commodities
    (C) Faster than stocks
    (D) Slower than other investments

71. Which of the following is not true regarding an option?
    (A) An optionee must give valuable consideration
    (B) A separate sales agreement must be binding
    (C) If the optionee does not exercise the option, he forfeits the thing of value given to the optionor as consideration
    (D) An option on a business opportunity can also include the site on which the business operates

72. A seller employed a broker through an authorization to sell, which included an authorization to accept deposits. Upon accepting a deposit from a potential buyer, and before presenting the offer to the seller, the broker misappropriated the money. The risk of loss is:
    (A) The buyer's because the broker was acting as his agent in handling the deposit
    (B) The seller's because he had given the broker specific permission to accept deposits
    (C) Both the buyer and the seller, because neither was at fault
    (D) The buyer, because he could have avoided any misappropriation by making his check out to an independent escrow company of the seller

73. A listing agent gave part of his commission to the buyer. He:
    (A) Must disclose this to the seller
    (B) Is guilty of criminal action
    (C) Is guilty of committing a civilly wrong act
    (D) May be disciplined by the Real Estate Commissioner

74. What essential element is necessary between a broker and a principal when dealing with the title, right, or interest in real property?
    (A) Written contract of employment
    (B) Broker has the right to draw up a purchase offer
    (C) Broker has the right to accept a deposit
    (D) Establish the rights of commission between the parties by law

75. A broker was instructed not to present any offers unless accompanied by a deposit. A buyer brings in an offer without a deposit. With regard to the offer:
    (A) The broker must present it
    (B) The broker should not present it
    (C) The broker should go back to the offeror and request the deposit
    (D) The broker cannot present it

Tax Implications of Real Estate Ownership (8%)

76. Smith buys an apartment building for $100,000. He keeps it for 10 years and sells it for $100,000. He had depreciated the improvements $40,000 over his period of ownership. As to his income tax position:
    (A) He has no recognized gain
    (B) His gain is taxable as ordinary income
    (C) His gain may be deferred
    (D) He has to pay capital gains on the amount of the depreciation

77. The county maintains an assessment roll that includes the assessed value of property. The purpose of this assessment roll is:
    (A) Establishment of the tax amount
    (B) Equalizing of assessments
    (C) Setting of the tax rate
    (D) Establishing the assessment for the tax base

78. An investor owned a commercial building with a market value of $85,000 with a cost basis of $65,000. If he exchanged it for a farm with a market value of $55,000 and received $20,000 in cash and a promissory note of $10,000, which of the following statements is true?
    (A) The transaction is taxed as ordinary income
    (B) He had a recognized gain of $30,000
    (C) He had a recognized gain of $20,000
    (D) He had a realized gain of $30,000 and it was all reportable in the year of the exchange

79. An investor owns a property free and clear valued at $320,000 with a book value of $220,000. If he or she exchanges for another property, also free and clear valued at $365,000 and pays no boot, the book value of the second property will be:
    (A) $365,000
    (B) $220,000
    (C) $585,000
    (D) Cannot be computed with the facts given

80. A property owner had the following monthly payments; principal $402, interest $202; real property taxes $104; fire insurance $21. For federal income tax purposes, how much could be deducted as expenses of ownership?
    (A) $306
    (B) $202
    (C) $104
    (D) $3,672

81. A man purchased a lot for $100,000 cash. In order to construct a building valued at $500,000, he took out a loan of $400,000 at 11% per annum and put down $100,000 in cash. For income tax purposes, what amount could he depreciate over the life of the building?
    (A) $400,000
    (B) $500,000
    (C) $600,000
    (D) $100,000

82. Points paid in obtaining a loan are treated in what manner on the federal income tax return?
    (A) Points are always deductible
    (B) Points are deductible only if the loan is obtained through a state or federal bank
    (C) Points are always deductible if used for interest but not for specific services by a lender
    (D) The manner in which they are treated depends on what they are being used for

83. The purchaser in a sale-leaseback transaction would be least concerned with the:
    (A) Location of the property
    (B) Depreciated book value of the building
    (C) General credit of the lessee
    (D) Condition and construction of the improvements

27

Brokerage: Responsibilities and Functions of Salespersons (17%)
     For Brokers: Broker's Responsibility for Office Management (22%)

84. A broker was to receive a 6% commission from the sale of a property. His or her salesperson was to receive 45% of the 6% commission. The salesperson received $8100. What was the selling price of the property?
(A) $40,000
(B) $135,000
(C) $300,000
(D) $435,000

85. A home was sold for $162,500 and the two brokers who cooperated in the sale agreed to a 50/50 split of a 4.5% commission. One of the broker's salespersons was to receive 50% of the broker's commission. What amount did the salesperson receive?
(A) $1,828.13
(B) $3,656.26
(C) $7,312.50
(D) None of the above

86. The Real Estate Commissioner may require impounding of a purchaser's deposit in a subdivision when the blanket mortgage does not contain an unconditional release clause. This is for the benefit of:
(A) The owner of the subdivision
(B) The purchaser
(C) The mortgage holder
(D) The lender

87. A lot contains 21,780 square feet and is 140 feet deep. The lot originally cost $17,424 and the owner wishes to sell at a price that will give him 40% profit over the cost after paying the broker a 10% commission. This would require the land to sell for how much per front foot?
(A) $158
(B) $174
(C) $198
(D) $189

88. How many acres would be contained in a parcel 330 feet by 220 feet?
(A) 3/4 acre
(B) 1 2/3 acres
(C) 1 acre
(D) 1 3/5 acres

89. All of the following statements pertaining to equal housing opportunities are correct except:
    (A) All prospects are entitled to full information concerning availability of home financing
    (B) "Blockbusting" or "panic selling" generally does not occur in a transaction between a broker and a buyer unless the buyer is also a seller
    (C) Unless they insist, white prospects need not be shown homes in racially transitional neighborhoods
    (D) The Federal Fair Housing Law equally applies to recreational and second home purchases

90. At 10:00 A.M. a broker receives an offer that meets full price and all terms of the listing. At noon, before he or she could submit the first offer, he or she receives a second offer on the same property for less money but all cash. The broker decides to submit the first offer and, if it is rejected, to submit the second offer. Which is true:
    (A) This is proper since second offer was for less than the listed price
    (B) This is proper since one should submit offers in the order received
    (C) The broker could be disciplined by the Real Estate Commissioner
    (D) This is improper since the broker owes a fiduciary relationship to both buyers

91. A property was purchased for $300,000 with $75,000 cash down payment. If the property increased in value by 10% this would increase the owner's equity by which of the following amounts?
    (A) 10%
    (B) 20%
    (C) 30%
    (D) 40%

92. A planned development could be which of the following?
    (A) Residential
    (B) Commercial
    (C) Industrial
    (D) Any of the above

93. Jones was paying $550 per month to the bank. After the bank deducted interest, $43.85 was applied to the principal. If the outstanding loan balance was $56,500, what was the rate of interest on Jones' loan?
    (A) 8 %
    (B) 9 %
    (C) 10 %
    (D) 11 %

94. A real estate broker cannot accept a listing from a minor appointing the broker as an agent because:
    (A) A minor is incapable of appointing an agent
    (B) A minor does not have the capacity to enter into contracts
    (C) A minor has the right to disaffirm the listing contract during his minority
    (D) The broker would breach the fiduciary relationship by misrepresenting a minor who is incapable of making adult decisions

95. Mr. Jones had broker Smith negotiate a new $2,500 second trust deed on a home with a term of 2 years. What is the maximum costs and commission Mr. Jones will have to pay?
    (A) $125
    (B) $250
    (C) $375
    (D) $640

96. Johnson, who owns a ranch, gave Broker Otis an exclusive listing to sell his property. Johnson also advanced Otis $100 to advertise the sale of this ranch in a brochure published by Otis. The real estate law requires that brokers must account for such funds by complying with which of the following?
    (A) Place the $100 in the broker's trust account in order that the money may be returned to the seller if the property is not sold
    (B) Place this advance fee in the broker's personal office account and spend it only for advertising the property
    (C) Place the $100 in the broker's trust account, expend from the trust account only for advertising the property, and provide a report to the seller that will itemize all expenditures made
    (D) Place the $100 in the broker's trust account in case the seller defaults

97. With regards to blind advertising:
    (A) It is permitted with the owner's permission
    (B) It is permitted when a broker deems that it will increase exposure of the property to potential buyers
    (C) It is not permitted. The advertisement would require the salesperson's name
    (D) It is not permitted. The advertisement must include the name and address of the broker

98. A broker refers all of his clients and customers to West Hills Title Insurance Company. The title company gives the broker a $10 fee for each referral. This practice is:
    (A) Permissible
    (B) Acceptable if the seller is paying for the policy and agrees
    (C) Acceptable if both buyer and seller are aware that broker is receiving a fee and agree
    (D) Forbidden

99. A lessor is renting a furnished apartment from period to period. Under the Fair Housing Law, he may do all of the following except:
    (A) Make credit checks and verify income
    (B) Check with former landlords for references
    (C) Require only single tenants to have co-signors for leases
    (D) Collect the first, second and last month's rent

100. In a sales transaction, an agent is paid by both parties but did not reveal the dual agency. What could happen in these circumstances?
    (A) The agent would be subject to discipline by the Real Estate Commissioner
    (B) The sale could be rescinded
    (C) The agent may not be able to enforce payment of his commission
    (D) All of the above

Practice Tests

This next series of seven practice tests will provide you with an opportunity to study separately the seven major subject areas that will make up the California qualifying examination. Each question asks about a point that has been the subject of an exam question that has been asked in the past and may appear again on a future exam. The exams are arranged in the most logical learning order.

° Carefully studying the explanation of every question you missed or have doubts about is the most effective and most efficient studying you can do.
° Use the pullout exam answer sheets at the back of this book.
° Repeat each test as many times as necessary.
° Wait a few days before retesting.
° Reach approximately 80% on all seven areas for salespersons (70% passing).
° Practice test score of at least 85% for brokers (75% passing).

Exam 3 - Real Property and Laws Relating to Ownership

1. The personal revocable and unassignable permission or authority to do one or more acts on the land of another without possessing any interest therein, is the definition of:
    (A) License
    (B) Easement
    (C) Encroachment
    (D) Option

2. Which of the following constitutes a lien?
    (A) Homestead
    (B) Easement
    (C) Mortgage
    (D) All of the above

3. Police Power is a governmental right and would result in:
    (A) The taking of private property for the construction of a highway
    (B) Zoning standards
    (C) Judgments
    (D) Deed restrictions in a subdivision

4. An owner of property located near a local airport was constantly bothered by the noise of low-flying aircraft. If the owner were to bring suit to force the city to condemn his or her property because of the noise, this would be an example of:
    (A) Condemnation
    (B) Inverse condemnation
    (C) Eminent domain
    (D) Equitable severance

5. To achieve planning goals, local, state and federal governments have the authority to regulate the use of or to purchase private property. In its broadest definition the source of this authority is known as:
    (A) Master planning
    (B) Zoning
    (C) Police power
    (D) Eminent domain

6. All of the following are characteristics of a fee simple estate except:
    (A) Free of all encumbrances
    (B) Freely inheritable
    (C) Freely transferable
    (D) Of indefinite duration

7. The date of priority of a mechanic's lien on any construction project is:
    (A) Date of commencement of construction
    (B) Date of completion of construction
    (C) Date of acceptance by owner
    (D) Date of occupation by owner

8. A flooring contractor is employed to install a hardwood floor in a new house. Generally speaking, the mechanic's lien date begins:
    (A) At the beginning of construction of the house
    (B) At the beginning of installation of hardwood floor
    (C) Upon completion of the house
    (D) Upon completion of installation of hardwood floor

9. An appurtenant easement involves two parcels of land. The owner of the dominant tenement may:
    (A) Have ingress and egress only
    (B) Retain the benefits and the burdens of the easement
    (C) Not retain easement rights with the transfer of the parcel
    (D) Transfer the interest independently of the land

10. Which of the following is the highest form of ownership?
    (A) Tenancy at will
    (B) Incorporeal freehold
    (C) Fee simple defeasible
    (D) Fee simple absolute

11. Which of the following is a difference between a mechanic's lien and a judgment lien:
    (A) Mechanic's liens are created by statute
    (B) Mechanic's liens may take priority before the recording date
    (C) Judgment liens are not effective until recorded
    (D) Judgment liens are involuntary liens

12. An estate that will continue for a period of 6 months only, fixed in advance by contractual agreement of the parties is an:
    (A) Estate from period to period
    (B) Estate at will
    (C) Estate at sufferance
    (D) Estate for years

13. An easement could be terminated by which of the following?
    (A) Prescription
    (B) Abandonment
    (C) Nonuse
    (D) Both (B) and (C)

14. The most common method of establishing deed restrictions in a new subdivision is:
    (A) Including the restrictions in the deed to each parcel
    (B) Recording the restrictions with the County Recorder's Office with a mention thereto appended to the deed of each buyer
    (C) Publishing the restrictions in a newspaper of general circulation
    (D) Including the restrictions in the Commissioner's final public report

15. The lien of a recorded deed of trust is removed from the records:
    (A) By recordation of a grant deed
    (B) When final payment has been made by trustor
    (C) By posting of a surety bond
    (D) When reconveyance deed is recorded

16. Riparian Rights refer to:
    (A) Rivers
    (B) Streams
    (C) Watercourses
    (D) All of the above

17. A recorded notice of lis pendens:
    (A) Does not directly affect the title to property of a person not directly a party to the court action
    (B) Can be filed on any type of lawsuit
    (C) Would make it difficult to convey title
    (D) Can be removed from the records only by an order of the court

18. A "percolation test" is used to determine:
    (A) Depth of footings
    (B) Size of the cistern needed for a given building
    (C) Quantity and potability of water
    (D) Capacity of soil to absorb water

19. A lessee renting for a period of six months would have what type of interest?
    (A) Estate for years
    (B) Period to period
    (C) Estate at sufferance
    (D) Estate at will

20. The customary procedure used to enforce private restrictions on real property is:
    (A) Judgment
    (B) Injunction
    (C) Indictment
    (D) Desist and refrain order

21. Which of the following is a requirement of joint tenancy?
     (A) Husband and wife relationship
     (B) The words "taken in joint tenancy" next to the names of the joint tenants
     (C) Each party has an equal interest
     (D) All of the above

22. Personal property presents certain problems to a broker. It becomes difficult to ascertain its ownership because it can:
     (A) Become real property
     (B) Be alienated
     (C) Be hypothecated
     (D) All of the above

23. The Master Plan prepared by a Planning Commission would cover which of the following?
     (A) Highways and streets
     (B) Commercial and industrial districts
     (C) Seismic safety
     (D) All of the above

24. Private restrictions placed by a landowner may be in the form of covenants or conditions restricting or limiting the use of the land. Private restrictions may be created by:
     (A) Deed only
     (B) Deed or written agreement
     (C) Written agreement or zoning ordinance
     (D) Deed or written ordinance

25. Restrictions on purchasing real property are placed on all of the following except:
     (A) An alien
     (B) A convict
     (C) An unemancipated minor
     (D) A minor who is a ward of the court

26. One who takes in severalty most generally takes title:
     (A) In common
     (B) In joint tenancy
     (C) In partnership
     (D) As sole owner

27. Anderson, Baker, and Carroll own property as joint tenants. Anderson dies:
     (A) Baker and Carroll receive Anderson's share through survivorship as tenants in common
     (B) Baker and Carroll receive Anderson's share through succession
     (C) Anderson's interest terminates
     (D) None of the above

28. A builder bought a parcel of real estate that had an old home on it. The builder later removed the dilapidated old home, had the lot graded, and immediately obtained a construction loan secured by a deed of trust. During the construction period a painter was unpaid and filed a mechanic's lien. Which of the following is correct?
    (A) The trust deed takes priority because it was recorded before construction was completed
    (B) The mechanic's lien applies secondarily to the trust deed
    (C) The mechanic's lien takes priority over the trust deed because the priority dates back to the time of start of construction
    (D) Mechanic's liens always take priority over trust deeds

29. The power of eminent domain can be exercised by:
    (A) Cities
    (B) Public utilities
    (C) Public education institutions
    (D) All of the above

30. "A charge imposed upon real property as security for a specific act" is a definition of:
    (A) Restrictive covenant
    (B) Easement
    (C) Lien
    (D) Encumbrance

31. Which of the following can "run with the land"?
    (A) Easements
    (B) Covenants that benefit the land
    (C) Stock in a mutual water company
    (D) All of the above

32. The basic legal tool a city will use for a layout plan is:
    (A) Exceptions to general land usage
    (B) Conditional use permit
    (C) Zoning
    (D) Variance

33. A fee simple estate, held in severalty, is real property in which the tenancy is:
    (A) Simple, absolute
    (B) Defeasible
    (C) Sole Ownership
    (D) Held in common with others

34. In ridding an area of nonconforming uses, rezoning ordinances may require that certain conditions be met. These would include all of the following except:
    (A) Prohibition of rebuilding
    (B) Prohibition of expansion
    (C) Retroactive zoning ordinances
    (D) Allowing a reasonable time (amortized period) within which the abuses may be eliminated

35. A court order affecting all the property held in the county by an owner is called:
    (A) A specific lien
    (B) A general lien
    (C) A lis pendens
    (D) An attachment

35

36. Davidson has an easement on Parkins' property. If Davidson is not a property owner, the easement is:
    (A) A restrictive easement
    (B) A non-possessory encroachment
    (C) An easement in gross
    (D) An appurtenant easement

37. A builder submitted building plans that included design specifications and materials for approval. When reviewing these plans, the building inspector determined some of the proposed materials were not in accordance with local building codes but that the use of these materials would not constitute a safety hazard and therefore approved the plans. This is an example of:
    (A) An exception
    (B) A variance
    (C) A permit
    (D) An infraction

38. With regard to local building codes (for example in Los Angeles), vs. the Federal Uniform Building Code, which would prevail?
    (A) Local building codes always take precedence over the Federal Uniform Building Code
    (B) Federal codes always take precedence
    (C) The Federal Uniform Building Code applies only to general codes while local codes are more specific
    (D) Whichever has the higher standards of health and safety will prevail

39. Which of the following is a correct statement in respect to encumbrances on real property?
    (A) A specific lien is always a voluntary lien
    (B) Encumbrances are liens but not all liens are encumbrances
    (C) Title companies will not insure encumbered property
    (D) It is common practice for a buyer to accept a deed to encumbered property

40. A commercial property no longer has a conforming use because it exists in an area where the zoning has been changed. The owner of this property has suffered a hardship because of the zoning change. Which of the following could the owner obtain as an exception to this new zoning that would be a benefit to him?
    (A) Spot zoning
    (B) A Conditional Use Permit
    (C) A Variance
    (D) Any of the above

41. The distinguishing characteristic of real property as distinct from personal property is:
    (A) Long-term asset
    (B) High cost of acquisition
    (C) Can be depreciated over useful life
    (D) Immovable

42. Quiet enjoyment usually refers to which of the following circumstances?
    (A) Neighbors creating a nuisance
    (B) Possessory interest of a tenant given by the owner of the paramount title
    (C) Noise abatement
    (D) None of the above

43. Four people own a property as joint tenants. If two joint tenants die, which of the following would be a true statement?
    (A) The devisees and heirs could rent the property as tenants in common with the other two
    (B) One title will be held by the remaining joint tenants
    (C) Each survivor would own a separate and divided interest
    (D) A separate legal title to a tenancy in common would be held

44. State enabling legislation gives cities and counties various controls over real property. The enabling legislation gives to cities and counties all but which of the following:
    (A) Subdivision and land use regulations
    (B) Local planning and zoning ordinances
    (C) Lien and attachment laws
    (D) Rent control and city codes

45. A money judgment of the court when recorded is always:
    (A) A voluntary lien
    (B) An involuntary lien
    (C) A superior lien
    (D) An equitable lien

46. An easement on real property may be terminated by the owner of the dominant tenement by filing:
    (A) A defeasance clause
    (B) A deed of reconveyance
    (C) A statement of nonresponsibility
    (D) A quitclaim deed

47. A person who has been judicially declared incompetent and who was bequeathed three properties by his brother:
    (A) Cannot receive title to real property because of his incompetency
    (B) Cannot receive title to real property but can receive title to personal property
    (C) Can accept title to real property given to him in a will
    (D) Can accept title only if it is placed with a trustee.

48. Which of the following does not affect the physical nature or use of real property?
    (A) A specific lien
    (B) Conditions that benefit the property
    (C) Restrictions
    (D) Covenants

49. A money judgment given by a court is effective to create a lien:
    (A) In all of the state by filing with the Clerk of the Court
    (B) In the county where the judgment is obtained
    (C) If recorded in the county where the defendant's property is located
    (D) Anywhere in the United States

50. An easement created by which of the following would be easiest to terminate by nonuse?
    (A) Deed
    (B) Prescription
    (C) Implication
    (D) None of the above

51. In the absence of court approval, a minor or incompetent:
    (A) Can receive a deed to a property through gift or inheritance
    (B) Can encumber real property through a power of attorney
    (C) Can convey property through a guardian
    (D) All of the above

52. An easement that is strictly personal in nature may best be described as:
    (A) Benefiting the dominant tenement
    (B) Burdening the servient tenement
    (C) Not capable of being owned by any other person
    (D) A non-transferable fee interest

53. Less-than-freehold estates consist of estates owned by:
    (A) Beneficiaries of trust deeds
    (B) Holders of easements
    (C) Lessees
    (D) Grantees of life estates

54. In addition to municipal or county controls imposed through zoning ordinances and the Subdivision Map Act, other government controls are exercised by:
    (A) Health, fire, and safety requirements
    (B) California Department of Real Estate
    (C) Agencies which insure and guarantee FHA and VA loans
    (D) All of the above

55. Which of the following is considered real property?
    (A) A stud in the wall of a house
    (B) Fixtures removable by a tenant
    (C) Fruit that was to be picked after the sale, as agreed upon by both the buyer and seller
    (D) Shrubs to be planted around a yard

56. An owner of a parcel of real property may have all of the following rights except:
    (A) Riparian rights
    (B) Littoral rights
    (C) Severance
    (D) Eminent Domain

57. Able had a 10-year lease from Jones on Blackacres. Smith owned Brownacres and wanted an easement from Able. Which of the following is a true statement?
    (A) Able can grant the easement but only for the term of the lease
    (B) Able can give the easement, but only with the owner's ratification
    (C) If the lease is recorded, Able would have the same property rights as Jones
    (D) An easement can be given only by the fee owner

58. A husband and wife hold title to some real property as community property. They wish to change their title to a mode that will provide the right of survivorship. To achieve this objective they could deed the property to themselves to hold in:
    - (A) People cannot deed property to themselves
    - (B) Severalty
    - (C) Joint tenancy
    - (D) Tenancy in common

59. Which of the following does not constitute an estate in real property?
    - (A) Remainder
    - (B) Deed of trust
    - (C) Reversion
    - (D) Leasehold

60. Zoning regulations are legally enforceable because:
    - (A) Of local planning agencies
    - (B) Of the police power of government
    - (C) Of the ease of enforcement
    - (D) They do not affect interstate commerce

61. Local zoning ordinances determining use of land and building may also determine?
    - (A) Size
    - (B) Setbacks
    - (C) Location of buildings
    - (D) All of the above

62. The most distinguishable characteristic of personal property is:
    - (A) Mobility
    - (B) Being incidental or appurtenant to land
    - (C) Anything affixed to land as a permanent part of the land
    - (D) All of the above

63. Which is real property?
    - (A) Land and buildings
    - (B) Natural and artificial barriers immovable by law
    - (C) Easements and rights-of-way to an adjoining property
    - (D) Any of the above

64. A specified charge against real property that is used as security is defined as:
    - (A) An easement
    - (B) Subdivision restrictions
    - (C) A lien
    - (D) Zoning

65. The Pacific and Great Western Telephone Company has an easement on a property being sold by Broker Root, but is not mentioned in the deed. The easement is:
    - (A) A specific lien
    - (B) A general lien
    - (C) An encumbrance
    - (D) An attachment

66. Which of the following is not a specific lien?
    (A) Unrecorded property tax lien delinquent from prior years
    (B) Judgment lien
    (C) Mechanic's lien
    (D) Blanket mortgage

67. Smith had the XYZ Swimming Pool Company install a pool. After completion of construction, a lien was filed on behalf of the XYZ Company to collect the amount of the contract. The lien filed was:
    (A) A general lien
    (B) A specific lien
    (C) A voluntary lien
    (D) None of the above

68. In California, estates at will are created by:
    (A) A properly written and executed document
    (B) Express agreement
    (C) Operation of law
    (D) Either (B) or (C)

69. Deed restrictions for a subdivision are created by:
    (A) Local building commission
    (B) Planning commission
    (C) Local building statutes
    (D) Developer or grantor

70. George Nordling subdivided a large section of a hillside location. In the deeds to individual lots, he placed a restriction requiring a 15,000 square foot minimum lot size. Subsequently, the local authorities succeeded in reducing the requirements of the zoning laws to a minimum requirement of a 10,000 square foot minimum lot size. Which requirement for minimum lot size takes precedence?
    (A) Zoning laws as they are based on police power
    (B) The original deed restriction
    (C) Precedence would require arbitration by local planning commission
    (D) The subdivider would be compelled to amend his restriction to conform to zoning laws

71. Under common law, it is necessary to give notice to terminate which of the following?
    (A) Estate for years
    (B) Estate at sufferance
    (C) Estate at will
    (D) None of the above

72. With regard to a limited partnership, which of the following statements is not correct?
    (A) A limited partner's liability is limited to the debts of the partnership
    (B) It must consist of one or more limited partners and one or more general partners
    (C) A limited partner cannot make decisions affecting management policies
    (D) A limited partner can lose all he invested in the partnership

73. Deed restrictions are:
    (A) Encumbrances
    (B) General liens
    (C) Constructive liens
    (D) All of the above

40

74. Which of the following are not liens?
    (A) Taxes
    (B) Trust Deeds
    (C) Judgments
    (D) Private Restrictions

75. Tenancy in common interests have a unity of:
    (A) Time
    (B) Title
    (C) Interest
    (D) Possession

76. Which of the following "runs with the land"?
    (A) Covenants
    (B) Stock in a mutual water company
    (C) Appurtenant easements
    (D) All of the above

77. Which of the following is considered real property?
    (A) Trade fixtures that can be removed without any damage to the property
    (B) A bearing wall
    (C) A refrigerator in a mobilehome that is not permanently affixed
    (D) Growing grapes that have been pre-contracted before harvest

78. Which of the following *is correct* with regard to an estate?
    (A) Title to an estate must be transferred by deed
    (B) A life estate is a less-than-freehold estate
    (C) An estate cannot be created by a lease
    (D) More than one estate can exist in the same property

79. Mr. Green owned stock in a mutual water company. This interest was appurtenant to the land. Green sold his property to Smith. Under these circumstances:
    (A) A separate contract must be written for the purchase of the stock
    (B) Property cannot be purchased in California without water rights
    (C) Nothing additional would have to be done regarding this purchase because stock in a mutual water company is an appurtenance to the land
    (D) None of the above

80. Who can initiate zoning changes?
    (A) Developer
    (B) Private person
    (C) City or county governments
    (D) All of the above

41

Exam 4 - Transfer of Property

1. Which of the following documents is almost never recorded?
    (A) A promissory note secured by a deed of trust
    (B) A notice of completion
    (C) A conditional sales contract
    (D) A trustee's deed

2. If a change of ownership is not filed, how many days after the change does an owner have to inform the County Tax Assessor about a change of ownership?
    (A) 15 days
    (B) 30 days
    (C) 45 days
    (D) 60 days

3. An escrow company received two termite reports in which the estimates of cost of the work differed. Under these circumstances:
    (A) The seller and broker must decide which report to use
    (B) The seller and broker should present both reports to the buyer
    (C) The least expensive report should be used
    (D) The most expensive report should be used

4. All of the following are required for acquiring title by adverse possession except:
    (A) Open and notorious use
    (B) Confrontation with the owner
    (C) Hostile to the true owner's title
    (D) It must be under a claim of right or color of title

5. A young person, single and unemancipated, sold a home and the transaction was completed and escrow closed. There was no court appointed guardian. In order for the transaction to be valid the young person must be at least _____ years old.
    (A) 16
    (B) 18
    (C) 19
    (D) 21

6. A quitclaim deed releases present claim, rights and title of the:
    (A) Grantor
    (B) Grantee
    (C) Servient tenement
    (D) Property

7. Who would provide a quitclaim deed to "quiet" a title?
    (A) Grantor
    (B) Trustor
    (C) Grantee
    (D) None of the above

8. Regarding a structural pest control certification report, licensees must know that this report must be given to:
   (A) The owner of the property
   (B) The buyer of the property
   (C) The lender on the property
   (D) All of the above

9. Trustee will deliver to the trustor:
   (A) A grant deed
   (B) A quitclaim deed
   (C) A reconveyance deed
   (D) A trustee's deed

10. A deed was given by "A" to "B" with oral instructions not to record the deed until "A's" death. The deed was:
    (A) Valid
    (B) Void
    (C) Voidable
    (D) Illegal

11. A broker lists and negotiates the sale of a home for Mr. "B," a young married man. At the time of the sale the broker was not concerned with the age of his client. After the deed had been signed and escrow closed, the title company informs the broker that the seller is under 18 years of age. The deed is:
    (A) Valid
    (B) Voidable
    (C) Outlawed
    (D) Illegal

12. A structural pest control report must be delivered to the:
    (A) Lender
    (B) Broker
    (C) Escrow company
    (D) Buyer

13. Which of the following would not be covered by a CLTA policy that would be covered by an ALTA policy?
    (A) Mistakes in liens and documents of record
    (B) Capacity of the grantee of a deed of reconveyance
    (C) Property lines accurately established by a survey
    (D) Discrepancies found in documents of record

14. Which of the following is not a means of creating an interest in real property?
    (A) Deed
    (B) Bill of sale
    (C) Mortgage
    (D) Lease

15. Which of the following would make a deed void?
    (A) Grantee is not named but is sufficiently described
    (B) Signature of grantor is spelled differently from the typed spelling on the deed
    (C) Grantor is set forth and has signed under a name not his own
    (D) Made to a fictitious grantee

43

16. In California a buyer of real property is most likely to seek title protection through:
    (A) Policy of title insurance
    (B) Certificate of title
    (C) Recording of title
    (D) Abstract of title

17. A buyer purchased a property using a recorded conditional sales contract and later defaulted on the payments. If a quitclaim deed was used to clear the cloud on title, it would be executed by:
    (A) Buyer
    (B) Seller
    (C) Both Buyer and Seller
    (D) None of the above

18. An escrow company can:
    (A) Order a termite report and authorize the work to be done
    (B) Change the amount of the broker's commission
    (C) Tell the buyers where to obtain the best available financing
    (D) Request funding of the buyer's loan

19. Able died leaving no heirs but had willed Blackacre Ranch to a Baker. Talbot was in possession of Blackacres under an existing lease that had two years to run. During the probate of Able's estate, the court found the will to be invalid. Under these circumstances, title to Blackacres would:
    (A) Pass to Baker since it was Able's intent
    (B) Pass to Talbot since he is in possession
    (C) Pass by statutory provisions by a court of proper jurisdiction
    (D) Pass through an action by one or more of the heirs for declaratory relief

20. Which of the following would create an interest in property with possessory rights but no form of title?
    (A) Mortgage
    (B) Easement
    (C) Sublease
    (D) Land contract

21. When an owner receives money for a property that has been destroyed or condemned, this is an example of:
    (A) Subrogated redemption
    (B) Involuntary conversion
    (C) Extinguishable conveyance
    (D) Depreciable obsolescence

22. Escrow companies are subject to the Corporations Commissioner's Regulations. Who would not be exempt?
    (A) Attorney at law
    (B) Broker escrowing property of other brokers
    (C) Broker not accepting a fee and handling his own escrow
    (D) Broker accepting a fee and handling his own escrow

23. Tooly, a 15-year-old minor, inherited some land that he deeded to a non-profit organization. The organization recorded the deed and put a building on the land. At 18, Tooly changed his mind and decided he wanted the property back.
    (A) Recording created an estoppel and prevented Tooly from having claim to the property
    (B) The deed was void because Tooly was a minor
    (C) Because of the time lapse between 15 and 18, Tooly was unable to reclaim the property
    (D) Tooly could claim the property if he reimbursed the organization for the cost of the building

24. In an assignment of a lease, the assignee becomes the:
    (A) Vendee
    (B) Vendor
    (C) Sublessee
    (D) Tenant

25. All of the following instruments are used to transfer an interest in real property *except*:
    (A) Trust deed
    (B) Mortgage
    (C) Bill of sale
    (D) Agreement of sale

26. Which of the following would hold equitable title:
    (A) Trustor under a deed of trust
    (B) Vendee under a land sales contract
    (C) Both (A) and (B)
    (D) Neither (A) nor (B)

27. A deed is void at its inception if:
    (A) The grantee is a minor
    (B) The grantor is legally incompetent
    (C) The grantee takes title under an assumed name
    (D) None of the above

28. In a certain county the Documentary Transfer Tax is $.55 per $500, or fraction thereof, of equity transferred. A property sold for $150,000 with $125,000 being subject to the transfer tax. This tax most nearly amounted to:
    (A) $27.50
    (B) $138.00
    (C) $165.00
    (D) $185.00

29. The first installment of real property taxes had been paid by the seller for the current fiscal year. Property taxes for the current fiscal year amounted to $1,200. If escrow closed on February 1, what amount of prorated taxes would the seller be required to pay?
    (A) $100
    (B) $200
    (C) $600
    (D) $1,200

30. James, an 11-year-old minor, owned a farm and asked his father to contract a broker to sell the farm. The father listed the property with a broker. The farm was sold and the deed was signed. James later changed his mind and wanted the farm. This transaction was:
(A) Valid because the father was acting for his son
(B) Void because James was a minor
(C) Void because the father arranged the sale through a broker
(D) Rescinded simply because James changed his mind

31. A property is purchased by Joan Barry, a single woman, and a deed executed in her name. Later, she married John Roberts and executed a new deed to the property acquired before her marriage, changing the grantee to read "Joan Roberts, a married woman." This action:
(A) Is immaterial as long as the property is adequately described
(B) Creates a cloud on title
(C) Will be corrected after being made of record for one year
(D) Could cause a problem as the separate property could become a joint tenancy

32. A tenant would be justified in abandoning a property in all of the following situations except when:
(A) Dilapidated conditions are created by the tenant
(B) Property is taken by eminent domain or condemnation
(C) The landlord threatens expulsion
(D) Excessive or unwarranted changes or alterations in the property made by the landlord

33. The real property taxes for the current fiscal tax year had been paid and amounted to $1,380.00. The property was sold and the escrow closed on May 1st. How much did the buyer have to pay in escrow?
(A) $115.00
(B) $230.00
(C) $460.00
(D) $1,150.00

34. All of the following can be assigned unless there is an agreement to the contrary except:
(A) Lease
(B) Fire insurance policy
(C) Option
(D) Trust deed

35. In the purchase of a residence, the buyer conditioned the sale upon the seller's providing the buyer with a certified inspection report from a licensed pest control operator showing the property to be free of wood destroying organisms. The seller contracted the Apex Termite Control Company who, upon inspection, reported termite damage and estimated the repairs would cost $500. The seller then had Apex repair the damage and the seller made payment directly to the contractor for the work that had been done. With respect to the report of work accomplished, which of the following is true?
   (A) No report need be made to the buyer since the seller had the work done, paid for it and the residence is now free of termites
   (B) The escrow officer would ensure the buyer has received a copy of the report since escrow cannot close until this has been accomplished
   (C) Either the broker or the seller would be responsible for delivering a copy to the buyer
   (D) The Apex Termite Company would be required to deliver a copy to the buyer

36. In making a title search, a title company would most likely search the records of the:
   (A) Federal Land Office
   (B) County Recorder's Office
   (C) County Clerk
   (D) All of the above

37. A proper acknowledgment may be taken by a notary public who is:
   (A) The grantee of a deed
   (B) The mortgagee of a mortgage
   (C) An employee of a corporation for which the instrument needs to be acknowledged if he has no interest in the property
   (D) The grantor of a deed

38. Carson acquired title to several properties before his arrest. While in prison, he wanted to convey one property to his son, and sell another. How would being in prison affect his ability to convey?
   (A) It would be hard to acquire title insurance
   (B) He must first get permission from California Adult Authority
   (C) He can dispose of his property as he pleases
   (D) His conveyance must be approved by an officer of the Department of Corrections

39. Two pest control inspection companies submitted pest control reports on the same property during escrow. The escrow officer should:
   (A) Use the report that requires the least work to be done
   (B) Request one of the pest control companies to withdraw its report
   (C) Return the reports to the broker and request written instructions from the seller as to which report to use
   (D) Return the reports to the broker and have him get written instructions from the seller and buyer as to which report to use

40. Buyer and seller sign escrow instructions that the broker takes to the escrow agent. The escrow agent discovered discrepancies between the escrow instructions and purchase contract. Which of the following is true?
    (A) The purchase contract would prevail because it is the original document
    (B) The escrow instructions generally prevail because it is the most recent document
    (C) The purchase contract must be redrafted to agree with the escrow instructions
    (D) The escrow agent and the broker must resolve the conflict

41. During escrow, if an unresolved dispute should arise between the seller and buyer preventing the close of escrow, the escrow holder may legally:
    (A) Act as a neutral arbitrator
    (B) Rescind the transaction and return all monies to both parties
    (C) Sue for specific performance
    (D) Enter court action with buyer and seller in an action of interpleader

42. All of the following can be prorated on a closing statement except:
    (A) Insurance
    (B) Taxes
    (C) Rents
    (D) Non-secured loan for which seller was in arrears in principal and interest payments

43. Documentary transfer tax is 55 cents per $500, or fraction thereof, of equity transferred. A property sold for $90,750 with a $30,000 loan being assumed by the buyer. Which was most nearly the tax?
    (A) $66.00
    (B) $67.00
    (C) $90.55
    (D) $100.10

44. Which of the following would never appear as a debit to the buyer on a closing statement?
    (A) Tax prorations
    (B) Interest on an assumed loan
    (C) FHA discount points on an FHA loan
    (D) Insurance prorations

45. A buyer of a property fails to examine public records on the property. The buyer is considered to have:
    (A) Actual notice
    (B) Constructive notice
    (C) Assumed notice
    (D) Conditional notice

46. An escrow can be terminated by which of the following?
    (A) Incapacity or death of either party
    (B) Mutual consent of the parties
    (C) An attorney-in-fact acting for one of the principals
    (D) Revocation by the broker

47. A standard policy of title insurance insures against:
    (A) Defects in the title known to the purchaser but not to the title company as of the date of the policy
    (B) Lack of capacity of persons having to do with title
    (C) Unrecorded easements
    (D) Eminent domain

48. Recording of a document affecting title to real property gives all of the following except:
    (A) Constructive notice of the contents of the document
    (B) Constructive notice of the existence of the rights conveyed in the document
    (C) Actual notice of the contents of the document
    (D) None of the above

49. Which of the following is normally in the weakest position against loss of property due to a claim by an outsider?
    (A) Holder of a certificate of title
    (B) Holder of an unrecorded deed who occupies the property
    (C) Holder of a recorded deed who rents the property
    (D) Holder of an unrecorded quitclaim deed who does not occupy the property

50. The purchase price of a property amounted to $100,000 with the buyer assuming an existing $60,000 loan. If the documentary transfer tax is $.55 for each $500 or fraction thereof, what was the tax paid on the transaction:
    (A) $55.00
    (B) $44.00
    (C) $33.00
    (D) $22.00

51. Which one of the following would cause a deed to be void?
    (A) The name on the deed is entirely different from the person's actual name
    (B) The person is not adequately designated
    (C) The person has a married name
    (D) The person's name is spelled differently

52. A proper acknowledgment may be taken by a notary public who is:
    (A) A grantee in a deed
    (B) A mortgagee in a mortgage
    (C) An employee of a corporation for which the instrument must be acknowledged if the employee has no interest in the property
    (D) A grantor of a deed

53. Middleton is a 15-year-old emancipated minor who hired a broker to sell her property. Middleton gave this broker her emancipation documents. After the broker procured a buyer, to whom should the broker deliver these documents?
    (A) The escrow company
    (B) The buyer
    (C) The title insurer
    (D) The buyer's lender

54. By which of the following means can a person gain title to real property?
    (A) Riparian rights
    (B) Littoral rights
    (C) Accession
    (D) Appurtenance

55. Which of the following would never be a way an individual could acquire an interest or estate in real property?
    (A) Prescription
    (B) Escheat
    (C) Succession
    (D) Accession

56. A landlord sued his tenant in small claims court because his tenant did not give notice before leaving. The tenant said that he had told the landlord of plumbing problems that the landlord did not repair. Which of the following is true?
    (A) The tenant would be compensated by the court
    (B) The landlord would get money from the court because the tenant should have repaired the plumbing and deducted it from his rent
    (C) The landlord would not get money from the court because either party could rescind the contract
    (D) The failure to repair the plumbing was a default on the landlord's part

57. Which of the following is an incorrect statement:
    (A) A deed of reconveyance must be recorded
    (B) A trust deed does not have to be recorded
    (C) A trust deed can be recorded in more than one county
    (D) A promissory note is not eligible for recording

58. There are different types of title insurance. The major differences between the owner's title insurance policy and the lender's title insurance policy include:
    (A) A lender's insurance covers the interest of the seller but owner's insurance covers the title
    (B) A lender's insurance covers the interests of the mortgagee
    (C) An owner's insurance covers the water and mining rights that the owner can claim
    (D) A lender's insurance extends coverage on easements and possession that is difficult to ascertain at time of purchase

59. In the absence of a special agreement to the contrary, a trust deed normally having highest priority is one that was:
    (A) Executed first
    (B) A construction mortgage
    (C) Recorded first
    (D) Executed and delivered first

60. Which of the following documents might be used to convey possessory rights in real property without conveying ownership rights?
    (A) License
    (B) A mortgage
    (C) A sub-lease
    (D) Grant of easement

61. A summary and digest of all transfers, conveyances, legal proceedings and any other facts relied on as evidence of title, showing continuity of ownership, together with any other elements of record which impair title, is a definition of a/an:
    (A) Abstract of Title
    (B) Certificate of Title
    (C) Chain of Title
    (D) Boilerplate form

62. The main purpose of a deed is to:
    (A) Show a change of real property transfer
    (B) Provide evidence of a change of title or transfer of an interest in real property
    (C) Identify the parties in the transfer of title of real property
    (D) Provide a legal document eligible for recording

63. A lessee may be justified in abandoning a rented dwelling if there is constructive eviction by the landlord. All of the following would be constructive eviction except:
    (A) Failure of the landlord to repair excessive wear and tear to property caused by the tenant
    (B) Condemnation of the entire property in eminent domain proceedings
    (C) An eviction notice is tendered by the landlord
    (D) Unwarranted delays by the landlord after notice to make repairs of damages that have made the property unfit for occupancy

64. The remedy of unlawful detainer is most commonly used by offended:
    (A) Trustors
    (B) Holders of notes in default
    (C) Lessors
    (D) Grantors

65. Which of the following is a benefit of extended coverage title insurance over standard coverage?
    (A) Protection against forged deeds
    (B) Protection against capital improvements being on your neighbor's property
    (C) Protection against recorded instruments
    (D) Protection against lack of capacity

66. The requisites of a grant deed differ from those of a land contract in which of the following ways?
    (A) Warranties to purchaser
    (B) Signature of principals
    (C) Designation of price
    (D) All of these

67. Which of the following items would most likely be short rated in escrow?
    (A) Insurance
    (B) Trust deed
    (C) Real estate taxes
    (D) Interest

68. When handling an escrow for both parties, the escrow holder is acting as:
    (A) Employee
    (B) Independent contractor
    (C) Agent
    (D) Advocate

69. Escrow companies normally base their prorations on a year of:
    (A) 350 days
    (B) 355 days
    (C) 360 days
    (D) 365 days

70. Of the following, who is entitled to examine the records of the county recorder, without being an employee of the county recorder's office?
    (A) A bank employee
    (B) Any interested citizen
    (C) Employees of the Office of the County Recorder
    (D) Any of the above

71. Which of the following is most frequently employed to assure title to real property for a grantee?
    (A) Certificate of title
    (B) Title insurance
    (C) Recordation of trust deed
    (D) Warranty deed

72. In determining whether to insure title, the title company would rely most on documents found in the:
    (A) Chain of Title
    (B) Title Report
    (C) Title Search
    (D) Title Guarantee

Exam 5 - Financing Real Estate

1. In real estate finance, a Beneficiary Statement refers to:
    (A) Amount of profit realized by a lender
    (B) The amount of principal due on a loan
    (C) Terms of a lease
    (D) Amount of money an heir would inherit

2. Mr. Chan borrowed $85,000 from the Rainbow National Bank and is required to leave $8,000 on deposit with the bank for the full term of the loan. This is defined as:
    (A) Spreading
    (B) Prepayment balance
    (C) Surplus balance
    (D) Compensating balance

3. If the Federal Reserve Bank tightens reserve requirements of member banks, it would usually result in:
    (A) Fewer number of private second trust deeds
    (B) Favorable news from a broker's standpoint
    (C) Greater number of private second trust deeds
    (D) Making more marginal loans available

4. When a deed of trust is foreclosed by court sale, the action:
    (A) Is the same as a foreclosure by trustee's sale
    (B) Provides for a one year redemption period in some cases
    (C) Is not legal in California
    (D) Bars the possibility of a deficiency judgment

5. The nominal rate of a loan is the:
    (A) Actual interest paid
    (B) Amount of projected interest calculated by the lender
    (C) Interest rate indicated on the note
    (D) The term used by lenders when the maximum rate of interest allowed by law is obtained on financing a property

6. Which of the following lenders:

    Participates and supervises construction loans

    Solicits loans from anyone

    Involves itself in the secondary money market

    Represents other lending institutions
    (A) Mortgage company
    (B) Insurance company
    (C) Commercial bank
    (D) Savings and loan association

7. Which of the following would be included in an FHA loan?
   (A) Prepayment penalty
   (B) Secondary financing
   (C) Mortgage life insurance
   (D) Schedule of payments

8. A buyer assumes an FHA mortgage with the lender's approval and pays the seller's equity in cash and the lender charges the buyer a $30 fee. This fee is known as:
   (A) An assumption fee
   (B) A novation
   (C) Points
   (D) An origination fee

9. What is the lender's best protection against default if the purchaser makes no downpayment?
   (A) Low interest rate
   (B) Length of loan
   (C) Appreciation of the property
   (D) Low monthly payments

10. What is the most important influence affecting the interest rates on trust deed loans?
    (A) Exchange rate overseas
    (B) Gross National Product
    (C) Supply and demand of funds
    (D) None of the above

11. Which of the following is an advantage to the seller of real property in using a conditional sales contract in the sale of property instead of giving a grant deed and taking back a large trust deed?
    (A) The seller can prohibit the vendor from recording the contract if the contract includes a clause prohibiting such recording
    (B) A deficiency judgment can be obtained in the event of default
    (C) Foreclosure proceedings are faster thereby permitting the vendor to recover possession quickly from the buyer
    (D) None of the above

12. The document used when the seller extends credit to the buyer and the buyer receives equitable title is identified as:
    (A) Mortgage
    (B) Grant deed
    (C) Conditional/installment contract
    (D) None of the above

13. In a real estate transaction, a prepayment penalty may be paid by the:
    (A) Seller
    (B) Buyer
    (C) Lender
    (D) None of the above

14. The factor that exerts the greatest influence on mortgage interest rates is:
    (A) The condition of the money market
    (B) The value of the property
    (C) The term of the loan
    (D) The offsetting influence of conservative vs. nonconservative lenders

15. In qualifying a borrower for an FHA loan the lender would be most interested in which of the following?
    (A) Credit characteristics of the borrower
    (B) Ethnic background of the borrower
    (C) Purchase price of the property
    (D) Marital status of the borrower

16. A borrower who is financing the purchase of a property with an FHA insured loan would contact:
    (A) A broker
    (B) An arranger of credit
    (C) A mortgagee
    (D) FHA

17. A due on sale clause, whether it is enforceable or not, contained in a mortgage or trust deed is a type of:
    (A) Defeasible clause
    (B) Acceleration clause
    (C) Executed clause
    (D) Legally enforceable clause

18. A client contacts you to take a listing. You look at the papers and discover that the property is being purchased on a contract of sale. The contract contains no alienation clause and there are no restrictions in the contract of sale prohibiting resale or assignment. One of the following is the most nearly correct statement. Your client could:
    (A) Sell the interest in the property but only after paying off the existing contract of sale
    (B) Assign the contract but remain primarily liable unless released from the liability
    (C) Properly give a warranty deed to the property to the purchaser providing the deed recited "subject to the existing contract of sale"
    (D) Properly give a grant deed to the property to the purchaser providing a recorded purchase money second trust deed is given to make payments due on the original contract

19. Which of the following might be used as a security device to encumber real property?
    (A) Mortgage
    (B) Trust deed
    (C) Land contract
    (D) Any of the above

20. In an advertisement, *only* the annual percentage rate is mentioned. What else must also be disclosed in the ad?
    (A) Monthly payments required
    (B) Amount of loan
    (C) Amount of downpayment required
    (D) No further disclosures necessary

21. Which of the following is a unique feature of a VA loan as compared to a conventional loan?
    (A) VA downpayment of 3% of the purchase price
    (B) VA downpayment is determined by the Certificate of Reasonable Value
    (C) VA downpayment is 5% of the appraised value
    (D) A VA loan requires no downpayment

22. What type of mortgage loan would a mortgagor have if he were able to acquire more money before his mortgage term matured without any rewriting of the contract?
    (A) Subordination mortgage
    (B) Blanket mortgage
    (C) Closed end mortgage
    (D) Open end mortgage

23. Which of the following statements regarding a prepayment penalty in Cal-Vet financing is correct effective 1998?
    (A) The prepayment is 2% of the current loan balance
    (B) If a Cal-Vet loan is paid off within 2 years of inception it requires a 2% penalty based on the current loan balance
    (C) If a Cal-Vet loan is paid off within the first five years there is a prepayment penalty based on the original loan amount
    (D) There is no prepayment penalty for an early payoff on a Cal-Vet loan

24. In the brokering of loans, an amortization table is used to determine:
    (A) Annual Percentage Rate
    (B) Monthly payments
    (C) Interest rate
    (D) Term of repayment

25. Some real estate loans are written so that, if there are changes in the money market, the interest rate on the loan may be changed. This is:
    (A) A fluctuating money market loan
    (B) A variable interest rate loan
    (C) An interim loan
    (D) A loan secured by a short-term Land Contract of Sale

26. Which of the following would be covered by the Real Estate Settlement Procedures Act (RESPA)?
    (A) 40 acres of land for development
    (B) An addition to a duplex
    (C) An initial lien on a 1- to 4-family dwelling
    (D) A commercial building project

27. Which of the following would be covered by the Real Estate Settlement Procedures Act (RESPA)?
    (A) Land for development
    (B) An addition of a room in a single-family residence
    (C) An initial lien on a 1-4 residential unit building
    (D) A commercial building

28. Interest rates will normally decline when:
   (A) Inflationary trends accelerate
   (B) There is an excess of mortgage funds available
   (C) The Federal Reserve Board increases reserve requirements
   (D) The federal budget deficit is high

29. The clause in a trust deed by which the balance of the debt becomes immediately due and payable is called:
   (A) An alienation clause
   (B) A subordination clause
   (C) An acceleration clause
   (D) A release clause

30. Which of the following loan costs are not required to be disclosed as a finance charge to the customer under Federal Truth in Lending rules?
   (A) Buyer's points
   (B) Time-price differential
   (C) Credit investigation
   (D) Finder's fees

31. The National Housing Act of 1934, in addition to providing for the insuring of loans, has had a number of secondary benefits. These would include all of the following except:
   (A) Establishing maximum standards of construction
   (B) Comprehensive system of valuing property and rating mortgage risk
   (C) Stimulating mortgage investment on a nationwide basis
   (D) Scientific subdivision planning to reduce neighborhood deterioration

32. Which of the following is a correct statement?
   (A) The effective interest rate is the interest rate paid and the nominal interest rate is the minimal rate that is charged
   (B) The effective interest rate is the percentage of interest that is actually paid by the borrower and the nominal interest rate is the percentage of interest that is stated in the loan
   (C) The nominal interest rate is the percentage of interest that is actually paid by the borrower and the effective interest rate is the percentage of interest that is stated in the loan
   (D) The nominal interest rate is the same as the annual percentage rate (APR)

33. Which of the following is included as part of the finance charge in a Truth-in-Lending disclosure statement?
   (A) Appraisal fee
   (B) Recording and document fees
   (C) Title insurance fees
   (D) Assumption fee

34. In the processing of a real estate loan, a loan officer will correlate the characteristics of the borrower, the loan characteristics, and the characteristics of the property offered. The summary prepared after completion of the study is called:
   (A) A property appraisal
   (B) A mortgage evaluation
   (C) An offset statement
   (D) A credit rating

35.   Lenders frequently will lend up to 95% on conventional residential mortgages due to the availability of:
    (A)   Guaranteed Mortgage Insurance
    (B)   Mortgage Cancellation Insurance
    (C)   Private Mortgage Guaranty Insurance
    (D)   Fannie Mae Insurance

36.   The term "default" in most mortgages commonly means that the mortgagor:
    (A)   Is delinquent in monthly payments
    (B)   Is not using the property for its intended purpose
    (C)   Failed to maintain the property
    (D)   Any of the above

37.   In a period of inflation, the Federal Reserve Board would take which of the following actions to curb inflation:
    (A)   Reduce reserve requirements
    (B)   Lower discount rates
    (C)   Raise discount rates and buy bonds
    (D)   Raise reserve requirements and sell bonds

38.   Broker Wilson sells a house, and a loan for the buyer is secured through a savings and loan association. Wilson carefully explains all loan costs to the buyer. According to the Real Estate Settlement Procedures Act (RESPA), which of the following is true?
    (A)   Broker Wilson would not have to provide an estimate of settlement costs to the buyer because he had explained all costs
    (B)   Broker Wilson must provide the buyer with an estimate of settlement costs within one week
    (C)   The lender must provide an estimate of settlement costs to the buyer immediately
    (D)   The lender must provide the buyer with an estimate of settlement costs within 3 days

39.   Mr. Jones made application to Federal Pacific Bank for a loan November 1st. The loan was approved on November 5th. Mr. Jones waived his right to a Uniform Settlement Statement under RESPA in writing and escrow closed on November 15th. The lender must supply the Uniform Settlement Statement:
    (A)   To FHA only
    (B)   On November 15th, the settlement date
    (C)   Three days after the settlement date
    (D)   As soon as practical after the close of escrow

40.   Under the Real Estate Settlement Procedures Act (RESPA) lenders are required to give borrower:
    (A)   A Bill of Sale
    (B)   A good faith estimate
    (C)   The amount of mortgage interest
    (D)   An invoice not exceeding $10.00 for the special information booklet

41. Under the provisions of the Real Estate Settlement Procedures Act, which of the following would not be considered a violation?
    (A) Kickbacks
    (B) Unearned fees
    (C) Seller designating title insurance company
    (D) Buyer designating lender

42. In which of the following situations could a beneficiary of a trust deed acquire an interest in an after-acquired title?
    (A) Trustor added improvements to the property
    (B) Trustor purchased additional property
    (C) Personal property later became affixed to the real property
    (D) All of the above

43. A person purchased a property for $70,000 and made a $14,000 downpayment. If they borrowed the balance of the purchase price, it would be considered a purchase money trust deed if they received this amount from:
    (A) A lender
    (B) A friend
    (C) The seller
    (D) Any of the above

44. The Jacksons bought a residence with a first trust deed loan from a savings and loan. The Londons bought a residence with a first trust deed loan from a bank. The Londons refinanced, obtaining a first trust deed loan from a savings and loan, to get money for a business opportunity. Which of the following is correct?
    (A) Neither has the right of rescission
    (B) Both have the right of rescission
    (C) Jacksons do not have the right of rescission, the Londons do
    (D) Londons do not have the right of rescission, the Jacksons do

45. Which of the following is not a result of a subordination clause?
    (A) Permits a first trust deed to be refinanced and extended without losing priority
    (B) Allows for a construction loan to take priority
    (C) More of a risk to seller and may cause increased cost of the land and more stringent release clause
    (D) It causes hardship on the buyer by placing the lender of a larger sum in the favored position

46. A borrower would not prefer a straight note loan compared to an installment note loan at the same interest rate because:
    (A) The monthly payments on the straight note would be higher
    (B) The loan costs of an installment note would be lower
    (C) An installment note is not for a short time
    (D) The borrower could use the money borrowed for his business

47. Regarding "warehousing" operations with respect to real estate finance, which of the following would apply?
    (A) Contract for sale
    (B) The mortgage banker collecting loans prior to sale
    (C) Long term debentures insured collaterally by real estate loans
    (D) Holding notes for investment

59

48. Truth-in-Lending advertising that mentions graduated monthly payments, should include:
    (A) Location of the property
    (B) Broker's name
    (C) Schedule of monthly payments
    (D) Name and address of lender

49. From the lender's point of view, the most significant factor concerning a purchase money first mortgage is that it takes priority over:
    (A) Any liens against the seller at the time of sale
    (B) Real property tax liens
    (C) Any liens against the purchaser at the time of purchase
    (D) All liens at the time of sale

50. A trustor must get the permission of the beneficiary when which of the following occurs?
    (A) Boundary changes
    (B) Restriction agreement
    (C) Consolidation agreement
    (D) All of the above

51. Life insurance companies do not like to deal directly with trustors, but prefer to pay mortgage preparation and service fees to which of the following to handle their loans indirectly?
    (A) Cal-Vet
    (B) VA/FHA
    (C) Mortgage Bankers
    (D) All of the above

52. Under the Truth-in-Lending Law, the 3-day right of rescission would begin with which of the following events, if they occurred on different days in the sequence stated:
    (A) The date the loan application is made
    (B) The date the disclosure statement is delivered
    (C) The date the note is signed
    (D) The date the funds are disbursed

53. In setting up a release schedule under a blanket encumbrance the beneficiary will usually require a disproportionate amount of money to release a particular lot:
    (A) To have better security on the remaining lots
    (B) Because the best lots usually sell first
    (C) To protect the investment as individual lots are sold
    (D) All of the above

54. A real estate broker selling a property would have to ascertain that which of the following was not present in order to make sure that the existing loan could be assumed or paid off with no change in the interest rate or a penalty?
    (A) Acceleration clause
    (B) Acquisition clause
    (C) Subordination clause
    (D) Option clause

55. In which of the following situations would a "package mortgage" be used?
    (A) When including the obligations of a first and second trust deed under one instrument
    (B) When encumbering real property and using personal property as additional collateral
    (C) When covering more than one parcel of land in a subdivision
    (D) When securing additional financing from the lender at a later date without rewriting the mortgage

56. Which of the following words placed in a promissory note would commit all the borrowers for repayment?
    (A) Jointly
    (B) Individually and severally
    (C) Jointly and severally
    (D) Individually

57. A developer wants to purchase land and later secure financing for improvements. What clause is most beneficial to the developer in the original trust deed used to purchase the land?
    (A) Acceleration clause
    (B) Alienation clause
    (C) Exculpatory clause
    (D) Subordination clause

58. An acceleration clause was inserted in a negotiable note. The inclusion of the acceleration clause would:
    (A) Not have any effect on its negotiability
    (B) Cause it to lose its negotiability
    (C) Make it less negotiable
    (D) Not have any effect on its negotiability nor would it be of any benefit

59. In the event a trustor defaults on loan payments under a trust deed note, the lender has the right to call the entire loan due and payable. Should a lender take such an action, he would exercise which of the following?
    (A) Alienation clause
    (B) Release clause
    (C) Subordination clause
    (D) Acceleration clause

60. Who benefits most from a subordination clause in a trust deed?
    (A) Trustee
    (B) Trustor
    (C) Beneficiary
    (D) None of the above

61. A builder is selling a house that he had built under a blanket encumbrance. Under normal procedure, the instrument which would be requested of the beneficiary would be a:
    (A) Grant deed
    (B) Warranty deed
    (C) Partial reconveyance deed
    (D) Quitclaim deed

62. A subordination clause in a trust deed:
    (A) Permits the obligation to be paid off before the end of the term of the loan
    (B) Prohibits the trustor from obtaining another loan before the original loan is paid off
    (C) Places the loan in an inferior position in regard to other liens and encumbrances on the property
    (D) Allows readjustment and rescheduling of the terms as stated in the trust deed

63. If one property is not sufficient collateral for a loan, the lender would use which one of the following?
    (A) Open-end mortgage
    (B) Closed-end mortgage
    (C) Blanket mortgage
    (D) All-inclusive deed or trust

64. A clause in a second trust deed that permits the first trust deed to be refinanced without affecting its priority would be known as a(n):
    (A) Subordination clause
    (B) Alienation clause
    (C) Acceleration clause
    (D) Lien waiver

65. A statement provided by the payor on a promissory note that would list payments, term period of the note, principal balance, interest etc., is called:
    (A) Offset Statement
    (B) Beneficiary Statement
    (C) Release clause
    (D) Request for Partial Reconveyance

66. If the holder of a note wished to endorse the note and did not want to be liable for payment, he would use which of the following endorsements:
    (A) In blank
    (B) Qualified
    (C) Restrictive
    (D) None of the above

67. The person who would benefit the most from appreciation of a mortgaged property would be which of the following?
    (A) Trustee
    (B) Beneficiary
    (C) Trustor
    (D) None of the above

68. A lender has the following lending policies and characteristics:
    Makes many loans on commercial properties
    Makes relatively few construction loans
    Usually seeks to avoid administering loans
    Prefers to make long-term loans

    This describes which of the following lenders:
    (A) Life insurance companies
    (B) Federal savings and loans
    (C) Mortgage companies
    (D) Savings and loan associations

69. All of the following are secondary benefits of the Federal Housing Administration as established by the National Housing Act of 1934 except:
    (A) A loan amount appropriate for borrower's income
    (B) Elimination of short-term financing
    (C) Mortgage guarantee insurance with low premiums to protect the borrower
    (D) Establishment of improved building standards

70. If the Federal Reserve Board wanted to create a tight money market, it would:
    (A) Lower discount rates
    (B) Raise discount rates
    (C) Raise discount rates and buy bonds
    (D) Lower discount rates and sell bonds

71. Which of the following types of financing would least likely create a need for a cash down payment from a borrower?
    (A) FHA
    (B) Conventional
    (C) VA
    (D) Cal-Vet

72. Jensen purchased a house on which there was a mortgage loan. After two years she wants to refinance. What is the most probable reason for her wishing to do this?
    (A) The first loan was a short-term loan
    (B) There was no subordination clause
    (C) Small equity invested in the home
    (D) Loan had been discounted and sold

73. Crall is selling a house to Thomas. In order to consummate the deal, Crall must take back a note from Thomas secured by a second deed of trust. Of the following, which would most likely be the reason for this?
    (A) The sale is being conventionally financed
    (B) The initial financing is VA guaranteed
    (C) The current money market is tight
    (D) The rate on the second will have a low discount rate

74. Junior loans that are available today can be secured through:
    (A) Commercial banks
    (B) Individual lenders or private lenders
    (C) Savings and loans
    (D) All of the above

75. A woman purchased a home for $80,000 and executed a mortgage for $70,000. The balance she paid in cash. Subsequently, a period of slow economic inflation sets in. This would benefit:
    (A) Beneficiary
    (B) Trustor
    (C) Trustee
    (D) Neither the beneficiary nor the trustor

76. Which of the following is not included in the total finance charge under truth in lending?
    (A) Appraisal and credit report fees
    (B) Points paid by the buyer on a FHA/VA loan
    (C) Premium for mortgage guaranty or similar insurance
    (D) Finder's fee and similar charge

77. In making a decision with regard to a proposed real estate loan for a borrower, a lender normally seeks to minimize:
    (A) A borrower's difficulties with regard to the results of divorce, death, or unforeseen events
    (B) Overall net yield
    (C) Loan to value ratio
    (D) The number of substandard loans in his portfolio

78. When a home is mortgaged, the equity belongs to:
    (A) Trustor
    (B) Trustee
    (C) Beneficiary
    (D) None of the above

79. When a home appreciates in value, the major benefit goes to the:
    (A) Trustor
    (B) Trustee
    (C) Beneficiary
    (D) Mortgagee

80. A buyer bought a unit of real property for $300,000 with a $75,000 downpayment and a $225,000 mortgage. The value of the property soon increased by 10%. The owner's equity increased by 40% due to the use of:
    (A) Leverage
    (B) Inflation
    (C) Influence
    (D) Amortization

81. Arnold took out a $14,000 loan for 90 days. He paid $420 interest. What was the annual interest rate?
    (A) 9%
    (B) 10%
    (C) 11%
    (D) 12%

82. On FHA loans, mutual mortgage insurance:
    (A) Insures mortgagees against fire
    (B) Pays off the mortgage if the mortgagor dies
    (C) Insures the mortgagee against loss through foreclosure
    (D) Is paid for by the mortgagee

83. A land sales contract is sometimes referred to as a substitute for a note and trust deed when discussing financing. In this context, a land sales contract is considered:
    (A) An option
    (B) A security device
    (C) Identical to a mortgage
    (D) The same as a lease

84. The interest rate for an FHA loan is negotiated by:
    (A) Agreement between seller and buyer
    (B) Agreement between borrower and lender
    (C) FHA
    (D) Lender

85. A developer bought ten lots valued at $1,000 each, with a 20% downpayment, and the seller carried back the mortgage. The developer wants additional financing from a lender for construction purposes. Which of the following would least likely protect the lender of the construction loan?
    (A) Physical inspection of the property
    (B) A posted notice of non-responsibility
    (C) A subordination agreement in the purchase money deed of trust
    (D) An ALTA title insurance policy

86. Which of the following relates specifically to the secondary money market?
    (A) Junior loans
    (B) Discounting of mortgages
    (C) First mortgages
    (D) Purchase money

87. A mortgage loan is identified as which of the following?
    (A) A promissory note
    (B) An unsecured note
    (C) A loan collateralized by real property
    (D) Any recorded instrument related to financial transfer

88. A low loan to value ratio indicates:
    (A) A large loan
    (B) A high equity
    (C) A low downpayment
    (D) A government guaranteed loan

89. A hard money cash loan is generally made by:
    (A) A conventional lender
    (B) A savings and loan association
    (C) A private lender
    (D) Any of the above

90. When referring to real estate finance, the term "impounds" most nearly means:
    (A) Moratorium
    (B) Reserves
    (C) Attachment
    (D) Penalty

91. Depending on the availability of funds and market rates, the rate of interest most likely to be charged is:
    (A) A fluctuating money market rate
    (B) A variable interest rate
    (C) An interior loan rate
    (D) The rate charged on a short-term land contract of sale

92. The loan to value ratio in a mortgage is defined as:
    (A) Monthly payment of the loan on a mortgage
    (B) Amount of a loan as a percentage of the purchase price
    (C) Amount of a loan as a percentage of the appraised value
    (D) Amount of a loan as a percentage of the assessed value

93. Reserves or impound accounts are borrower's funds held by lenders in a reserve account to assure future payments for all of the following except:
    (A) Specific improvements/annual assessments
    (B) City/county taxes
    (C) Insurance premium
    (D) Monthly interest on a mortgage

94. The lender under a trust deed is called:
    (A) Trustee
    (B) Beneficiary
    (C) Trustor
    (D) Mortgagee

95. A borrower would not prefer a straight note loan compared to an installment note loan at the same interest rate because:
    (A) The monthly payments on the straight note would be higher
    (B) The loan costs of an installment note would be lower
    (C) An installment note is not for a short time
    (D) He or she could use the borrowed money for their business

96. When is there a late charge permitted on a mortgage payment on a home?
    (A) Right after the due date
    (B) When 15 days late
    (C) On the 10th day
    (D) After 10 days beyond the due date

97. Which of the following does not represent a demand source of mortgage money?
    (A) Sales financing
    (B) FNMA
    (C) Construction
    (D) Refinancing

98. Under Truth-in-Lending, a "Notice of Cancellation" could be given when:
    (A) The loan was used for business expansion
    (B) The loan was secured by the owner's residence
    (C) The loan was more than $25,000 and was not secured
    (D) The loan was secured by a commercial building

99.   There was a second trust deed for $5,000. The holder sold it to a friend for $3,500. In the language of real estate practice, this would be known as:
(A) Liquidating
(B) Hypothecation
(C) Depreciation
(D) Discounting

100.   A trustor, under a deed of trust, defaults on a note and refuses to reinstate the loan. The most expedient thing for the beneficiary to do is to institute a:
(A) Judicial foreclosure
(B) Lien sale
(C) Foreclosure sale
(D) Sheriff's sales

101.   On a conventional loan the rate of interest is generally:
(A) Less than on an FHA loan
(B) Greater than on an FHA loan
(C) The same as any loan source
(D) The maximum the law will allow

102.   Impounds are used as a safety measure to insure payment of certain recurring bills. A lender might require a borrower to make deposits into an impound account with each monthly payment. Which of the following would least likely be part of the impound deposit?
(A) Property taxes
(B) Mortgage interest
(C) Homeowner's association fees
(D) Assessment bond payments

103.   Discount points on financing under the California Farm and Home Purchase Act are paid by which of the following?
(A) The state
(B) The buyer
(C) The seller
(D) No one

104.   The minimum crawl space under a single-family residence according to FHA regulations is:
(A) 16"
(B) 18"
(C) 20"
(D) 24"

105. Under which of the following loan transactions would the lender have the best opportunity to secure a deficiency judgment in the event of a default and foreclosure?
      (A) A first trust deed and note executed in favor of a conventional lender, the proceeds being used to purchase a single-family residence
      (B) A first trust deed and note executed in favor of a private lender to secure a loan, the proceeds of which were used to purchase an automobile
      (C) A second trust deed and note executed by the buyer in favor of the seller of a ten-unit apartment
      (D) A first trust deed and note taken back by a subdivider as part of the purchase price of an unimproved lot

106. As the first line of defense in lending money on a residential property, a lender would look to which of the following?
      (A) Income of the borrower
      (B) Loan to value ratio
      (C) Property value
      (D) Installment payments of the amortized loan

107. In accordance with the Truth-in-Lending law, which of the following must be included in the advertisement for a graduated payment mortgage loan?
      (A) The location of the property
      (B) The address of the lender
      (C) The name of the broker
      (D) The amounts of different monthly payments

108. In a purchase of real property in which a land sales contract is used, the buyer has:
      (A) An estate of inheritance
      (B) A fee simple estate
      (C) Possessory rights
      (D) All of the above

Exam 6 - Valuation/Appraisal of Real Property

1.   Effective gross income reflects:
   (A)   Vacancies and credit losses
   (B)   Management expenses
   (C)   Taxes
   (D)   Depreciation

2.   All of the following would be considered substandard in a building except:
   (A)   Inadequate heating
   (B)   Dampness of rooms
   (C)   Electrical wiring that is not up to code, but was up to code at the time of construction and is safe
   (D)   Defect in exterior surface coverings

3.   A property was purchased for $193,000 at $4.40 per square foot. The depth of the property was 200 feet. What was the cost per front foot?
   (A) $220
   (B) $440
   (C) $880
   (D) $960

4.   An appraiser was employed by a buyer to appraise a commercial property that had some improvements that were affixed in such a manner as to have implications of questionable legality. The appraiser should:
   (A)   Appraise the property ignoring the improvements in question
   (B)   Appraise the property including the improvements in question because these improvements will be transferred in the sale with other improvements along with the land
   (C)   Appraise the property, try to ascertain the legality of the improvements, and state the reasons in his report
   (D)   Refuse to appraise this property for the buyer

5.   If the surface of a partition wall feels to be about the same temperature as the interior surface of an exterior wall this would indicate:
   (A)   There was adequate insulation
   (B)   Warm air is seeping through the walls
   (C)   Warm air is escaping through the vents
   (D)   Heating ducts are improperly installed

6.   Economic Obsolescence would include a loss of value due to:
   (A)   Over improvement by the property owner
   (B)   Oversupply of properties
   (C)   Poor layout
   (D)   Lack of parking

7. In the appraisal of a residential property, the appraiser would give the most consideration to which of the following?
   (A) Marketability and acceptability
   (B) Square footage and acceptability
   (C) Cost
   (D) Assessed value

8. The total square footage of the house in the illustration most nearly is:
   (A) 1440 sq. ft.
   (B) 1530 sq. ft.
   (C) 1700 sq. ft.
   (D) 2100 sq. ft.

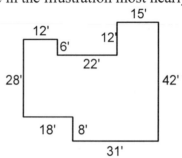

9. In an operating statement taxes and insurance would be:
   (A) Fixed expenses
   (B) Operating expenses
   (C) Variable expenses
   (D) Reserves for replacement

10. To determine the square footage of a house:
    (A) Measure the inside dimensions of rooms
    (B) Measure the outside of house as a whole
    (C) Measure the outside of house and garage
    (D) Measure the inside of the house

11. The fluctuations (activities) of the money market are extremely important to the real estate business. When interest rates go up and the income of a property is fixed, capitalized value of the property will:
    (A) Increase
    (B) Be unaffected in a short term
    (C) Decrease
    (D) Tend to stabilize

12. Amenities of residential real estate are:
    (A) Measurable on the market
    (B) Its capacity to provide shelter effectively
    (C) The property's physical attributes
    (D) Not considered by appraisers because they are intangible qualities

13. In determining the market value of a property, the appraiser considers:
    (A) Physical land and improvements thereon
    (B) Utility
    (C) Bundle of rights
    (D) All of the above

14. Which of the following is not true with respect to depreciation as determined by an appraiser?
    (A) It is loss of value from any cause
    (B) It is inherent in the property and not created by outside influences
    (C) It can be computed for both past and future
    (D) It can be determined by more than one method of appraisal

15. When determining the market value of real property, an appraiser considers the value of which of the following?
    (A) Physical land and improvements thereon
    (B) Utility
    (C) Bundle of Rights
    (D) All of the above

16. To analyze a leased property, an appraiser would consider:
    (A) Rent and other charges, date, parties, security and term
    (B) Covenants, right of assignment, option for renewal and provisions for disaster, condemnation, improvements and repairs
    (C) Both (A) and (B)
    (D) None of the above

17. A kiosk is:
    (A) A roof style
    (B) A method of home cooling
    (C) An information booth in a mall
    (D) A popular garden ornament

18. A salesperson obtained a listing and the salesperson stated that his broker will later appraise the property to verify the listing price. Which of the following statements is correct?
    (A) The broker cannot legally appraise the property
    (B) The broker may make an appraisal only if the broker is also a state-licensed or state-certified appraiser
    (C) The broker can make the appraisal but must charge a separate fee for this activity
    (D) The broker can make the appraisal if he prepares a narrative report that sets forth his extensive qualifications

19. For purpose of determining effective gross income of an apartment building, the appraiser would deduct from gross income all of the following except:
    (A) Collection losses
    (B) Rent concessions
    (C) Vacancies
    (D) Past contractual rent

20. Which of the following is improved value?
    (A) Market value of land and improvements
    (B) Market value divided by total rents
    (C) Difference between economic and contract rent
    (D) Cost of reproduction less depreciation

21. Which of the following reduces the usefulness of the market data approach to appraisal?
    (A) Rapid change in financing terms
    (B) Positive and negative effects of the comparison approach
    (C) Varied differences between financing terms
    (D) Rapidly fluctuating economy

22. Two houses were built on two adjacent lots of equal value. Construction costs and maintenance were the same. One house is appraised to be of higher value. What is most likely the reason?
    (A) One house had more economic obsolescence
    (B) One house had more wear and tear
    (C) One house was considered to have functional obsolescence
    (D) Both houses were across the street from a non-conforming house that resulted in economic obsolescence

23. A commercial development in a straight line along a major arterial street would identify:
    (A) A neighborhood shopping center
    (B) A commercial center
    (C) A strip commercial development
    (D) A commercial line

24. The gross multiplier is least likely to be used in the appraisal of:
    (A) Commercial property
    (B) Apartment buildings
    (C) A residence
    (D) Vacant land

25. The amount an appraiser charges for an appraisal is established by the:
    (A) Agreement between the appraiser and the client
    (B) Federal Housing Authority
    (C) Real Estate Commissioner
    (D) Office of Real Estate Appraisers

26. An appraiser would consider all of the following as contributing to the stability of a neighborhood except:
    (A) Homogeneity of buildings, people, and uses
    (B) Many families with children going to school
    (C) Increased density and rapid turnover of population
    (D) Residence in the path of urban directional growth

27. The value measure unit applied by an appraiser to express rental value of a warehouse space most likely is which of the following?
    (A) Front foot
    (B) Square foot
    (C) Cubic foot
    (D) Relationship between the size of the building and the size of the lot

28. An investor was going to have a building constructed that was to cost $300,000 and could, when completed, be leased for $5,000 per month. The annual operating expenses for the property would be $12,000. The amount the investor could invest in the land to realize a 12% return would be:
    - (A) Nothing since it is not economically feasible
    - (B) $12,000
    - (C) $100,000
    - (D) $300,000

29. In the capitalization of net income, the most difficult item for an appraiser to establish is the:
    - (A) Selection of a capitalization rate
    - (B) Effective gross income
    - (C) Determination of Net income
    - (D) Determination of Gross income

30. The standards that a state licensed or certified appraiser must follow are found in the:
    - (A) URAR
    - (B) MAI
    - (C) USPAP
    - (D) NAR

31. If an appraiser is using the Property Residual method, the unknown and desired result is:
    - (A) Land value
    - (B) Net income
    - (C) Property value
    - (D) Capitalization rate

32. A fee appraiser:
    - (A) Assesses land for the government
    - (B) Works full-time for a broker
    - (C) Is a self-employed appraiser who appraises property for a fee
    - (D) Works full-time for a lender

33. In the valuation process, an appraiser would be least concerned with:
    - (A) The identification of real estate
    - (B) The identification of the property rights being appraised
    - (C) The assessed value
    - (D) The definition of value

34. An appraiser, when making an appraisal of real property, would be least concerned with which of the following?
    - (A) Assessed value
    - (B) Sale price
    - (C) Replacement cost
    - (D) Comparable sales

35. The principle of value, which affirms that a purchaser will buy goods and services at the lowest cost available, is:
    - (A) Regression
    - (B) Inflation
    - (C) Retribution
    - (D) Substitution

36. Quality, quantity, and durability are considered in the appraisal of an income property. An appraiser takes into account the quality of income by means of which of the following?
    (A) Capitalization rate
    (B) Q, Q, and D
    (C) Capitalized income
    (D) Depreciation

37. The maximum possible income an income property can yield is:
    (A) Gross scheduled income
    (B) Effective gross income
    (C) Net income
    (D) Net spendable income

38. Which of the following is an indirect method of calculating accrued depreciation?
    (A) Age-life
    (B) Breakdown
    (C) Capitalized income
    (D) Engineering

39. Gross income $25,000
        Fixed expenses   7,000
        Operating expenses 8,000
        Total expenses   - 15,000
        Net income $10,000

    Above is an abbreviated operating statement of an apartment building. Based on other apartment houses in the area, the owner was advised that if he raised his rent by 10% his net income would be increased by:
    (A) $1,000
    (B) Proportionately
    (C) 20%
    (D) 25%

40. In planning a shopping center in a suburban community, which of the following would be the most important consideration?
    (A) Location
    (B) Amenities
    (C) Proximity of shipping and warehousing facilities
    (D) Purchasing power

41. The easiest way for an appraiser to calculate the present value of a building would be by:
    (A) A quantity survey
    (B) A unit-in-place cost method
    (C) A review of the building permit records
    (D) Market data

42. In the narrative form of appraisal report, where would the property value be stated?
    (A) Description of use
    (B) Description of the neighborhood
    (C) Purpose of the appraisal
    (D) Legal description of the property

74

43. Which of the following is the most expensive and difficult type of appraisal?
    (A) Unit-cost-in-place
    (B) Quantity survey
    (C) Square foot cost
    (D) Development

44. The gross rent multiplier is developed by:
    (A) Dividing the sales price by the gross monthly income
    (B) Dividing the gross monthly income by the sales price
    (C) Dividing the gross monthly income by the assessed value
    (D) Dividing the gross monthly income by the market value

45. An appraiser is employed to advise an apartment owner of the economic feasibility of construction of a swimming pool. The appraiser would be most concerned with which valuation principle?
    (A) Principle of Regression
    (B) Principle of Contribution
    (C) Principle of Integration
    (D) Principle of Substitution

46. In the sales comparison approach, the adjusted sales price of the comparable property is:
    (A) The only indication of the market value
    (B) Indicated by agreement between the buyer and the seller
    (C) An estimate of value of the comparable property with similar prominent characteristics to the subject property
    (D) A direct relationship to market value

47. An investment that would best hold its value as a hedge against inflation would be:
    (A) A no risk investment
    (B) An income producing investment that would maintain its value
    (C) An investment similar to an annuity
    (D) an investment that has a high degree of liquidity

48. When comparing physical life to economic life, the economic life is usually:
    (A) The same
    (B) Lesser
    (C) Greater
    (D) Depends on the improvement

49. In appraisal, the following are recognized methods for the valuation of land except:
    (A) Comparative method
    (B) Equity method
    (C) Abstraction method
    (D) Development method

50. All of the following statements about depreciation are true except:
    (A) It is a loss of value from any cause
    (B) It can be a loss of value due to wear and tear
    (C) It includes all influences that reduce the value of property below replacement cost
    (D) It always is concerned with intrinsic factors but never with extraneous factors

51. An appraiser wants to appraise a property using comparable sales prices of similar homes. Adjustments for difference between the home and comparables will be made by adjusting:
    (A) Comparables to the normal
    (B) Comparables to the subject property
    (C) Subject property to the normal
    (D) Subject property to the comparables

52. If an appraiser was appraising a residence built in 1910, which of the following would he use?
    (A) Cost-of-living index of 1910
    (B) Original cost of materials in 1910
    (C) Cost-of-living index that increased from 95 to 128
    (D) Today's cost of reproduction

53. Which of the following would least likely affect the stabilization of value on a single-family residence in a residential neighborhood?
    (A) Zoning
    (B) Newness
    (C) Private restrictions
    (D) Availability of public transportation

54. If the gross income on a commercial property is $265,000 on a quarterly basis and the expenses are 32% of the gross annual income, what is the net annual income?
    (A) $720,800
    (B) $1,060,000
    (C) $143,000
    (D) $339,200

55. It is known that a prudent buyer will not pay more for a property than he could purchase another suitable property for if there is no undue delay in acquiring the other property. This is considered the principle of:
    (A) Substitution
    (B) Anticipation
    (C) Competition
    (D) Contribution

56. The basic economic characteristic that best expresses real estate value is:
    (A) High replacement cost
    (B) Proximity to high rentals
    (C) Prospect of speculative gain
    (D) Maximum utility of available resources

57. These paragraph headings, Introduction, Description of General Neighborhood, Market Value and Economic Factors, and Final Estimate of Value, would be present in which type of appraisal?
    (A) Form (summary)
    (B) Letter (restricted)
    (C) Narrative (self-contained or summary)
    (D) None of the above

58. Wall studs are placed on and secured to which of the following?
    (A) Joist
    (B) Sole plate
    (C) Girders
    (D) Sub-flooring

59. The Principal of Substitution applies to:
    (A) Structural design
    (B) Income
    (C) Use
    (D) All of the above

60. An appraiser may apply the Principle of Substitution in which of the following appraisal methods?
    (A) Market Data approach
    (B) Income approach
    (C) Cost approach
    (D) Any of the above

61. When must an appraiser be licensed or certified by the state?
    (A) In a federally related transaction
    (B) To appraise real property
    (C) To call themselves an appraiser
    (D) To collect a fee

62. Depth tables are prepared and used by:
    (A) Mutual water companies to show the depth where water is found in desert areas
    (B) Appraisers to determine the value of property where lots vary in depth
    (C) Accountants to facilitate the figuring of interest payments on declining balances
    (D) The Department of Recreation in connection with beach properties in relation to high tides

63. The expansion and contraction of available space is due to market fluctuations of:
    (A) Prices and rents
    (B) Elasticity of demand
    (C) Permanence of residence
    (D) Financing terms

64. If the gross annual income is $56,400 and the yearly net income is 15% of that amount, the monthly net income is:
    (A) $683.00
    (B) $819.00
    (C) $705.00
    (D) $638.00

65. An owner has a 100-unit apartment house. Which of the following items would be deductible from the gross income in determining net operating income?
    (A) Depreciation
    (B) Income tax
    (C) Mortgage payments of principal and interest
    (D) Wages for part-time gardeners and maintenance personnel

66.   Usefulness of the cost approach is limited when appraising:
        (A)   An older property with many functional deficiencies
        (B)   A new structure on an appropriate site
        (C)   In an unusually active real estate market
        (D)   For construction

67.   In establishing an estimate of value by appraisal, it is very important to differentiate between the purpose of the appraisal and:
        (A)   The principles of appraisal
        (B)   Function for which the appraisal is being made
        (C)   Amenities to the owner
        (D)   The appraisal process

68.   On hot days, customers prefer to walk in the shade. Certain locations, due to the sun's fading effect on display window clothing, are the least desirable. Which of the following is the least desirable side of the street for a clothing retailer.
        (A)   Northeast
        (B)   Southwest
        (C)   Southeast
        (D)   Northwest

69.   An appraiser using the replacement cost approach on an older residential property would use all of the following except:
        (A)   Depreciation
        (B)   Capitalization of income
        (C)   Land value
        (D)   Cost of improvements new

70.   Why are more buildings torn down than fall down?
        (A)   Taste and environmental changes occur faster than buildings wear out
        (B)   Newly constructed buildings are being built better than before
        (C)   The scope of urban renewal is expanding rapidly
        (D)   Zoning is no longer an effective means of controlling land use

71.   There are three main causes of depreciation. Which one of these finds its origin in social sources which is the basis for the old axiom, known in social circles, that "more houses are torn down than fall down"?
        (A)   Economic obsolescence
        (B)   Functional obsolescence
        (C)   Straight-line depreciation
        (D)   Physical deterioration

72.   An apartment house under construction has many prospective renters. The city now wants to widen the street. This change results in a 10% loss of renters. This loss would be an example of:
        (A)   Economic obsolescence
        (B)   Functional obsolescence
        (C)   Physical obsolescence
        (D)   Physical deterioration

73. Which of the following is an indirect method to determine accrued depreciation?
    (A) Age-life method
    (B) Capitalized income
    (C) Cost approach
    (D) Engineering method

74. A roof which slopes upward from all four sides and is joined at the ridge is called a:
    (A) Gable roof
    (B) Gambrel roof
    (C) Mansard roof
    (D) Hip roof

75. Among the following, the best definition of capitalization is:
    (A) The highest rate of return on an investment
    (B) The minimum rate of return on an investment
    (C) The result of dividing net income by a percentage rate of return to determine value
    (D) The relationship between value and net worth

76. Which of the following would not be used to determine net income for an income property?
    (A) Vacancies
    (B) Management fees
    (C) Mortgage interest
    (D) Maintenance costs

77. While appraising a single-family residence that is renting for $640 per month, the appraiser finds that the home across the street recently sold for $90,000 and had been renting at the time of sale for $600 per month. Based on this data, the appraised value would be:
    (A) $90,000
    (B) $96,000
    (C) $110,000
    (D) $124,000

78. A prudent buyer would not pay more for a parcel of real estate than he would have to pay for another similar parcel based on the Principle of:
    (A) Balance
    (B) Supply and demand
    (C) Highest and best use
    (D) Substitution

79. An income property showed a value of $800,000 when capitalized at a rate of 9%. A new investor wishing to purchase the same property engaged an appraiser who used a capitalization rate of 12%. According to the appraiser, the value would be:
    (A) $800,000
    (B) $600,000
    (C) $300,000
    (D) $224,000

80. In which of the following appraisal approaches may an appraiser be asked to predict the future value of a property?
    (A) Market
    (B) Cost
    (C) Capitalization
    (D) Summation

81. If there is a transition from a buyer's market to a seller's market, which of the following would be the result?
    (A) It would have no effect on the price
    (B) Sales prices would increase because of an increase in demand and a lag in supply
    (C) Sales prices would decrease because of a decrease in demand and an increase in supply
    (D) It would cause a decrease in land development and construction of new homes

82. An investor who owned a 40-unit apartment building found that his vacancy factor had increased by $400 per month. If the property is capitalized at 12%, what is the loss in value of the property due to the increased vacancy factor?
    (A) $4,000
    (B) $4,800
    (C) $40,000
    (D) $400,000

83. The most difficult step for an appraiser in the gain over the Sales Comparison Approach is to:
    (A) Collect data
    (B) Analyze data
    (C) Adjust the comparable to the subject property
    (D) Average data

84. What is the indicated value of a property that produces a gross monthly income of $2,400 and the appropriate multiplier is 10.72?
    (A) $25,000
    (B) $108,000
    (C) $225,000
    (D) $308,000

85. Smith built a $250,000 house in a neighborhood in which houses are valued between $75,000 and $85,000. Any resulting loss of value would be an example of:
    (A) Physical depreciation
    (B) Functional obsolescence
    (C) Economic obsolescence
    (D) Physical obsolescence

86. The recognized definition of highest and best use includes the term:
    (A) Net return
    (B) Effective gross income
    (C) Multiple units
    (D) Income production

87. A lot on which there was a structure of no value was appraised for highest and best use. The appraiser would:
    (A) Appraise the value of the land and deduct the cost of demolition
    (B) Ignore the structure's salvage cost
    (C) Appraise the value of the land and add the cost of demolition
    (D) Appraise the value of the land and ignore the cost of demolition

88. A recommendation for the best appraisal method to be used to estimate the value of a vacant parcel of land would be:
    (A) Income approach
    (B) Cost approach
    (C) Sales comparison approach
    (D) An average of the first two methods

89. An owner of an apartment building under construction has many prospective renters. The city now wants to widen the street by 15 feet. The result is a 10% loss of prospective renters. This loss would be an example of:
    (A) Physical deterioration
    (B) Physical obsolescence
    (C) Functional obsolescence
    (D) Economic obsolescence

90. An appraiser determines the accrual for depreciation in the use of:
    (A) Sales comparison approach
    (B) Cost approach
    (C) Income approach
    (D) None of the above

91. Under the cost approach, the replacement cost is distinguished from the reproduction cost because replacement cost is defined as the cost of constructing an improvement with:
    (A) Substantially the same utility as the property being appraised
    (B) The same materials as were used in the original construction
    (C) Either (A) or (B)
    (D) Neither (A) nor (B)

92. Smith owns an older apartment building and is considering the merits of an expensive remodeling plan. The deciding factor that would be instrumental on his final decision would be the:
    (A) Cost of the plan
    (B) Wishes of the tenants
    (C) Potential increases in the real property taxes
    (D) Effect of the plan on the net income

93. An appraiser would most likely use a depth table in appraising which of the following types of property?
    (A) Residential
    (B) Commercial
    (C) Rural
    (D) Industrial

94. The appraiser is called upon to estimate a value to real property based upon its future utility by forecasting. In the appraisal process, "forecasting" consists of:
    (A) Taking the past as a guide to the future with no modification or justification for the projection other than the historical pattern of past developments
    (B) Taking the past as a guide to the future together with judgments for the projection of the future
    (C) Projecting into the future with absolute certainty
    (D) None of the above

95. In the appraisal of a residential property, the appraiser would give the most consideration to which of the following?
    (A) Marketability and availability
    (B) Square footage—total and living
    (C) Cost
    (D) Assessed valuation

96. Which of the following would contribute to the functional obsolescence of a building?
    (A) Declining neighborhood
    (B) Adverse zoning across the street from the property
    (C) Massive cornices on a building
    (D) Rotten mudsills

97. To find the details of the subfloor, such as size and dimensions of concrete piers, footings, and other detailed construction measurement, a real estate licensee would examine which of the following?
    (A) Floor plan
    (B) Plot plan
    (C) Foundation plan
    (D) Elevation plan

98. Which of the following would least likely protect a single-family residential neighborhood from losing value?
    (A) Introduction of average-priced homes in an area of better quality properties of the same type
    (B) Residents in the area have the same income
    (C) Minor change in zoning regulations
    (D) Most families are from the same religious and ethnic group

99. An appraiser using the land residual approach is attempting to determine:
    (A) Building value
    (B) Land value
    (C) Capitalization rate
    (D) Income

100. The fluctuation (activities) of the money market is extremely important to the real estate business. When interest rates go up and income of a property is fixed, capitalized value of the property will:
    (A) Increase
    (B) Be unaffected in a short term
    (C) Decrease
    (D) Tend to stabilize

101.   In order to arrive at an effective gross income for rental properties, an appraiser should deduct which of the following from gross income?
(A)   Real property taxes
(B)   Repairs
(C)   Vacancies and collection losses
(D)   Depreciation

102.   An appraiser in evaluating a residence will consider all of the following to be signs of economic obsolescence except:
(A)   A residence near an airport with constant noise of take-offs and landings
(B)   An air-condition/heating system that does not work
(C)   Adverse zoning
(D)   Proximity of a nuisance

103.   In appraising a property using the market data approach, how would an appraiser treat the value of a feature found in the comparable property but not found in the subject property?
(A)   Add the value of the amenity to the subject property
(B)   Subtract the value of the amenity from the sales price of the comparable property
(C)   Disregard the value of the feature, as no two properties are exactly alike
(D)   Treat the amenity as not included in the valuation

104.   If an appraiser does not adhere to appraisal standards (USPAP) for the purpose of defrauding an FDIC insured lender, the appraiser could be guilty of:
(A)   A misdemeanor
(B)   Violating Department of Real Estate Rules and Regulations
(C)   An ethics violation
(D)   A felony

Exam 7 - Real Estate Practice

1. An agency contract can be created by all of the following except:
    (A) Appointment by the principal
    (B) Implied contract in law
    (C) Oral contract
    (D) Voluntary offer by the agent

2. A Fictitious Business Name Statement must be renewed and filed with the County Clerk in the county where the business is located and operated:
    (A) Never, unless abandoned
    (B) Every five (5) years, by December 31st of said year
    (C) By June 30th
    (D) One (1) year from original filing

3. Termination of an agency may occur by all of the following except:
    (A) Extinction of the subject matter of the agency
    (B) Renunciation of the agency by the broker
    (C) Mutual abandonment of the agency by all parties
    (D) Revocation by the principal if the agent has an interest in the subject matter of the agency

4. At what point would an individual be considered incapable of handling his own affairs because of mental incompetence?
    (A) An individual voluntarily commits himself to a mental institution for psychiatric treatment
    (B) After proper procedures are followed, an individual is committed to a mental hospital for psychiatric treatment
    (C) An individual goes to work every day, visits a psychiatrist twice a week, but is unable to perform his duties at work
    (D) A conservator is appointed by a court to oversee an individual's business affairs.

5. A selling agent who is the exclusive agent for the buyer can do all of the following except:
    (A) Submit his client's offer to the seller and seller's agent with the seller's approval
    (B) Personally submit the buyer's offer to the seller
    (C) Withhold negative information about the buyer
    (D) Act as the seller's agent since the seller is the one paying the commission

6. An executed contract is a contract:
    (A) Completed and fully performed by both parties
    (B) Under the jurisdiction of the probate court
    (C) Signed, notarized and recorded
    (D) To be rewritten

7. Which of the following new laws became effective on January 1, 1988?
    (A) Mortgage Loan Disclosure Law
    (B) Agency Relationships in Residential Real Property Transactions Law
    (C) Real Estate Settlement Procedures Act
    (D) Truth In Lending Law

8. All of the following can sue for specific performance except:
   (A) Purchaser of a residential property
   (B) Seller of a large tract of land
   (C) An Attorney-in-fact acting for the principal
   (D) A broker acting as the agent for the principal

9. The quickness with which assets can be converted into cash is known as:
   (A) Yield
   (B) Leverage
   (C) Liquidity
   (D) Risk

10. When is the best time for a seller to obtain a termite report?
    (A) Before determining the sales price
    (B) Before putting the house on the market
    (C) Before opening escrow
    (D) After the lender's appraisal

11. Broker Wilson did not present a second offer on a particular property but rather held it as a backup offer while the seller was considering the first offer.
    (A) This was permissible
    (B) This is not permissible since he should present all offers
    (C) This was not permissible, as the second offer should be returned so the offeror can make a larger offer
    (D) This is not permissible, as the second offer should be returned to the offeror so that he might look at other property

12. Which of the following elements is not necessary in the formation of a contract?
    (A) Offer
    (B) Acceptance
    (C) Consideration
    (D) Performance

13. An agent may collect a commission for a negotiated sale after the term of the listing contract expired if:
    (A) There is an alienation clause
    (B) Agent sues the principal for liquidated damages
    (C) Agent signs a release clause
    (D) The contract contains a protection period clause

14. A listing agreement is a(n):
    (A) Promise for a promise
    (B) Employment contract
    (C) Bilateral executory contract
    (D) All of the above

15. When dealing with the public, a broker must:
    (A) Not refuse to take a listing
    (B) Delegate responsibilities to another person
    (C) Disclose all material facts known only to him or her
    (D) All of the above

16. When a business is sold with real property:
    (A) One deposit receipt must be used
    (B) The same escrow and title company must be used for both the sale of the business and the sale of the real property
    (C) Two deposit receipts may be used
    (D) An escrow need not be used in the sale of the business

17. There are several reasons why a contract can be voidable. However, a voidable contract is binding on the parties until it is:
    (A) Discovered
    (B) Invalidated
    (C) Rescinded
    (D) Qualified

18. A written statement that is sworn to or affirmed in the presence of a notary is:
    (A) An allocation
    (B) A ratification
    (C) An affidavit
    (D) An estoppel

19. If you, as a broker, are the buyer's agent, you will want others to know:
    (A) After the offer is accepted
    (B) Before the close of escrow
    (C) After you get your commission
    (D) As soon as possible

20. A contract providing for the payment of commission to the broker regardless of who sells the property, including the owner, is:
    (A) A net listing
    (B) An open listing
    (C) An exclusive agency listing
    (D) An exclusive authorization and right to sell listing

21. Investors would place their money into which of the following as a hedge against inflation?
    (A) Trust deeds and mortgages
    (B) Equities
    (C) Savings accounts
    (D) Government bonds

22. The clause which provides that the broker is eligible for a commission after the termination of an authorization to sell is the:
    (A) Liquidated damages clause
    (B) Probate clause
    (C) Protection clause
    (D) Anti-theft clause

23. The most common listing agreement allows the broker to:
    (A) Find a purchaser, obtain an offer, and bind the principal to that offer
    (B) Guarantee the purchaser will accept
    (C) Find a purchaser, fill out the deposit receipt, obtain an offer and present it
    (D) Convey title

24. An offer is terminated by:
    (A) Revocation by the offeree
    (B) Rejection by the offeror
    (C) Rejection by the offeree
    (D) A change in the offer made by the offeror

25. The broker who most likely has earned a commission is the one who has:
    (A) Communicated acceptance by seller to buyer
    (B) Communicated buyer's offer to seller
    (C) Secured acceptance of an offer
    (D) Secured a substantial deposit with an offer

26. A portfolio risk manager should be concerned with which of the following?
    (A) Liquidity
    (B) Reserves
    (C) Diversification
    (D) All of the above

27. Equity in real estate is commonly referred to as:
    (A) The difference between market value and outstanding liens
    (B) Downpayment
    (C) The difference between market value and loan amount
    (D) All of the above

28. Two parties entered into a contract, but one of the parties had previously been adjudged incompetent. The other party to the contract was not aware of this fact. What is the status of this contract?
    (A) Void
    (B) Illegal
    (C) Voidable
    (D) Enforceable if the seller could prove there was no coercion involved

29. Which of the following would be included in a bona fide listing agreement?
    (A) Commission, sales price, signatures, address, terms of the sale
    (B) Financing terms, sales price, commission, address, signature of one party
    (C) Sales price, commission, sales costs, address, signature of the broker
    (D) Signatures of both sellers, address, financing terms, condition of terms, sales price

30. Broker Rowe negotiated an exchange agreement between Hansen and Crowley. Hansen and Crowley signed agreements independent of each other to pay a commission. Later, in escrow Crowley breached the contract. Hansen then sold the property through another broker with whom Hansen had previously had the property listed. A court action by Rowe against Crowley for a commission would most likely result in:
    (A) A judgment against Crowley for full payment of a commission per terms of the contract
    (B) A judgment against Crowley and Rowe for payment of both commissions
    (C) A judgment against Crowley only if Rowe fails to join with Hansen as defendants in the suit
    (D) A judgment against Crowley for both commissions with right of contribution against Hansen for one half of the judgment amount

31. A real estate broker, as an agent, must follow the lawful instructions of his principal in a real estate transaction. Failing to do so, the broker:
    (A) Is liable for damages to the principal as a result
    (B) Is subject to loss of license in a court of jurisdiction
    (C) Is subject to a fine or imprisonment according to the law
    (D) Any of the above

32. Before the purchaser is advised of the seller's acceptance of an offer, the purchaser can withdraw his offer:
    (A) Provided the offer is not irrevocable
    (B) Provided the offeree has breached the offer
    (C) Provided the offer is breached by the seller
    (D) For any reason

33. All of the following are necessary for the creation of an agency agreement except:
    (A) Consideration
    (B) Mutual agreement of the parties
    (C) Competency of the seller
    (D) Fiduciary relationship

34. A real estate broker could be held liable to a buyer if he or she:
    (A) Unknowingly makes a misrepresentation to the buyer based on false information given by the seller
    (B) Executes an agreement with the buyer on behalf of the seller under a power of attorney granted by seller
    (C) Acts in excess of the authority given by the seller under a listing agreement
    (D) Retains the buyer's check at the seller's request after the seller has accepted an offer and acceptance has been communicated to the buyer

35. A real estate licensee negotiated the sale of a farm for a seller. The agent's commission can be paid in which of the following forms?
    (A) Assignment of funds from buyer to seller
    (B) Assignment of existing note
    (C) Check or cash
    (D) Any of the above

36. In order for a contract for the transfer of real property to be binding on the buyer and seller, it must:
    (A) Be recorded
    (B) Have an offer and acceptance
    (C) Be acknowledged
    (D) Satisfy all of the above

37. An attorney-in-fact is:
    (A) An attorney or executor of an estate
    (B) A principal in a transaction
    (C) A legally competent person acting on behalf of another
    (D) All of the above

38. All of the following would terminate an offer except:
    (A) A counteroffer by the offeree
    (B) A party to the offer dies
    (C) Revocation of the offer by the offeror after the offeree posted legal notice of acceptance
    (D) The offeror revokes the offer before acceptance is communicated to him

39. Broker Hardy received a listing from Watson to sell Watson's commercial property, along with an option for Hardy to purchase within 30 days. After 27 days, Hardy decided to exercise his option and purchase the property. The broker must:
    (A) Inform Watson of all material facts concerning the property
    (B) Disclose his potential profit and obtain the written consent of the principal approving the amount of such profit
    (C) Present all outstanding offers to Watson
    (D) All of the above

40. What binds buyer and seller in a contract?
    (A) Recording
    (B) Offer and acceptance
    (C) Acknowledgment
    (D) Title insurance

41. Why is a legal description recommended in a sales contract?
    (A) To help cooperating salespersons to find the property
    (B) The lender requests it
    (C) The seller may have other properties in the area
    (D) For the title company to locate the property

42. Under authority of a signed exclusive agency listing, Broker Davis diligently advertised for sale the $165,000 home of owner Johnson. Prior to the expiration date of the listing, Johnson sold the home to a friend. Davis was refused payment of any commission whatsoever. Davis is legally entitled to receive from Johnson:
    (A) No commission
    (B) One-half commission
    (C) All expenses incurred in advertising the home
    (D) Full commission

43. A contract signed under duress would be:
    (A) Void
    (B) Unenforceable
    (C) Voidable
    (D) Illegal

44. Which of the following requires the Real Estate Transfer Disclosure Statement?
    (A) Foreclosure of 1-4 residential units
    (B) Sales transaction of 1-4 residential units
    (C) Transfer of 1-4 residential units in bankruptcy
    (D) All of the above

45. Which of the following is not essential in the creation of an agency:
    (A) Fiduciary relationship
    (B) Capacity of parties
    (C) Lawful object
    (D) Payment of consideration

46. A broker who is not authorized to accept deposits in his listing agreement must inform the offeror that:
    (A) No deposits will be accepted
    (B) It is implied by law that if authorized by the seller, deposits can be accepted
    (C) An agent must accept all deposits
    (D) The risk of loss lies solely with the buyer. The seller will not be liable in event of loss of the deposit

47. A wife signs an agreement to sell community real property. The contract as it applies to them is:
    (A) Void
    (B) Enforceable
    (C) Unenforceable
    (D) Illegal

48. A real estate broker is most likely to receive a commission from both parties when involved in which of the following transactions?
    (A) The selling of a business opportunity
    (B) A short-term lease
    (C) Tax-free exchange
    (D) Negotiation of a loan

49. John and Mary Jackson gave broker Jones a $500 deposit to cover closing costs and signed an offer to purchase a home for $65,000 provided they could obtain a loan for the full price of the home. Included in the offer to purchase was a clause which read, "Subject to buyers obtaining a VA loan in the amount for $65,000, secured by subject property, payable over a period of 30 years at 11 1/2% interest with monthly payments to be approximately $644 per month, plus taxes and insurance." Which of the options below most nearly represents what was intended by the clause?
    (A) If the full $65,000 loan is not obtainable, buyers and seller may renegotiate the sale on different terms
    (B) If the $65,000 loan is not obtainable, the buyers may cancel their offer and recover the $500 deposit
    (C) If the maximum loan available is $63,000 buyers may pay the difference of $2,000 and proceed with purchase
    (D) Any of the above

ASSOCIATION OF REALTORS

REAL ESTATE PURCHASE CONTRACT AND RECEIPT FOR DEPOSIT
THIS IS MORE THAN A RECEIPT FOR MONEY. IT IS INTENDED TO BE A LEGALLY BINDING CONTRACT. READ IT CAREFULLY.
CALIFORNIA ASSOCIATION OF REALTORS® (CAR) STANDARD FORM

DATE: _Feb. 2,_ , 19 _95_ AT _Sacramento,_ , California,
RECEIVED FROM _John J. Smith and Mary Smith, husband and wife_ ("Buyer")
THE SUM OF _Four Thousand_ Dollars $ _4,000_

as a deposit to be applied toward the
PURCHASE PRICE OF _one hundred twenty-five thousand_ Dollars $ _125,000_
FOR PURCHASE OF PROPERTY SITUATED IN _Sacramento_ , COUNTY OF _Sacramento_ , California,
DESCRIBED AS _123 Happy Valley Lane_ ("Property").

1. **FINANCING: THE OBTAINING OF THE LOAN(S) BELOW IS A CONTINGENCY OF THIS AGREEMENT.** Buyer shall act diligently and in good faith to obtain all applicable financing.

   A. FINANCING CONTINGENCY shall remain in effect until (Check ONLY ONE of the following):
      1. ☐ (If checked). The designated loan(s) is/are funded and/or the assumption of existing financing is approved by Lender.
      OR 2. ☑ (If checked). _60_ calendar days after acceptance of the offer. Buyer shall remove the financing contingency in writing within this time. If Buyer fails to do so, then Seller may cancel this agreement by giving written notice of cancellation to Buyer.

   B. OBTAINING OF DEPOSIT AND DOWN PAYMENT by the Buyer is NOT a contingency, unless otherwise agreed in writing.

   C. DEPOSIT to be deposited ☑ with Escrow Holder, ☐ into Broker's trust account, or ☐ _____ $ _4,000_
      BY ☑ Personal check, ☐ Cashier's check, ☐ Cash, or ☐ _____,
      PAYABLE TO _Broker_
      TO BE HELD UNCASHED UNTIL the next business day after acceptance of the offer, or ☐ _____

   D. INCREASED DEPOSIT, within _7_ calendar days after acceptance of the offer, to be deposited ☑ with Escrow Holder,
      ☐ into Broker's trust account, or ☐ _____ $ _16,000_

   E. BALANCE OF DOWN PAYMENT to be deposited with Escrow Holder on demand of Escrow Holder . . . . $ _5,000_

   F. FIRST LOAN IN THE AMOUNT OF . . . . $ _85,000_
      ☐ NEW First Deed of Trust in favor of ☐ LENDER, ☐ SELLER; or
      ☐ ASSUMPTION of existing First Deed of Trust; or ☑ _Buyer to take title subject to existing loan_
      encumbering the Property, securing a note payable at approximately $ _723_ per month (☑ or more), to include
      ☑ principal and interest, ☐ interest only, at maximum interest of _8_ % ☑ fixed rate, ☐ initial adjustable rate, with a maximum
      lifetime interest rate increase of _NA_ % over the initial rate, balance due in _± 20_ years. Buyer shall pay loan fees/points not to
      exceed _$600_

   G. SECOND LOAN IN THE AMOUNT OF . . . . $ _15,000_
      ☐ NEW Second Deed of Trust in favor of ☑ LENDER, ☐ SELLER; or
      ☐ ASSUMPTION of Existing Second Deed of Trust; or ☐ _____.
      encumbering the Property, securing a note payable at approximately $ _318.75_ per month (☑ or more), to include
      ☑ principal and interest, ☐ interest only, at maximum interest of _10_ % ☑ fixed rate, ☐ initial adjustable rate, with a maximum
      lifetime interest rate increase of _NA_ % over the initial rate, balance due in _5_ years. Buyer shall pay loan fees/points not to
      exceed _$650_

   H. TOTAL PURCHASE PRICE, not including costs of obtaining loans and other closing costs . . . . $ _125,000_

   I. LOAN APPLICATIONS: Buyer shall, within the time specified in paragraph 26B(1), submit to lender(s) (or to Seller for applicable Seller financing), a completed loan or assumption application(s), and provide to Seller written acknowledgment of Buyer's compliance. For Seller financing: (1) Buyer shall submit a completed loan application on FNMA Form 1003; (2) Buyer authorizes Seller and/or Broker(s) to obtain, at Buyer's expense, a copy of Buyer's credit report; and (3) Seller may cancel this purchase and sale agreement upon disapproval of either the application or the credit report, by providing to Buyer written notice within 7 (or ☐ _____) calendar days after receipt of those documents.

   J. EXISTING LOANS: For existing loans to be taken over by Buyer, Seller shall promptly request and upon receipt provide to Buyer copies of all applicable notes and deeds of trust, loan balances, and current interest rates. Buyer may give Seller written notice of disapproval within the time specified in paragraph 26B(5). Differences between estimated and actual loan balance(s) shall be adjusted at close of escrow by:
      ☐ Cash downpayment, or ☑ _Seller will pay_
      Impound account(s), if any, shall be: ☐ Charged to Buyer and credited to Seller, or ☐ _____

   K. LOAN FEATURES: LOANS/DOCUMENTS CONTAIN A NUMBER OF IMPORTANT FEATURES AFFECTING THE RIGHTS OF THE BORROWER AND LENDER. READ ALL LOAN DOCUMENTS CAREFULLY.

Buyer and Seller acknowledge receipt of copy of this page, which constitutes Page 1 of _____ Pages.
Buyer's Initials (___) (___) Seller's Initials (___) (___)

OFFICE USE ONLY
Reviewed by Broker or Designee _RKM_
Date _Feb 3, 19XX_

EQUAL HOUSING OPPORTUNITY
M-PM-8/93

BROKER'S COPY
REAL ESTATE PURCHASE CONTRACT AND RECEIPT FOR DEPOSIT (DLF-14 PAGE 1 OF 6)

Reprinted by Permission California Association of Realtors®. Endorsement Not Implied

Questions 50 through 57 refer to the Deposit Receipt on the previous page.

50. If the second trust deed of $15,000 cannot be obtained because the debt ratio is not sufficient for the lender, then what happens to the deposit/downpayment?
    (A) The total deposit/downpayment would be returned to the buyer
    (B) None of the deposit/downpayment would be returned to the buyer
    (C) Half of the deposit/downpayment would be retained and half returned to the buyer
    (D) Any seller's cost incurred would be subtracted and the seller reimbursed; the rest of the deposit/downpayment would be returned to the buyer

51. Prior to acceptance of the offer the buyer informs the broker that they wish to cancel. Under these circumstances, the buyer would:
    (A) Forfeit the downpayment and deposit
    (B) Keep the deposit but forfeit the downpayment
    (C) Have the uncashed deposit check returned
    (D) Have the broker request that a $4,000 check be issued to the buyer by the escrow company

52. The $15,000 second trust deed loan the buyer is to obtain will be secured by a trust deed in favor of the lender. This type of security is a:
    (A) General lien
    (B) Specific lien
    (C) Blanket lien
    (D) None of the above

53. Within how many days after seller's acceptance of this offer must buyer remove the financing contingency?
    (A) A reasonable amount of time
    (B) 30 days
    (C) 60 days
    (D) At any time before close of escrow

54. What is the total amount of the downpayment?
    (A) $4,000
    (B) $5,000
    (C) $16,000
    (D) $25,000

55. If the beneficiary statement for the first trust deed loan shows a balance due of $3,000 more than shown on the deposit receipt, this will be handled in which of the following ways?
    (A) Seller and buyer will share the cost
    (B) Seller will pay
    (C) The amount will be added to the buyer's cost
    (D) Escrow will be put on hold until the buyer and seller agree on how it will be paid

56. Buyer is taking title subject to the first trust deed lien. Who is liable for the loan in the event of default.
    (A) Buyer
    (B) Seller
    (C) Both buyer and seller
    (D) Neither A nor B

57. The monthly payment of $723 on the first trust deed loan includes:
    (A) Interest and principal
    (B) Taxes and insurance
    (C) Both A and B
    (D) Neither A nor B

58. Certain contacts to be held enforceable in court under the Statute of Frauds must be in writing. Which of the following would be required to be in writing?
    (A) Employment of a real estate broker to sell stock-in-trade and goodwill of a business
    (B) Employment of a real estate broker to find a business to purchase
    (C) Employment of a real estate broker to negotiate one-year leases on business property
    (D) Any agreement not to be performed within one year

3. **ESCROW:** Escrow instructions shall be signed by Buyer and Seller and delivered to _ABC Escrow Company_, the designated Escrow Holder, within _30_ calendar days after acceptance of the offer (or ☐ at least _NA_ calendar days before close of escrow). Buyer and Seller hereby jointly instruct Escrow Holder and Broker(s) that Buyer's deposit(s) placed into escrow or into Broker's trust account will be held as a good faith deposit toward the completion of this transaction. Release of Buyer's funds will require mutual, signed release instructions from both Buyer and Seller, judicial decision, or arbitration award. Escrow shall close ☐ on _NA_, 19___, or ☑ within _60_ calendar days after acceptance of the offer. Escrow fee to be paid as follows: _Seller to pay 50% and Buyer to pay 50%_.

4. **OCCUPANCY:** Buyer ☑ does, ☐ does not intend to occupy Property as Buyer's primary residence.

5. **POSSESSION AND KEYS:** Seller shall deliver possession and occupancy of the Property to Buyer ☑ on the date of recordation of the deed at _11:00_ AM/PM, or ☐ no later than _NA_ calendar days after date of recordation at _NA_ AM/PM, or ☐ _NA_. Property shall be vacant unless otherwise agreed in writing. If applicable, Seller and Buyer shall execute Interim Occupancy Agreement (CAR FORM IOA-14) or Residential Lease Agreement After Sale (CAR FORM RLAS-11). Seller shall provide keys and/or means to operate all Property locks, mailboxes, security systems, alarms, garage door openers, and Homeowners' Association facilities.

6. **TITLE AND VESTING:** Buyer shall be provided a current preliminary (title) report at _Buyer's_ expense. Buyer shall, within the time specified in paragraph 26B(5), provide written notice to Seller of any items reasonably disapproved. (A preliminary report is only an offer by the title insurer to issue a policy of title insurance and may not contain every item affecting title.) At close of escrow: (a) Title shall be transferred by grant deed; (b) title shall be free of liens, except as provided in this agreement; (c) title shall be free of other encumbrances, easements, restrictions, rights, and conditions of record or known to Seller, except for: (1) all matters shown in the preliminary (title) report which are not disapproved in writing by Buyer as above, and (2) _none other_; (d) Buyer shall receive a California Land Title Association (CLTA) policy issued by _ABC Title Insurance Co_ Company, at _Buyer's_ expense. (An ALTA-R policy may provide greater protection for Buyer and may be available at the same or slightly higher cost than a CLTA policy. The designated title company can provide information, at Buyer's request, about availability and desirability of other types of title insurance.) For Seller financing, paragraph 1L(5) provides for a joint protection policy. Title shall vest as designated in Buyer's escrow instructions. **(THE MANNER OF TAKING TITLE MAY HAVE SIGNIFICANT LEGAL AND TAX CONSEQUENCES; THEREFORE, BUYER SHOULD GIVE THIS MATTER SERIOUS CONSIDERATION.)**

Reprinted by Permission California Association of Realtors®. Endorsement Not Implied

Questions 59 through 63 are based on the portion of the deposit receipt above.

59. If the seller insists that this escrow be held at XYZ Escrow Company, where will the escrow be held?
    (A) ABC Escrow Company because the buyer has the right to choose the escrow company
    (B) XYZ Escrow Company because the seller has the right to choose
    (C) At a neutral site selected by the broker
    (D) None of the above

60. If this offer is accepted, which of the following will be true?
    (A) The buyer does not intend to occupy the property
    (B) The property cannot qualify as the buyer's principal residence
    (C) The property will qualify as the buyer's personal residence
    (D) All of the above

61.   Escrow fees will be paid as follows:
       (A)   Seller will pay the full fee
       (B)   Buyer will pay the full fee
       (C)   Seller and buyer will each pay one-half the fee
       (D)   The escrow fee will be included in the title insurance cost

62.   Title is to be transferred by:
       (A)   Real property sales contract
       (B)   Warranty deed
       (C)   Quitclaim deed
       (D)   Grant deed

63.   Buyer's title shall vest as follows:
       (A)   As community property if buyers are husband and wife
       (B)   As joint tenants if buyers are not husband and wife
       (C)   In whatever mode that seller and buyer agree upon
       (D)   As designated in the buyer's escrow instructions

64.   Under what circumstances may a broker fill-out the seller's Real Estate Transfer
       Disclosure Statement?
       (A)   When instructed to do so by the seller
       (B)   When the seller is out of town
       (C)   If authorized by the escrow agent
       (D)   Never

65.   A seller's transfer disclosure statement provides that a broker do which of the following?
       (A)   Visually inspect the property and advise of any pertinent information
       (B)   Physically inspect inaccessible areas and report findings to the buyer
       (C)   Pay for the pest control inspections
       (D)   Inspect condominium common areas

30. **BROKERS:** (If initialled.) Any Broker who initials below agrees to (a) mediate any dispute or claim with Buyer, Seller, or other initialling Broker, arising out of this contract or any resulting transaction, consistent with paragraph 28, and (b) arbitrate any dispute or claim with Buyer, Seller, or other initialling Broker arising out of this contract or any resulting transaction, consistent with paragraph 29. However, if the dispute is solely between the Brokers, it shall instead be submitted for mediation and arbitration in accordance with the Board/Association of REALTORS® or MLS rules. If those entities decline to handle the matter, it shall be submitted pursuant to paragraphs 28 and 29. The initialling of this paragraph shall not result in any Broker being deemed a party to the purchase and sale agreement. As used in this paragraph, "Broker" means a brokerage firm and any licensed persons affiliated with that brokerage firm.

Selling Broker
By: _____

Listing Broker
By: _____

_____ (Initials)   _____ (Initials)

31. **LIQUIDATED DAMAGES:** (If initialled by all parties.)

Buyer's Initials _____   Seller's Initials _____   Buyer and Seller agree that if Buyer fails to complete this purchase by reason of any default of Buyer:
   A. Seller shall be released from obligation to sell the Property to Buyer.
   B. Seller shall retain, as liquidated damages for breach of contract, the deposit actually paid. Buyer and Seller shall execute RECEIPT FOR INCREASED DEPOSIT/LIQUIDATED DAMAGES (CAR FORM RID-11) for any increased deposits. However, the amount retained shall be no more than 3% of the purchase price if Property is a dwelling with no more than four units, one of which Buyer intends to occupy as Buyer's residence. Any excess shall be promptly returned to Buyer.
   C. Seller retains the right to proceed against Buyer for specific performance or any other claim or remedy Seller may have in law or equity, other than breach of contract damages.
   D. In the event of a dispute, Funds deposited in trust accounts or escrow are not released automatically and require mutual, signed release instructions from both Buyer and Seller, judicial decision, or arbitration award.

32. **ATTORNEY'S FEES:** In any action, proceeding, or arbitration between Buyer and Seller arising out of this agreement, the prevailing party shall be entitled to reasonable attorney's fees and costs, except as provided in paragraph 28.

33. **MULTIPLE LISTING SERVICE:** If Broker is a Participant of a multiple listing service (MLS), Broker is authorized to report the sale, price, terms, and financing for publication, dissemination, information, and use of the MLS, its parent entity, authorized members, participants, and subscribers.

34. **OTHER TERMS AND CONDITIONS:** Buyer to pay broker 2.5% of the selling price
Seller to pay broker 2.5% of the selling price

35. **TIME OF ESSENCE; ENTIRE CONTRACT; CHANGES:** Time is of the essence. All prior agreements between the parties are incorporated in this agreement, which constitutes the entire contract. Its terms are intended by the parties as a final, complete and exclusive expression of their agreement with respect to its subject matter and may not be contradicted by evidence of any prior agreement or contemporaneous oral agreement. The captions in this agreement are for convenience of reference only and are not intended as part of this agreement. This agreement may not be extended, amended, modified, altered, or changed in any respect whatsoever except by a further agreement in writing signed by Buyer and Seller.

36. **AGENCY CONFIRMATION:** The following agency relationship(s) are hereby confirmed for this transaction:

Listing Agent: __Charles McCarthy__ is the agent of (check one):
(Print Firm Name)

☐ the Seller exclusively; or ☑ both the Buyer and Seller.

Selling Agent: _____ (if not same as Listing Agent) is the agent of (check one):
(Print Firm Name)

☐ the Buyer exclusively; or ☐ the Seller exclusively; or ☐ both the Buyer and Seller.

(IF THE PROPERTY CONTAINS 1-4 RESIDENTIAL DWELLING UNITS, BUYER AND SELLER MUST ALSO BE GIVEN ONE OR MORE DISCLOSURE REGARDING REAL ESTATE AGENCY RELATIONSHIPS FORMS (CAR FORM AD-11).)

37. **OFFER:** This is an offer to purchase the Property. All paragraphs with spaces for initials by Buyer and Seller are incorporated in this agreement only if initialled by both parties. If only one party initials, a Counter Offer is required until agreement is reached. Unless acceptance is signed by Seller and a signed copy delivered in person, by mail, or facsimile, and personally received by Buyer or by __NA__, who is authorized to receive it, by __Jan. 8__, 19 XX at __11:00__ AM/PM, the offer shall be deemed revoked and the deposit shall be returned. Buyer and Seller acknowledge that Broker(s) is/are not a party(ies) to the purchase and sale agreement. Buyer has read and acknowledges receipt of a copy of the offer and agrees to the above confirmation of agency relationships. This agreement and any supplement, addendum, or modification, including any photocopy or facsimile, may be executed in two or more counterparts, all of which shall constitute one and the same writing.

Receipt for deposit is acknowledged:
BROKER __Charles McCarthy__
By _____

BUYER __Grace Fields__
BUYER __Chester Fields__
Address __24 Wistful Vista__
__City, California__
Telephone __555-1234__   Fax _____

Reprinted by Permission California Association of Realtors®. Endorsement Not Implied

95

Questions 66 through 70 are based on the portion of the deposit receipt reproduced on the opposite page.

66. The buyer who has put up a deposit of $30,000 in escrow toward the purchase price of $195,000 breached the contract and demanded a refund of the deposit. According to the terms of the liquidated damages clause, the buyer would be entitled to a refund of:
    (A) $24,150
    (B) $28,150
    (C) $58,500
    (D) $ 5,850

67. If, after the offer is accepted, the buyer learns that he might have to re-locate because of his job, how would a monetary dispute over the deposit be resolved?
    (A) Buyer would have to go to court to recover deposit
    (B) Buyer could appeal to the Real Estate Commissioner
    (C) The broker could get a third party to resolve the dispute
    (D) Escrow could resolve the disagreement

68. According to the terms of the deposit receipt, the listing broker could legally act on behalf of:
    (A) Both the buyer and the seller
    (B) Seller
    (C) Buyer
    (D) The broker can't be a dual agent unless it was specifically written into the contract

69. What would be the amount of the broker's commissions if the selling price of the property were $195,000?
    (A) $4,875
    (B) $9,750
    (C) $5,850
    (D) $11,700

70. Buyers made an offer on the property January 2. On January 8, the buyers called the listing office to see if the sellers had accepted their offer. The buyers were told that the sellers would not respond until January 10th. Under these circumstances, the buyers could:
    (A) Not demand a return of their deposit because the sellers were going to respond on January 10th
    (B) Terminate the offer and demand the return of the deposit
    (C) Revoke the offer but would only be entitled to 1/2 of the deposit
    (D) Demand specific performance

Exam 8 - Tax Implications of Real Estate Ownership

1. A married couple purchased a principal residence for $350,000 and sold it four years later, in July of 1998, for $650,000. Taking into account all exemptions, on how much of the gain will they have to pay taxes?
    (A) $300,000
    (B) $50,000
    (C) Nothing
    (D) Nothing, if they re-invest in another residence of equal or greater value

2. A capital gain exclusion on a principal residence is:
    (A) $250,000
    (B) $250,000 for an individual or $500,000 for a married couple once in a lifetime
    (C) $250,000 for an individual or $500,000 for a married couple once in a lifetime if one of them is over 55 years of age
    (D) $250,000 for an individual or $500,000 for a married couple every two years

3. Which of the following has the responsibility for assessing for real property tax purposes?
    (A) Board of Equalization
    (B) Assessor's Office
    (C) Both (A) and (B)
    (D) Neither (A) nor (B)

4. Which of the following statements regarding a tax-free exchange is true?
    (A) Each party must trade for like property of equal value with a smaller mortgage and receive boot
    (B) To be eligible, a property must be held for income or investment or for use in trade or business
    (C) A party to the exchange can deduct a loss on the exchange
    (D) A rented house cannot be exchanged for an office building

5. All of the following are subject to property taxes except:
    (A) Real property in unincorporated areas
    (B) Intangible personal property
    (C) Possessory interest of lessees in tax exempt publicly owned properties such as the rights to leases of mineral, oil, and gas interests
    (D) Mobilehome that is on a permanent foundation

6. How much boot is necessary to effect the following exchange: NE ¼ of the NE ¼ of Section 9 at $800 per acre for the S ¼ of the NE ¼ of Section 2 at $500 per acre. (Both parcels are owned free and clear.)
    (A) $ 8,000
    (B) $40,000
    (C) $18,000
    (D) $24,000

97

7. Which of the following has the responsibility for determining property values for real property tax purposes?
    (A) Board of Supervisors
    (B) Board of Equalization
    (C) Assessor's Office
    (D) Tax Commissioner

8. A man owns a property free and clear valued at $660,000 with a book value of $440,000. If he exchanges for another property, also free and clear, valued at $730,000 and pays no boot, the book value of the second property will be:
    (A) $440,000
    (B) $660,000
    (C) $730,000
    (D) Cannot be determined with the facts given

9. Which of the following is an example of "boot" received for income tax purposes?
    (A) Increase in depreciation taken
    (B) Decrease in depreciation
    (C) Net debt relief in a tax deferred exchange
    (D) All of the above

10. A property in which the owner was delinquent in the real estate taxes will become a tax defaulted property as of:
    (A) December 10
    (B) January 1
    (C) April 10
    (D) July 1

11. All of the following are exemptions from local real property taxes except:
    (A) Senior citizens tax exemption
    (B) Veteran's exemptions
    (C) Homeowner's exemption
    (D) Low income homeowner's exemption

12. Which of the following defines the "marginal tax rate"?
    (A) It is the tax rate on the next dollar an investor would earn
    (B) A surtax charged by the federal government
    (C) A total tax paid to the state
    (D) A 28% tax on ordinary income

13. Hyde is exchanging a property valued at $155,000 which is owned free and clear for Foley's property which is also free and clear valued at $160,000. The book value of Hyde's property is $70,000 at the time of the exchange and Hyde pays Foley $5,000 as part of the exchange. Which of the following would be the most nearly correct statement?
    (A) Hyde has a $75,000 gain
    (B) Hyde has a recognized gain
    (C) Foley has a recognized gain
    (D) There is no gain realized by either party

14. The consistency of the property tax burden on a property is related to:
    (A) The assessment of similar properties in a nearby neighborhood
    (B) The tax rate applied to similar properties in a nearby neighborhood
    (C) The turnover and improvements of neighboring properties
    (D) The direct proportion to services rendered in that area

15. A homeowner may take advantage of an exclusion from capital gains on the sale of their principal residence:
    (A) Every two years
    (B) Only if they re-invest the proceeds into a new personal residence within a two year period
    (C) If the homeowner is over 55 years of age
    (D) Never

16. Mr. Newton owned a 6-unit dental building and lot valued at $225,000. The adjusted cost basis was $185,000 and the property was mortgaged for $137,000. He exchanged with the owner of a store building valued at $198,000 with a $125,000 mortgage. Newton also received $25,000 cash boot. What is Newton's actual and taxable gain?
    (A) $78,000—$54,000
    (B) $73,000—$43,000
    (C) $50,000—$37,000
    (D) $50,000—$13,000

17. Smith buys an apartment building for $300,000. She keeps it for 10 years, sells it for $300,000 since the land and the building value did not increase. She had depreciated $110,000 over his period of ownership. As to her tax position:
    (A) She has no recognized gain
    (B) Her gain is taxable as ordinary income
    (C) Her gain may be deferred
    (D) She has to pay capital gains on the amount of the depreciation

18. An owner believes that his property has been over assessed. He can appeal the assessment to the:
    (A) County Tax Collector's Office
    (B) Board of Supervisors
    (C) Department of Real Estate
    (D) Assessor's Appeal Board

19. The state fiscal year falls between the dates:
    (A) December 31 to January 1, midnight
    (B) January 1 to December 31
    (C) July 1 to June 30, midnight
    (D) June 30 to July 1

20. A city has sold an assessment bond for the improvement of streets in a certain area. Properties within that area are assessed:
    (A) In proportion to services or benefits that the land would receive
    (B) By the size of the lot
    (C) By the area
    (D) By the number of lots in the subdivision

21. Jones purchased a 4-acre parcel for $2,000 per acre in 1974. He or she subdivided this parcel into 4 lots and several years later sold each lot for $10,000. What was Jones' capital gain?
    (A) $46,000
    (B) $32,000
    (C) $ 6,000
    (D) Cannot be computed from the information given

22. Andrew purchased Bliss's ranch on May 1, 1995. The real property taxes for 1995-96 are:
    (A) Added to the purchase price for Andrew
    (B) A personal obligation of Andrew
    (C) A personal obligation of Bliss
    (D) A lien on the ranch

23. Smith owned a property that was valued at $160,000 and had a cost basis of $60,000. He or she exchanged this property for a property owned by Kent valued at $155,000. If Kent paid $5,000 into escrow to close the transaction:
    (A) Smith has a recognized gain
    (B) Kent has a recognized gain
    (C) Neither party has a recognized gain
    (D) None of the above

24. Smith sold a house under an installment sales agreement. The main advantage of this method is the ability to:
    (A) Choose which years in which to declare the gain
    (B) Postpone declaring the gain until the debt is fully repaid
    (C) Pro-rate the gain over the term of the installment contract
    (D) Declare the gain in the year of sale

25. Ms Johnson owns two personal residences. If she sells one residence, under what circumstances could she defer her gain?
    (A) She could defer her gain on the residence of greater value
    (B) She could defer her gain only if the property sold was her principle residence
    (C) She must sell both residences to defer the gain
    (D) She could defer her gain if she sold either residence

26. Which of the following statements with regard to real estate tax redemption is correct?
    (A) The most important factor in the tax-stamp sale is to start the redemption period running, but the delinquent owner's possession is undisturbed
    (B) If taxes are not paid after a one-year period, the property is deeded to the state
    (C) Delinquent owner may pay taxes and accrued penalties in monthly installments
    (D) If the delinquent owner alienates the property, the redemption period is terminated

27. What is the difference between real property taxes and assessment bonds?
    (A) Special assessments are levied by special improvement districts only
    (B) Assessments have superiority over property taxes
    (C) Special assessments are used for local improvements
    (D) Assessments are subordinate to real estate taxes

28.   A residential property is reassessed:
(A)   When the county government needs the money
(B)   When the property is destroyed by fire and then reconstructed
(C)   Every time the property is sold
(D)   Every three (3) years

29.   On which of the following could you take a capital gain or loss for income tax purposes?
(A)   Mortgaging property
(B)   Market value change at the date of sale
(C)   Liquidated damages on a breached contract
(D)   Discounts accrued on short-term notes

30.   The annual residential tax obligation is determined by:
(A)   County Assessor's Office
(B)   Board of Equalization
(C)   Board of Supervisors
(D)   Treasurer's Office

31.   For federal income tax purposes a property owner can deduct all of the following in computing annual net income, except:
(A)   Interest paid on a mortgage
(B)   Wooden fence
(C)   Depreciation
(D)   Manager's salary

32.   Which of the following is best described as "boot"?
(A)   Decrease in basis
(B)   Increase in basis
(C)   Net mortgage relief in an exchange
(D)   No change in basis

33.   In regard to property taxes, a tax lien would be:
(A)   Inferior to other private parties
(B)   On par with all others
(C)   Superior to mortgages
(D)   Inferior to mortgages

34.   A street is improved and paved under the 1911 Street Improvement Act. How many days are allowed, after the bill is presented to the property owners, before it goes to bond?
(A)   20
(B)   30
(C)   60
(D)   90

35.   What type of organization is formed in order to create a Real Estate Investment Trust (REIT)?
(A)   Corporation
(B)   Limited Partnership
(C)   General Partnership
(D)   Syndication

36. Jones has purchased a property and assumed a street assessment bond of $2,000 that had been initiated under the Street Improvement Act of 1911. This obligation would most properly be considered:
    (A) Part of the cost of the property
    (B) Payment usable for future taxes
    (C) Improvement of personal property
    (D) Special assessment that will have bearing on the value of the individual properties

37. A buyer purchased a condominium and now lives in it as his principal residence. For income tax purposes, the owner may deduct which of the following expenses.
    (A) Interest paid on a mortgage for the purchase of his condominium unit
    (B) Assessments for areas of common usage
    (C) Maintenance
    (D) All of the above

38. In federal income tax accounting, how would a capital improvement be treated?
    (A) A deduction from net income can be taken in the year of completion
    (B) An exemption of up to $1,000 can be taken on the capital improvement
    (C) The cost of the improvement can be added to the cost basis
    (D) None of the above

39. Mr. Adams purchased an income property for $380,000. The market value of the property was $390,000 and the tax assessor placed a value of $370,000 on it. If he pad $80,000 down and financed the balance, his basis for income tax purposes would be:
    (A) $80,000
    (B) $370,000
    (C) $380,000
    (D) $390,000

40. Realized gain includes:
    (A) That portion of the gain that is attributable to that tax year
    (B) That portion of the gain that does not have to be declared in the present
    (C) The total gain
    (D) All of the above

41. Assessed value for property tax purposes in California is the full cash value as of the tax roll for 1975-1976, plus a maximum annual inflationary factor increase up to:
    (A) 1%
    (B) 2%
    (C) 5%
    (D) 100%

42. Annual property taxes for a personal residence are:
    (A) 1% of the assessed value plus additional cost for bond indebtedness
    (B) 2% of cash value plus additional cost for bond indebtedness
    (C) 1% of appraised value
    (D) Determined by the assessments of the county assessor

43. The primary responsibility for reporting a real estate transaction to the IRS is on the:
    (A) Escrow company
    (B) Lender
    (C) Appraiser
    (D) Real estate agent

44.   Which of the following can be a federal income tax advantage from real estate ownership?
      (A)   Depreciation is deductible
      (B)   Capital gain may be reported over a number of years
      (C)   An exchange of certain properties can be tax free
      (D)   All of the above

45.   What effect does tax depreciation have on income producing property?
      (A)   The market value of the property decreases
      (B)   The value of the property increases
      (C)   The basis of the property is reduced
      (D)   The basis of the property is increased

46.   The expenditure of dollars necessary for the creation of an improved residential property is called its:
      (A)   Cost
      (B)   Price
      (C)   Investment
      (D)   Value

47.   In the sale of a business, sales tax would be paid on which of the following?
      (A)   Trade fixtures and furniture
      (B)   Inventory of goods on hand
      (C)   Goodwill
      (D)   Accounts

48.   What does ad valorem mean:
      (A)   According to value
      (B)   For life
      (C)   At will
      (D)   To the use and benefit

49.   Mrs. Marsh owned a commercial property with an adjusted basis of $175,000 that had a first trust deed of $147,000 outstanding. She exchanged this property for an apartment building valued at $187,000 and $18,000 in cash and assumed a first trust deed of $143,000 on the property acquired. Mrs. Marsh's tax consequences on this exchange would be how much actual and how much taxable gain?
      (A) $35,000—$4,000
      (B) $35,000—$18,000
      (C) $34,000—$22,000
      (D) $33,000—$4,000

50.   When property is declared in default by operation of law for delinquent taxes:
      (A)   All existing liens are extinguished
      (B)   The owner is required to vacate the property
      (C)   The state will sell the property to the highest bidder at auction
      (D)   The owner has a five-year period to bring the taxes current prior to auction

51. In leasing an apartment for 2 years, beginning September 1, 1995, the owner collected the last two months rent in advance. The prepaid rents received would be reported on his income tax for the year:
    (A) 1995
    (B) 1996
    (C) 1997
    (D) At the end of the lease period

52. The Assessment Roll reflects California policy of establishing real property assessed values as what percent of full cash value?
    (A) 1%
    (B) 10%
    (C) 25%
    (D) 100%

53. All of the following qualify for itemized deductions by the owner-occupant of a single-family residence in the appropriate tax year except:
    (A) Real property taxes
    (B) Interest on a deed of trust
    (C) The unreimbursed portion of a casualty or theft loss in excess of 10% of the adjusted gross income
    (D) The cost of painting a bedroom

Exam 9 - Brokerage: Responsibilities and Functions of Salespersons & For Brokers: Broker's Responsibility for Office Management

1. The sidewalks in a condominium are:
   (A) Made at least 4 feet wide
   (B) Tarmacs
   (C) Common areas
   (D) All of the above

2. Which area is the largest?
   (A) 2 sections
   (B) 10% of a township
   (C) 5,280' x 10,560'
   (D) 4 square miles

3. A buyer purchased a property at 20% less than the listed price and later sold it for the original listed price. What was the percentage of profit based on his cost?
   (A) 10%
   (B) 20%
   (C) 25%
   (D) 40%

4. In the negotiation for the purchase of a property, the broker failed to mention the installation of a septic tank. If the buyer finds that this material fact makes the property unacceptable, the buyer should:
   (A) Report this to the Health Department
   (B) Demand a percolation test and soil analysis
   (C) Ask for a rescission of the contract
   (D) Report this to the Real Estate Commissioner

5. The purpose of a trust account is to:
   (A) Keep the broker's funds and trust funds separated
   (B) Provide for the commingling of the trust funds and the broker's funds
   (C) Provide easy disbursement of funds
   (D) None of the above

6. Mr. Able borrowed money to build an apartment building and wanted to place advertising in the newspaper that would solicit the following: (1) Married Couples Only (2) No Minorities. He was correct in his advertising in:
   (A) 1 only
   (B) 2 only
   (C) Neither 1 nor 2
   (D) Both 1 and 2

7. A dual agency in the negotiation of a sale of real property is lawful if:
   (A) Both brokers agree
   (B) The broker of the seller agrees
   (C) Both buyer and seller agree
   (D) The escrow agent agrees

8. A person owns three-quarters of an acre that is rectangular in shape and 110' in depth. He or she paid $1,400 for an adjacent parcel of the same depth but which is two-thirds the area of the first parcel. They then subdivide the combined parcels into lots that are eighty-two and one-half feet across their frontages. After selling these lots for $750 each, they realize a 50% profit on the purchase price of his original parcels. What was the original cost of the three-quarter acre parcel?
   (A) $800
   (B) $1,600
   (C) $3,000
   (D) $3,100

9. A broker told a customer that if they purchased a lot, "it was a gold mine," and that it could be sold for four times what they paid for it by the end of two years. The customer bought the lot but did not attempt to sell it for four years. At that time, they discovered that the broker who had sold them the lot was now selling similar lots for less than the original price of their lot. What course of action could be taken against the broker?
   (A) Civil and disciplinary action could be taken against the broker
   (B) The broker was only "puffing," a common practice in selling real estate and could not be held liable to the buyer; however the broker could be disciplined by the Department of Real Estate
   (C) Nothing could be done about such oral statements, as the real estate market is speculative and always involves some risks for the purchaser
   (D) Nothing, as the Statute of Limitations applies

10. The Subdivision Map Act provides primary responsibility for the physical aspects of the subdivision to:
   (A) The Real Estate Commissioner
   (B) The governing bodies of cities and counties
   (C) The State Land Commissioner
   (D) The State Department of Public Health

11. Mr. Brown applied for a loan for the purchase of a house. The loan was denied due to an unfavorable credit report. He repeatedly asked for a copy of his credit report and was unable to get one from the credit-reporting bureau involved. Mr. Brown can do which of the following?
   (A) Recover enough money to compensate him for damage to his credit
   (B) Sue for attorney's fees and actual damages
   (C) Sue for punitive damages up to $5,000
   (D) Do any or all of the above

12. Percolation test refers to:
   (A) Water wells
   (B) Soil analysis
   (C) Sewage
   (D) Flood control

13. Which of the following is most nearly the number of townships in a parcel of land that is 28 miles square?
   (A) 28
   (B) 22
   (C) 17
   (D) 11

14. Which of the following is correct with regard to townships and ranges?
    (A) Ranges are numbered north and south from the base line
    (B) Township lines run east and west
    (C) Townships are numbered east and west from the principal meridian
    (D) Range lines run east and west

15. Which of the following is the largest parcel of land?
    (A) 5280' x 10,560'
    (B) 1/10 of a township
    (C) Four square miles
    (D) One mile by two miles

16. If you plan to build a single-family residence on a 50' x 150' lot and the city requires a 20' setback on the front and a 4' setback along the sides and back of the lot, the maximum square footage of the home would be?
    (A) 7,500
    (B) 6,500
    (C) 5,460
    (D) 5,292

17. Items that a landlord-owned apartment building and a condominium project would have in common would be:
    (A) Separate tax bills sent to each tenant
    (B) Occupants of both have estates in real property
    (C) After development of five units both would come under the subdivision law
    (D) Occupants of both have a fee interest

18. An estate in real property consisting of an undivided interest in common in a portion of a parcel of real property, together with a separate interest in space could be:
    (A) Residential
    (B) Industrial
    (C) Commercial
    (D) Any of the above

19. A plot plan:
    (A) Is used as a guide to the placement of structures and related improvements on the lot
    (B) Is used as an exact guide for construction of improvements
    (C) Shows exterior of structures to be built
    (D) Shows contour of the land

20. A person obtained a loan for $20,000 secured by a property. The borrower paid 4 discount points to obtain the loan and the payments were $163 per month including 8% interest. The terms of the note provided for a 2% prepayment penalty on the face amount of the loan. Five years later, the owner sold the property for cash. If during the term of the loan, the average balance had been $18,500, what amount did the lender make on the loan over the five-year period?
    (A) $1,200
    (B) $2,310
    (C) $8,600
    (D) $9,600

21.	Which of the following acts or statements might be a cause for disciplining a licensee?
(A)	A statement made to the seller that this is the highest offer the buyer will make
(B)	A statement to the buyer that this is the lowest offer a seller will accept
(C)	A statement to a buyer, "This is the best house on the street"
(D)	Misrepresentation that did not result in a loss to the principal

22.	To manage properties for the general public an individual must be a:
(A)	Certified Property Manager (CPM)
(B)	Licensed broker
(C)	Member of a rental service that lists apartments for rent
(D)	Nothing is required

23.	A real estate agent's license will be suspended when the Real Estate Fund pays a judgment creditor of the agent and will not be reinstated until the agent:
(A)	Reimburses the Recovery Account for one-half of all funds paid to the judgment creditor, plus interest
(B)	Pays back the Recovery Account with interest
(C)	Pays the judgment creditor all funds that were not paid from the Recovery Account, plus interest
(D)	Pays the judgment creditor and the Recovery Account plus interest

24.	A Mortgage Loan Disclosure Statement (Broker's Loan Statement) is required by law to be retained by the broker for:
(A)	2 years
(B)	3 years
(C)	4 years
(D)	5 years

25.	If a home sold for $76,000 that represented a 17% profit over the original purchase price, the original purchase price was
(A)	$63,250
(B)	$63,500
(C)	$64,957
(D)	$65,431

26.	A seller of a condominium must provide a buyer with copies of the:
(A)	CC&Rs
(B)	The latest financial statement
(C)	Bylaws
(D)	All of the above

27.	An agent is showing the home of an owner who has AIDS. Concerning the fact that the owner has AIDS, the agent should:
(A)	Disclose the fact only if someone inquires
(B)	Disclose the fact whether asked or not
(C)	Never disclose the fact
(D)	Disclose the fact if the buyer expects to obtain an FHA loan

28.	A house sold for $73,700, which represented a 17% profit over the original purchase price. The original purchase price was:
(A)	$61,170
(B)	$62,992
(C)	$71,570
(D)	$86,229

29. How many square miles are there in one township?
    (A) One
    (B) Six
    (C) Twenty-four
    (D) Thirty-six

30. Baker purchased 10 lots for $20,000 each with a cash downpayment of $20,000 and encumbered the balance with a blanket mortgage. On each $20,000 increment he paid he would get one lot free and clear. Later, Baker paid $40,000 on the mortgage and received two lots free and clear. After this transaction, Baker's percentage of equity in the remaining lots:
    (A) Increased
    (B) Decreased
    (C) Remained the same
    (D) Was eliminated

31. "A," an unlicensed person, offers "B" $1,000 an acre for 10 Acres. "B" accepts the offer not knowing that "A" already has an offer of $2,000 an acre for the same parcel. The deal goes through as stated. "B" can:
    (A) Sue and get his land back
    (B) Let the deal go through but "A" has to give "B" the excess profit
    (C) Do nothing. The transaction stands
    (D) Report "A" to the Real Estate Commissioner

32. A one-acre parcel is divided into four equal rectangular lots parallel to each other and each 240 feet in depth. What is the approximate width of each lot?
    (A) 280.0'
    (B) 181.5'
    (C) 45.4'
    (D) 87.8'

33. A fire insurance policy can be cancelled by the insurance company:
    (A) At any time without notice
    (B) If the company gives the insured notice within a reasonable time prior to cancellation
    (C) Without notice if the buyer has had excessive losses
    (D) Only after the company has given written notice and the insured has signed an acceptance

34. "Theft" as it relates to real estate includes all of the following except:
    (A) Entering and removing part of the realty
    (B) Defrauding by misrepresentation
    (C) Signing another person's name without his authorization
    (D) Taking away part of the security for a mortgage with the intent to defraud the mortgagee

35. Smith purchased a property for $72,000 with a $20,000 down payment and assumed a $52,000 mortgage with interest at 12% and payments of $520 per month plus interest. Before any payments were made, the property resold for twice the amount of the original purchase price. For every dollar invested, how many dollars did he receive in return?
    (A) $ 4.60
    (B) $ 8.50
    (C) $11.00
    (D) $18.00

36. A house sold for $40,000 on which the seller was to pay a 6% commission. His other costs were 1% prepayment penalty on his existing loan balance of $32,000, escrow fees of $92, title insurance of $328, and 5 points on a new $38,000 FHA loan. The seller's costs of sale would be what percent of his equity?
    (A) 63%
    (B) More than 30% but less than 50%
    (C) 84%
    (D) 105%

37. An owner of a small investment company advertised and sold properties for a commission. In his advertisements he did not indicate that he was as a licensee, and in fact, he was not. He also made false statements in his advertising. Since he failed to disclose material facts, who would prosecute this person?
    (A) Local law agencies
    (B) District Attorney
    (C) Real Estate Commissioner
    (D) Attorney General

38. In a transaction in which the sale of a property has resulted, the broker must keep a copy of the deposit receipt for three years from:
    (A) Date of deposit receipt
    (B) Date of acceptance of offer
    (C) Date of closing of transaction
    (D) Date of recording of grant deed

39. In accordance with the Real Estate Settlement Procedures Act, the lender must supply the borrower with a Uniform Settlement Statement:
    (A) 10 days after loan commitment
    (B) 3 days prior to settlement
    (C) 1 day prior to settlement
    (D) At or before closing

40. What is the best definition of "company dollar" with regard to a real estate office?
    (A) Office expenses
    (B) Gross income minus operating expenses
    (C) Gross income minus commissions
    (D) Cost to set-up the business for a specific length of time

41. A buyer made an earnest money offer to purchase property, and the broker placed the funds in his trust account. After the seller's acceptance but prior to opening of escrow, the buyer informs the broker that he has revoked his offer and demands the return of the deposit. The broker, not wanting to be involved in the conflict with respect to the disposition of the deposit funds, deposited them with the appropriate court. This would be an example of:
    (A) Assignment
    (B) Interpleader
    (C) Equitable disposition
    (D) Surrender

42. If an apartment owner is converting the building to a condominium project, each tenant must receive advance notice to vacate of how many days?
    (A) 90 days
    (B) 120 days
    (C) 180 days
    (D) 30 days

43. An investor bought a second trust deed in the face amount of $1,400 on which he was allowed a 15% discount. He received payments of $122 per month including 9% interest for 1 year. What was the percentage of return on his investment?
    (A) 40%
    (B) 31%
    (C) 23%
    (D) 25%

44. An investor purchases an investment property. An appraisal of the property showed a 12% return. The broker gives the buyer a financial report on the property but fails to take into consideration vacancies and management fees. The broker is guilty of:
    (A) Fraud
    (B) Caveat Emptor
    (C) Misrepresentation
    (D) False promises

45. A broker shows a house to a buyer after listing the house. The broker does not clearly disclose the agency relationship. The agency is:
    (A) Voidable
    (B) Listing only
    (C) Accidental dual agency
    (D) Ostensible agency

46. A parcel of ground measuring 110 yards by 220 yards contains how may acres?
    (A) ½ acre
    (B) 2 ½ acres
    (C) 5 acres
    (D) 7 ½ acres

47. An agent would be guilty of fraudulent misrepresentation when:
    (A) The representation was material and inconsistent with fact
    (B) The misrepresentation was given with knowledge of the truth
    (C) The misrepresentation caused the purchaser to enter into a contract
    (D) All of the above

48. According to Title VIII of the Civil Rights Act of 1968 and an 1866 law enacted by Congress, a person discriminated against in the purchase of a home because of race could go into court and the court could determine all of the following *except*:
    (A) Money damages for humiliation and embarrassment
    (B) Money damages and punitive damage to prevent a recurrence
    (C) Money damages and specific performance
    (D) Revocation and suspension of broker or salesperson's license if the court concludes he has discriminated

49. John Jones is a proprietary lessee in a stock cooperative apartment and makes monthly payments that include principal, interest, taxes, insurance, maintenance, and association fees. Which of the following is correct?
    (A) The tax collector will always issue a separate tax bill to each owner
    (B) The city will divide the cost of an assessment bond against the property among the owners
    (C) The owner may not deduct the amount of his property tax on income tax return
    (D) If other lessees fail to make payments, the owner can lose his equity through a foreclosure sale

50. A licensed real estate salesperson has been selling unimproved lots through the employing broker and receiving a finder's fee from a lender for referring the buyers to the lender. The broker discovers this and fires the salesperson and warned all the other salespeople not to be involved in this type of practice. If these facts come to the attention of the Real Estate Commissioner:
    (A) The Commissioner has no cause for disciplinary action even though it may be unethical
    (B) Both the broker and the salesperson may be disciplined
    (C) The broker and not the salesperson is subject to disciplinary action
    (D) The salesperson alone is subject to disciplinary action

51. Broker "A" had a listing and cooperated with Broker "B" on an offer from a buyer procured from Broker "B." Seller accepted buyer's offer and the transaction was placed in escrow. It is due to close within two or three days when Broker "A" learns that Broker "B" has arranged a sale of similar acreage at a considerably higher price to the same buyer. In these circumstances, what should Broker "A" do?
    (A) Do nothing because of the imminent closing
    (B) Attempt to renegotiate a higher price
    (C) Notify the seller of the higher price
    (D) File an interpleader action and obtain a writ of replevin

52. According to the Government Code, a person discriminated against when buying a home:
    (A) May purchase the home if it is still available
    (B) May purchase a similar home from the owner if one is available
    (C) May be awarded punitive and actual damages
    (D) Any of the above

53.   Mr. Applegate purchased a home in a subdivision through Broker Able. Applegate applied for a loan and on the loan application there were two boxes that he was asked to check. One box was for marital status and the other for race. Applegate may:
(A)   Refuse to answer the question on race and marital status
(B)   Be required to answer these two questions by the lender in order for the loan to be processed
(C)   Sue the broker arranging the loan and the loan officer for asking these questions on the loan application
(D)   File a complaint with the Real Estate Commissioner

54.   An owner bought a home for $63,360 and now wishes to sell and is informed that the cost of selling will amount to 12% of the selling price. The owner wishes to sell at a price so as not to have a loss. How much would the home have had to appreciate in order to offset the selling costs?
(A)   24%
(B)   112%
(C) $4,320
(D) $8,640

55.   In a real estate office, Workman's Compensation should be carried on:
(A)   Secretaries
(B)   Sales agents
(C)   Bookkeepers
(D)   All of the above

56.   The housing and construction industry in California is governed by those laws that include:
(A)   State Housing Law, Local Building Code, Real Estate Law
(B)   Health and Safety Code, State Housing Law, Real Estate Law
(C)   Housing and Community Development, Real Estate Law, Health and Safety Code
(D)   Contractor License Law, Local Building Code, State Housing Act

57.   A fire insurance policy began March 1, 20XX and cost $316.80 for 3 years of coverage. The insured cancelled the policy as of November 16 of the same year. What is the amount of the unused policy?
(A) $74.80
(B) $121.00
(C) $242.00
(D) $316.80

58.   The Alcoholic Beverage Control Act prohibits the issuance of an "on sale" general license to which of the following?
(A)   A club that has been in existence for 6 months
(B)   A cafeteria that has been in operation for 6 months
(C)   A hotel that has been operating for one year
(D)   A boat docked in San Francisco County

59.   What was the purpose of enactment of the Equal Credit Opportunity Act?
(A)   To minimize the cost of credit
(B)   To standardize the minimum requirement for obtaining credit
(C)   To prohibit discrimination by lenders based on sex or marital status
(D)   To regulate the amount of credit extended by a lender

60. A large cosmetics plant is being built in a small town. A developer plans to build a new subdivision to provide housing for the new workers who will be moving into town. He recognized that most of the employees of the cosmetics plant would be women. In setting up his sales programs, the developer gave instructions that (1) the advertising was to be pointed toward a preference for women buyers and (2) the properties should be sold equally to Caucasians, Blacks, Chicanos, and Asians. As the quota for each group was sold other members of that group would be discouraged from buying through increasing prices to them and advising them that no properties were available. Such instructions would be in violation of the Fair Housing Laws as follows:
    (A) Item (1) only
    (B) Item (2) only
    (C) Both item (1) and item (2)
    (D) Neither item (1) nor item (2)

61. Green paid $77,000 for a home in a real estate transaction. The lender would lend 80% of the $75,000 value. If the buyer was charged 3% of the selling price for closing costs and made a $1,200 cash down payment, what additional amount of money would the buyer need in order to complete the transaction?
    (A) $13,490
    (B) $15,800
    (C) $18,110
    (D) None of the above

62. The owner of an apartment building wished to rent to married couples only and planned to inquire on the rental application about the marital status of prospective tenants. The inclusion of this question on the application:
    (A) Is acceptable if the loan on the property was given by a private investor
    (B) Would be acceptable since there is no law prohibiting this
    (C) Is acceptable if the property in unencumbered
    (D) Is illegal

63. In doing a feasibility study for residential development, taking into consideration national economic conditions, all of the following items would be necessary except:
    (A) Analysis of economic basis
    (B) Target markets
    (C) Specific data related to the proposed project
    (D) Local zoning codes

64. Which of the following will have an impact on the real estate market in years to come?
    (A) Land use regulation
    (B) Consumerism
    (C) The real estate industry
    (D) All of the above

65. A seller asked his listing broker the ethnic background of a prospective buyer:
    (A) The broker must disclose this information
    (B) Disclosure is against the Rumford Act
    (C) Disclosure may be made but the broker must tell the seller it cannot affect his decision because of the California Fair Housing Law
    (D) The broker should ask the buyer's broker if it is all right to advise the seller of the buyer's ethnic background

114

66. A salesperson, canvassing a Caucasian neighborhood which was located near a minority neighborhood, contacted prospective sellers and informed them they should sell now before their property lost value due to minorities' entering into the area. Using these tactics he was successful in obtaining several listings. This action is considered to be:
    (A) Steering
    (B) Panic peddling
    (C) Block busting
    (D) Both (B) and (C)

67. A home was purchased for $90,000 with a 1/5th cash downpayment and the balance was financed with monthly payments of $606 that included 9 % interest to be paid in 30 years. By what percentage did the cost of the home increase because of the use of credit?
    (A) 78%
    (B) 147%
    (C) 160%
    (D) 162%

68. A $54,000 fire insurance policy began March 1, 20XX and cost $950.40 for three years of coverage. The insured cancelled the policy as of November 16 of the same year. What is the amount of premium for the unused portion of the policy?
    (A) $696.00
    (B) $726.00
    (C) $633.60
    (D) $950.40

69. Two lots sold for $9,430 that represented a 15% profit to the seller over the four-year period the properties were held. The interest loss was figured at 5% and the taxes were $164 per year. What was the net loss over the period of ownership?
    (A) $415.00
    (B) $816.00
    (C) $1,066.00
    (D) $2,070.00

70. Mr. Able owns an unencumbered lot and decided to build. On May 2nd, the lumber company delivered $1,000 worth of lumber to the property. On May 2nd, he obtained a construction loan for $30,000 from People's Savings and Loan Association. The loan was recorded after the lumber was delivered. In June, more lumber was delivered and the completed structure was painted. In August, Mr. Able moved into the house. The lumber company could not collect its balance of $2,000 and the painter could not collect $4,000 for the painting; they each filed a mechanic's lien. If the property is sold at a foreclosure sale and nets $30,000, the amount received by People's Savings and Loan would be:
    (A) $30,000
    (B) $29,000
    (C) $24,000
    (D) Nothing

71. In a sales transaction, an agent is paid by both parties but he did not reveal his dual agency. What could happen in these circumstances?
    (A) The agent would be subject to discipline by the Real Estate Commissioner
    (B) The sale could be rescinded
    (C) The agent may not be able to enforce payment of his commission
    (D) All of the above

72. Williams owned 40 acres of land in 1955 that she subdivided into 65 lots and placed a restriction in each deed that said these lots may "not be sold to non-Caucasians." This restriction is:
    (A) Prohibited by local, state, and federal statutes and regulations of all real estate commissions
    (B) Unenforceable through court action because it is a violation of the United States Constitution
    (C) Valid until Williams died
    (D) None of the above

73. A broker advertises in the paper that if a seller lists his property with the broker, the broker would credit the seller with $50 toward the commission to be paid. Also included in the advertisement is the statement that if a prospective buyer brings a copy of the advertisement to the broker, the buyer would be credited in the amount of $50 in escrow that would be applied to the purchase price of the property. Would the broker be subject to the discipline of the Real Estate Commissioner with regard to this advertisement?
    (A) The broker would be disciplined because his promises to sellers and buyers in the advertisement would constitute payments to unlicensed persons
    (B) The broker can credit the seller but cannot credit the buyer
    (C) The broker can credit the buyer but not the seller
    (D) The broker may pay the $50 to the seller and to the buyer

74. A licensee can legally do all of the following except:
    (A) Use an open listing without a final and definite termination date
    (B) Collect a commission or service a mortgage loan that he did not negotiate
    (C) Claim an income tax deduction for commission paid for the sale of his own property
    (D) Fail to use a termination date on an exclusive listing

75. A farm boundary runs 3,960' along a country road. At right angles to one end of this boundary, a second side extends 1,980'. Parallel to the short side is a third side that is 3,960' long. A concrete drainage ditch forming the fourth side connects the open sides. The enclosed farmland is how many acres?
    (A) 120 acres
    (B) 270 acres
    (C) 480 acres
    (D) 540 acres

76. When Atkins is selling his trade fixtures, which of the following instruments must he execute?
    (A) Chattel real
    (B) Bill of sale
    (C) Warranty Deed
    (D) None of the above

77. A real estate licensee went into a neighborhood and attempted to solicit a listing by stating to the property owner that "non-whites" would be moving into the neighborhood and that property values would thereby go down. Such conduct would be considered all of the following except:
    (A) Blockbusting
    (B) Panic selling
    (C) Illegal conduct
    (D) Legal but unethical

78. A broker had several agents working in his office. Two of his agents brought in offers on the same listing, one in the morning and one in the afternoon. The second agent's offer was $1,000 less than the first agent's. The broker held the second offer until the first offer was accepted or rejected. This was:
    (A) Permissible because the second offer was lower
    (B) Permissible because of the relationship between the broker and his sales agents
    (C) Forbidden because of the fiduciary relationship to both buyers
    (D) Forbidden in the above circumstances

79. It is improper for a salesperson to do which of the following?
    (A) Tell his principal that he has the nicest farm in the county
    (B) Keep the client's secret that the property has a leaky roof
    (C) Show the property only on sunny days
    (D) Submit verbal offers to the principal

80. The objective of the Subdivided Lands Law is to protect purchasers of property in new subdivisions from fraud, misrepresentation, or deceit in the marketing of subdivided lots, parcels, units, and undivided interests in the State of California:

    An owner of land wants to subdivide his property. What is the minimum number of parcels he would have to create in his new subdivision in order to fall under the Subdivided Lands Law?
    (A) 2 parcels
    (B) 3 parcels
    (C) 4 parcels
    (D) 5 parcels

81. Kent's ranch is 36 miles square. What is the number of townships contained in the ranch?
    (A) 36
    (B) 18
    (C) 24
    (D) 22

82. If a seller received a check from escrow in the amount of $111,561.30 and escrow had deducted a commission of 6% of the selling price and other expenses of $1,210.50 the gross selling price was:
    (A) $111,561.30
    (B) $110,067.30
    (C) $111,277.80
    (D) $119,970.00

117

83. Jones bought two lots for $36,000 each and divided them into three equal lots that he sold for $30,000 each. His percentage of profit was:
    (A) 15%
    (B) 20%
    (C) 25%
    (D) 40%

84. Mr. Ferguson purchased a property for $125,000 with 12% cash down. He financed the balance with equal monthly payment s of $1,048 that included 11% interest, and the loan would be fully amortized in 30 years. Mr. Ferguson sold the property for $139,750 before making any payments on the loan. What was his equity at the time of sale?
    (A) $15,000
    (B) $24,750
    (C) $29,750
    (D) None of the above

85. A seller takes back a note and second deed of trust for $11,220 and sells it immediately for $7,293. The amount of the discount on the note is most nearly.
    (A) 28%
    (B) 35%
    (C) 54%
    (D) 65%

86. Brown owned a parcel of land in a recreation area that was 395,340 square feet. The government retained ownership of a corner of the parcel that was 110 feet long and 30 feet wide. The land sold for $5,250 per acre. What was the value of the land owned by Brown.
    (A) $5,250
    (B) $47,250
    (C) $395,340
    (D) $442,590

87. Broker Thomas negotiated a 25-year lease with an annual rent of $30,000. The agreement was that Broker Thomas would receive a commission annually based on the following schedule:

    7% for the first year, 5% for the next 4 years, 3% for the next 15 years, and 1% for each year thereafter to the completion of the lease.

    How much commission will Broker Thomas have received at the end of the 19th year?
    (A) $20,700
    (B) $21,600
    (C) $22,200
    (D) $23,000

88. Brewer wants to purchase a home, but is denied financing because of an agency's credit report. Brewer has repeatedly tried to get a copy of this report, but the agency refuses to give it to him. Brewer can bring action under the California Civil Code to:
    (A) Recover enough money to compensate him for damage to his credit
    (B) Recover attorney fees and equitable damages
    (C) Recover punitive damages up to $5,000
    (D) Do any or all of the above

89. In a subdivision, who is generally responsible for assuring the installing of curbs, streets, and public utilities?
    (A) Developer
    (B) City or County
    (C) Department of Parks and Recreation
    (D) An incorporated group of homeowners

90. At the time an owner offers to list his or her property with a broker, the owner makes it a condition that it may not be disclosed that the home is in a slide area. What should the broker do?
    (A) The broker should advise the owner to sell the property himself
    (B) The broker should not take the listing
    (C) The broker should recommend that the owner list his property with someone else
    (D) The broker should accept the listing but disclose this information orally to any potential buyers

91. The required written agreement of broker-salesperson is a regulation of which of the following?
    (A) Real Estate Commissioner
    (B) N.A.R.
    (C) Real Estate Board
    (D) No one

92. An owner of a five-unit apartment complex intends to sell each unit to different individuals. He wants each to own an estate in each unit with ownership of structures and land in joint ownership. Under these circumstances, this plan would be considered a:
    (A) Subdivision
    (B) Partition
    (C) Lot-splitting
    (D) Variance

93. The year in which the U.S. Supreme Court barred racial discrimination, both public and private, in the sale or rental of real property was:
    (A) 1960
    (B) 1968
    (C) 1972
    (D) 1984

94. How many square miles are there in a section?
    (A) 1
    (B) 6
    (C) 24
    (D) 36

95. A bank made a loan and charged a 4-point loan fee. Later, the banker sold the note at a 3 point discount and received a check for $69,580. What was most nearly the face amount of the loan?
    (A) $70,000
    (B) $72,100
    (C) $73,000
    (D) $74,500

96. An individual borrowed $5,000 and made equal monthly payments over a 20-year period. If the interest rate was 5% and he paid the lender a total of $7,920, the principal payment in the first month was:
    (A) $33.00
    (B) $20.83
    (C) $53.83
    (D) $12.18

97. How many square miles are there in ½ of a standard township?
    (A) 9
    (B) 18
    (C) 24
    (D) 36

98. Mr. Sharp lists his house with Agent Long, who finds a buyer and induces Mr. Sharp to accept the buyer's offer by making a verbal promise to find Sharp another suitable residence before escrow closes on the sale. Escrow closed, and Long was unable to perform. It is most likely that:
    (A) Sharp will complain and charge Long with criminal negligence
    (B) Sharp will initiate civil court action
    (C) Since Long only made a verbal promise, he has no liability to perform
    (D) Sharp will withdraw his acceptance of the buyer's offer and not be liable

99. A licensee put a blind ad in a local newspaper. A blind ad:
    (A) Does not identify the broker
    (B) Does not give the address of the licensee
    (C) Does not give the address of the property
    (D) Does not disclose the selling price

100. A seller sued a real estate broker for misrepresentation of a material fact that the broker had made to him during the sale transaction. In defending the suit, the broker was able to prove that the listing contract with the seller had been an oral agreement. Under these circumstances:
    (A) This is a valid defense based upon the Statute of Frauds
    (B) The Statute of Frauds is not a bar in any real estate transaction litigation
    (C) This defense is not a bar because it was not the issue
    (D) The broker is only liable for misrepresentation to buyers

101. Mr. Jones had broker Smith negotiate a new $2,500 second trust deed on a home with a term of 2 years. What is the maximum costs and commission Mr. Jones will have to pay?
    (A) $195
    (B) $250
    (C) $415
    (D) $640

102. A man who owned a large tract of land wanted to subdivide it. Into how many interests would he have to divide the land before the subdivision comes under the Subdivision Map Act?
    (A) One interest
    (B) Two interests
    (C) Three interests
    (D) Five interests

103. A salesperson unlawfully takes "kickbacks" in connection with licensed real estate activities. The employing broker finds out about the kickbacks, fires the salesperson, and warns others in the office not to do this. Under these circumstances:
(A) Only the salesperson could be disciplined by the Real Estate Commissioner
(B) Only the broker could be disciplined by the Real Estate Commissioner
(C) Both the salesperson and the broker could be disciplined by the Real Estate Commissioner
(D) A court could revoke the salesperson's real estate license

104. The broker's "desk fee" would most likely be paid:
(A) By a new licensee
(B) In property management
(C) By an appraiser
(D) In a 100% brokerage

105. George Greedy owns a subdivision in Roughacres and intends to mail a promotional brochure to 1,000 persons. The brochure will offer gifts and prizes and state that winners will be property owners. The brochure does not state that a person must attend a sales seminar and tour the subdivision in order to be eligible for a gift or prize. Would this brochure be in violation of any law?
(A) No, it is not unlawful since he is not required to disclose that a person must attend a sales seminar in order to become eligible for a gift or prize
(B) No, it is not unlawful since each person who wins a prize is also a property owner.
(C) Yes, it is unlawful since he did not disclose that a person must be present and attend a sales seminar to be eligible for a gift or prize
(D) Yes, it is unlawful since you cannot win a prize and be a property owner.

106. A property that is referred to as "turnkey" is likely to be:
(A) A government subsidized low-income housing project
(B) Parcels on which the planning is complete and ready for building
(C) A contractor's package is completed and ready for occupancy
(D) Illegal ranch subdivision

107. The amount of interest most likely paid on a straight loan of $26,500 for 20 years at 15% interest is:
(A) $33,500
(B) $35,000
(C) $79,500
(D) $90,365

108. The receipt for a subdivision final report must be kept on file by the subdivider or his agent for:
(A) 1 year
(B) 2 years
(C) 3 years
(D) 4 years

109. A broker who negotiates a real estate loan to which the Brokers Loan Law is applicable must deliver the mortgage loan disclosure statement to the borrower:
   (A) Within 24 hours
   (B) Three days previous to signing
   (C) After close of escrow
   At signing

Exam 10 - Screening Exam A

This screening exam is designed to give you a mirror through which to look at yourself to get an objective measurement of your present position—your state of readiness at this time. With the results of this practice test you will be able to focus your further study onto any areas of weakness revealed in this test because this exam is balanced in subject matter in the same way your state test will be balanced.

o   Do not memorize the questions or answers.
o   Read for understanding the explanations of the answers. Wait a few days.
o   Repeat the entire exam until you are scoring 80 – 85%.
o   Use the pullout exam answer sheets at the back of this book.

1.   Which of the following is *always* considered real property?
   (A)   Cultivated crops sold but not yet harvested
   (B)   Extracted minerals
   (C)   Stock in a mutual water company
   (D)   Grapes on vines sold under contract

2.   With what type of estate is the phrase "of indefinite duration" most usually associated?
   (A)   Estate for years
   (B)   Estate period-to-period
   (C)   Estate of inheritance
   (D)   Less-than-freehold estate

3.   A holder of a life estate can do all of the following except:
   (A)   Rent or lease it
   (B)   Sell it
   (C)   Will it
   (D)   Encumber it further

4.   A lessor leased a property to a lessee for a five-year period. The lessor died. The lessee found out that the lessor had only a life estate in the property. The new owner wanted to cancel the lease:
   (A)   The lease expired at the death of the lessor
   (B)   The lease was valid because it did not have clauses allowing for the sale of the property
   (C)   The lease was valid for the entire length of the original lease
   (D)   The new owner of the property must renew the lease

5.   Eminent domain and police power are governmental rights established by law. Which of the following actions would not be considered police power?
   (A)   Condemnation
   (B)   Building regulations
   (C)   Zoning laws
   (D)   Subdivision development regulations

6. Which of the following relates to time, title, interest, and possession?
   (A) Severalty
   (B) Survivorship
   (C) Mortgage
   (D) Tenancy in common

7. In the event of a business failure, the creditors would look to the personal assets of any of the principals of a:
   (A) Corporation
   (B) Partnership
   (C) Limited partnership
   (D) None of the above

8. Which of the following is an important consideration in the exercise of the power of eminent domain?
   (A) The proposed use must be both practical and public
   (B) The owner's inconvenience must not be greater than the government's convenience
   (C) The proposed use must be practical and just compensation must be paid
   (D) The proposed use must be public, and just compensation must be paid

9. Joint tenancy and community property interests have which of the following in common?
   (A) Both involve the husband and wife
   (B) Survivorship
   (C) Same conveyance
   (D) Equal interests

10. Under a tenancy in common relationship:
    (A) There must be a unity of possession
    (B) Tenants have same rights of survivorship as in joint tenancy
    (C) Each has equal half interest
    (D) If one leases his half, he must pay rent to the other

11. A corporation cannot hold title to real property as a joint tenant because:
    (A) It is a violation of the Securities Act
    (B) Of its perpetual existence
    (C) It is difficult to list all stockholders in the deed
    (D) A corporation cannot convey title to real property

12. A license differs from an easement in that a license:
    (A) Must be in writing
    (B) May be assigned
    (C) Is a permanent right
    (D) Can be revoked

13. Jones is using Smith's swimming pool and suffers an injury. If Jones instituted court action and obtained a judgment against Smith for $2,500, it would be a:
    (A) Voluntary lien
    (B) General lien
    (C) Specific lien
    (D) Abstract lien

14. "A charge imposed upon real property as security for a specific act" is a definition of:
    (A) Restrictive covenant
    (B) Easement
    (C) Lien
    (D) Encumbrance

15. All of the following are true regarding an appurtenant easement except:
    (A) There must be at least two tracts of land under separate ownership
    (B) The dominant tenement must abut the servient tenement at the border
    (C) The easement would run with the land
    (D) The dominant tenement would benefit and the servient tenement would be burdened

16. An easement may be terminated by all of the following except:
    (A) Written release by the owner of the dominant tenement
    (B) Revocation by the owner of the servient tenement
    (C) Nonuse of a prescriptive easement for 5 years
    (D) Destruction of the servient tenement

17. What is the difference between real property taxes and assessment bonds?
    (A) Special assessments are levied by special improvement districts only
    (B) Assessments have superiority over property taxes
    (C) Special assessments are used for local improvements only
    (D) Assessments are subordinate to real estate taxes

18. The California sales tax applies to:
    (A) Real and personal property
    (B) Ad valorem taxation
    (C) Tangible personal property
    (D) All of the above

19. A man owns property free and clear valued at $320,000 with a book value of $220,000. If he exchanges for another property, also free and clear, valued at $365,000, and pays no boot, his book value on the second property will be:
    (A) $365,000
    (B) $585,000
    (C) $220,000
    (D) Cannot be computed with the facts given

20. What does ad valorem mean?
    (A) According to value
    (B) For life
    (C) At will
    (D) To the use and benefit

21. Which of the following would have the least effect on property taxes in a community?
    (A) Number of commercial buildings and high priced homes
    (B) Compactness of the community
    (C) Zoning and private restrictions
    (D) Homestead exemptions

22. The unadjusted basis of a taxpayer's property is best defined as:
    (A) Original cost of acquisition
    (B) Original cost plus capital improvement
    (C) Original cost minus allowable depreciation
    (D) Original cost plus capital improvements minus depreciation

23. Which of the following expenses on a personal residence may be deducted from ordinary income for tax purposes?
    (A) General upkeep
    (B) Depreciation
    (C) Property taxes and mortgage interest
    (D) Wear and tear

24. Mrs. Marsh owned a commercial property with an adjusted basis of $175,000 that had a first trust deed of $147,000 outstanding. She exchanged this property for an apartment building valued at $187,000 and $18,000 in cash and assumed a first trust deed of $143,000 on the property acquired. Mrs. Marsh's tax consequences on this exchange would be how much realized and how much recognized gain?
    (A) $34,000 – $12,000
    (B) $35,000 – $18,000
    (C) $34,000 – $22,000
    (D) $33,000 – $ 4,000

25. A homebuyer is aware that their new home will be reassessed as of the date of close of escrow. If they pay $120,000 for the home and the tax rate is 1.15%, their new monthly tax bill is most likely to be:
    (A) $115
    (B) $1,200
    (C) $1,380
    (D) Cannot be estimated accurately on the basis of the information given

26. Buyer purchased a property from Seller on August 15, 1998. Buyer was to take possession as of September 30, 1998, with all prorations to be as of the same date. On November 1, 1997, Seller had paid the taxes for the fiscal year of 1997–98. The escrow closing statement would show which of the following?
    (A) Buyer pays Seller for 3 months taxes
    (B) Seller pays Buyer for 3 months taxes
    (C) Buyer pays Seller for 9 months taxes
    (D) Seller pays Buyer for 9 months taxes

27. How much boot is necessary to effect the following exchange: NE ¼ of the NE ¼ of section 9 at $800 per acre for the S ¼ of the NE ¼ of section 2 at $600 per acre? (Both parcels are owned free and clear)
    (A) $16,000
    (B) $80,000
    (C) $32,000
    (D) $48,000

28.   Jones purchased an apartment building in 1995 for $300,000, paying $50,000 down and giving a note and deed of trust for the balance. The lot was valued at $50,000. Which of the following amounts should be depreciated over the useful life of the property?
    (A) $200,000
    (B) $235,000
    (C) $250,000
    (D) $300,000

29.   The prudent buyer, in purchasing a new home in a new subdivision tract, would most likely choose a home located:
    (A) On a key lot
    (B) In the center of the tract
    (C) Across from the shopping center
    (D) Near a bus stop

30.   While appraising a single-family residence that is renting for $950 per month, the appraiser finds that the home across the street sold recently for $139,500 and had been renting at the time of sale for $775 per month. Based on these data, the appraised value would be:
    (A) $113,800
    (B) $114,200
    (C) $171,000
    (D) None of the above

31.   The value measure applied by an appraiser to establish value of industrial land is which of the following?
    (A) Acre and square foot
    (B) Acre and front foot
    (C) Square foot and front foot
    (D) None of the above

32.   In the appraisal of property, the Principle of Substitution would apply to:
    (A) Sales Comparison approach
    (B) Cost approach
    (C) Income approach
    (D) Any of the above

33.   What is the first step in the appraisal process?
    (A) Define the appraisal problem
    (B) Make a preliminary survey and appraisal plan
    (C) Classify the data
    (D) Organize the data program

34.   The easiest method for an appraiser to use when calculating the replacement cost of an improvement would be:
    (A) A quantity survey
    (B) A unit-in-place cost method
    (C) A review of the building permit records
    (D) Comparative-unit method

35. An appraiser using the land residual approach is attempting to determine:
    (A) Building value
    (B) Land value
    (C) Capitalization rate
    (D) Income

36. A conduit in a new building would be installed by which of the following?
    (A) Carpenter
    (B) Electrician
    (C) Plumber
    (D) Roofer

37. An appraiser is employed to advise an apartment owner of the economic feasibility of construction of a swimming pool. The appraiser would be most concerned with which valuation principle?
    (A) Principle of Regression
    (B) Principle of Contribution
    (C) Principle of Integration and Disintegration
    (D) Principle of Substitution

38. The fluctuations (activities) of the money market are extremely important to the real estate business. When interest rates go up and the income of a property is fixed, the capitalized value of the property will:
    (A) Increase
    (B) Be unaffected in a short term
    (C) Decrease
    (D) Tend to stabilize

39. In which of the following approaches would the appraiser be least concerned with land value?
    (A) Replacement cost
    (B) Gross multiplier method
    (C) Capitalization of income
    (D) Land residual approach

40. An owner has a 100-unit apartment house. Which of the following items would be deductible from the gross income in determining net income:
    (A) Depreciation
    (B) Income tax
    (C) Mortgage payments of principal and interest
    (D) Wages for part-time gardeners and maintenance personnel

41. If an appraiser was appraising a residence built in 1910, which of the following would be used?
    (A) Cost of living index 1910
    (B) Original cost of materials in 1910
    (C) Original cost adjusted to today's cost of living index
    (D) Today's cost of reproduction

42. The value of income producing property is usually dependent upon:
    (A) Capitalization of future net income
    (B) Market value
    (C) Being proportional to structural soundness of the building
    (D) Being inversely proportional to the depreciation allowance on the remaining economic life

43. In order to arrive at an effective gross income for rental properties, an appraiser should deduct which of the following from gross income:
    (A) Real property taxes
    (B) Repairs
    (C) Vacancies and collection losses
    (D) Depreciation

44. The greatest cause of loss of value to real property and the improvements thereon is:
    (A) Deterioration
    (B) Wear and tear
    (C) Obsolescence
    (D) Lack of maintenance

45. Which of the following is improved value?
    (A) Market value of land and improvements
    (B) Market value divided by total rents
    (C) Difference between economic and contract rent
    (D) Cost of reproduction less depreciation

46. In doing a feasibility study for residential development, taking into consideration national economic conditions, all of the following items would be considered except:
    (A) Analysis of economic basis
    (B) Target markets
    (C) Specific data related to the proposed project
    (D) Local zoning codes

47. From an appraisal standpoint, market value is most closely related to:
    (A) Market price
    (B) Market cost
    (C) Utility
    (D) Assessed value

48. To an investor in real property, cash flow means:
    (A) Gross income less an allowance for vacancies
    (B) Net income used for capitalization purposes
    (C) Income left after deducting taxes from net income
    (D) Monies left after deducting operating expenses, interest and principal payments from gross income

49. Productivity is a direct function of:
    (A) Supply
    (B) Demand
    (C) Value
    (D) Use

50. Functional utility in a dwelling is dependent upon:
    (A) The desires of its occupants
    (B) Its floor plan and equipment
    (C) Zoning in the area
    (D) Condition of heating system

51. If a developer requested backfill he or she would be using it for:
    (A) Garden Landscaping
    (B) Roadways
    (C) Replacing excavated earth against foundation walls
    (D) Driveways

52. In the sale of real property, all of the following statements concerning financing are true except:
    (A) A mortgage is a lien on real property; an execution of a mortgage does not transfer title
    (B) An owner who borrows and executes a trust deed is a trustor
    (C) Selling a note for less than its face value is known as discounting
    (D) A promissory note is security for the trust deed

53. Jackson purchased a property for $70,000 and made a $14,000 downpayment. If he borrowed the balance of the purchase price, it would be considered a purchase money trust deed if he received this amount from:
    (A) A conventional lender
    (B) A friend or relative
    (C) The seller
    (D) Any of the above

54. The trustor under a trust deed is the party who:
    (A) Lends the money
    (B) Receives the note
    (C) Holds the property in trust
    (D) Signs the note as maker

55. When a trust deed is properly prepared and executed, the power of sale of the secured property is given by:
    (A) Beneficiary to seller
    (B) Buyer to trustor
    (C) Trustee to lender
    (D) Trustor to trustee

56. A deed of reconveyance would be signed by the:
    (A) Grantee
    (B) Beneficiary
    (C) Trustor
    (D) Trustee

57. Mr. and Mrs. Crest purchased a home two years ago, financing it with a long term first trust deed and note. They encountered some financial difficulty and were unable to make their payment for two consecutive months. As a result, the beneficiary initiated foreclosure proceedings and the Crests received a copy of the notice of default that had been recorded. Their best course of action at this time is to exercise their right of:
   (A) Redemption
   (B) Reinstatement
   (C) Loan moratorium
   (D) Refinancing

58. In new construction financing, the lender will usually release the final payment to the borrower when the:
   (A) Owner has accepted the property
   (B) Mechanic's lien period has expired
   (C) Work has been completed
   (D) Notice of completion has been recorded

59. Under the 1911 Street Improvement Act, funds may be raised by the local government, benefiting a subdivider, for all the following purposes except:
   (A) Purchase of land for a subdivision
   (B) Payment for streets, walks, and curbs
   (C) Payment for drainage system
   (D) Payment for offsite improvements

60. An owner wishes to sell the home and has arranged with a lender to finance the purchase, but has not yet obtained a buyer. This situation would be termed:
   (A) A firm commitment
   (B) A conditional commitment
   (C) An option
   (D) An interim commitment

61. A primary source of funds for residential financing is:
   (A) The Federal Home Loan Bank
   (B) The Federal Savings and Loan Insurance Corporation
   (C) A Federal Savings and Loan Association
   (D) The Federal Housing Administration

62. The lower the loan-to-value ratio the higher the:
   (A) Equity interest
   (B) Degree of risk
   (C) Loan amount
   (D) Rate of interest

63. Which of the following is the lender whose loan policies are characterized by:

   —A preference for short-term loans

   —A heavy reliance on its past association with the borrower

   —Loans on property situated close to the lender's office

   —Some interim construction loans
   (A) Commercial bank
   (B) Mortgage banker
   (C) Savings and loan associations
   (D) Insurance company

64. Smith asked a broker to help secure a $19,000 loan for 5 years using his house as collateral. The appraised value of the residence was $80,000 and was completely free of liens and encumbrances. The broker would likely fail to succeed if he attempted to secure the loan through:
   (A) Savings and loan
   (B) Insurance company
   (C) Private lender
   (D) Commercial bank

65. Impounds are used as a safety measure to insure payment of certain recurring bills. A lender might require a borrower to make deposits into an impound account with each monthly payment. Which of the following would least likely be part of the impound deposit?
   (A) Property taxes
   (B) Mortgage interest
   (C) Homeowner's association fees
   (D) Assessment bond payments

66. In real estate financing, reference is sometimes made to "take–out" loans. This refers to:
   (A) Net amount after points and prepaid interest are deducted
   (B) A blanket encumbrance
   (C) Construction loan
   (D) Long-term loan after construction

67. A buyer assumes an FHA mortgage with the lender's approval and pays the seller's equity in cash and the lender charges the buyer a $300 fee. This fee is known as:
   (A) An assumption fee
   (B) A novation fee
   (C) Points
   (D) An origination fee

68. Conventional loans differ from FHA insured loans in all of the following ways except:
   (A) Conventional loans generally have a smaller loan-to-value ratio
   (B) FHA loans require a loan impound account to pay taxes and insurance
   (C) Deficiency judgments are always permitted on conventional loans (unless barred by statute) and are never allowed on FHA loans
   (D) FHA loans generally allow for longer maturity dates

69. In a period of inflation the Federal Reserve Board would take which of the following actions to curb inflation:
(A) Reduce reserve requirements
(B) Lower discount rates
(C) Raise discount rates and buy bonds
(D) Raise reserve requirements and sell bonds

70. A salesperson takes a listing that requires that the buyer "assume" the existing loan. From the standpoint of the salesperson, the sale would be easiest if the existing loan is:
(A) A Cal-Vet loan
(B) A conventional loan
(C) An FHA loan
(D) An insurance company loan

71. Annual Percentage Rate is defined as:
(A) All loan costs, direct or indirect, expressed as a percentage rate
(B) Direct loan costs only
(C) Relative amount of credit cost expressed as a dollar total
(D) Direct and indirect costs plus taxes and closing costs

72. Savings and loan institutions obtain most of their money for making loans from:
(A) Individual savings
(B) Corporation savings
(C) Corporation profits
(D) FNMA

73. RESPA applies to certain federally-related loans secured by liens on owner-occupied one- to four-unit dwellings. Which of the following is federally-related under RESPA?
(A) A lender whose deposits are insured by a federal agency
(B) A seller taking back a note and deed of trust
(C) A private lender making a loan
(D) None of the above

74. Discount points on financing under The California Farm and Home Purchase Act are paid by which of the following?
(A) The state
(B) The buyer
(C) The seller
(D) No one

75. Liquidation of a financial obligation on an installment basis is which of the following?
(A) Acceleration
(B) Conventional
(C) Amortization
(D) Conversion

76. A conventional lender considering a real estate loan would be most concerned with which of the following?
(A) Federal and state regulations
(B) Degree of risk involved
(C) Amount of mortgage funds available
(D) Economic and financial conditions of the nation

133

77. All of the following may be negotiable instruments except:
    (A) Installment note
    (B) Bank Draft
    (C) Check
    (D) Mortgage securing a promissory note

78. Recording a deed would give:
    (A) Effective notice
    (B) Actual notice
    (C) Constructive notice
    (D) Right of possession

79. A Standard Policy of Title Insurance would insure against:
    (A) Forgery in the chain of title
    (B) Validity of a tenant's lease to be free of all liens and encumbrances
    (C) Items that the insured knew were faulty
    (D) All of the above

80. In California, the abstract of title has ultimately been replaced by:
    (A) Title guarantee
    (B) Certificate of title
    (C) Trust deed
    (D) Policy of title insurance

81. Recording a deed:
    (A) Transfers title
    (B) Gives actual notice
    (C) Raises presumption of delivery
    (D) Insures possession

82. All of the following are correct concerning probate sales of real property except:
    (A) Commissions for brokers negotiating sales are determined by the probate code according to prearranged schedules based on selling price
    (B) The representative of the estate may enter into an exclusive listing with the broker with the approval of the court
    (C) An offer can be accepted by the representative of the estate with the approval of the court
    (D) The first bid in a probate sale must not be less than 90% of the court's appraisal

83. Which of the following is correct with regard to an estate?
    (A) Title to an estate must be transferred by deed
    (B) A life estate is a less-than-freehold estate
    (C) An estate cannot be created by a lease
    (D) More than one estate can exist in the same property simultaneously

84. A lessee may be justified in abandoning a rented dwelling if there is constructive eviction by the landlord. All of the following would be constructive eviction except:
(A) Failure of the landlord to repair excessive wear and tear to property caused by the tenant
(B) Condemnation of the entire property in eminent domain proceedings
(C) An eviction notice is tendered by the landlord
(D) Unwarranted delays by the landlord after notice to make repairs of damages that have made the property unfit for occupancy

85. A joint tenancy can be created by deeds conveying undivided interests in which of the following?
(A) By transfer from a wife deeding her separate property to herself and husband as joint tenants
(B) By transfer from joint tenants deeding their interests to themselves and others as joint tenants
(C) By transfer from tenants in common deeding to themselves as joint tenants
(D) All of the above

86. The remedy of unlawful detainer is most commonly used by the offended:
(A) Trustors
(B) Holders of notes in default
(C) Lessors
(D) Grantors

87. An estate in real property consisting of an undivided interest in common in a portion of a parcel of real property, together with a separate interest in space in a residential, industrial, or commercial building is a partial definition of a:
(A) Planned development
(B) Community apartment
(C) Condominium
(D) Stock cooperative

88. In the absence of expressed provisions in the deed restrictions and plans, which of the following is part of a condominium unit?
(A) Bearing walls
(B) Central heating system
(C) Elevator
(D) None of the above

89. In most cases, the least satisfactory place to obtain a legal description of property is:
(A) Deed
(B) Real property tax bill
(C) Escrow instructions
(D) Preliminary title report

90. In accordance with the Real Estate Settlement Procedures Act, the lender must supply the borrower with a Uniform Settlement form:
(A) 10 days after loan commitment
(B) 3 days prior to settlement
(C) 1 day prior to settlement
(D) At or before closing

91. How much can a lender legally charge a borrower for the preparation of the Federal Uniform Settlement Statement?
    (A) Nothing
    (B) 1/2 of 1%
    (C) $25.00
    (D) 1%

92. An escrow agent is exempt from licensing requirements of the Corporations Commissioner in all but which of the following?
    (A) An attorney-at-law who is not actively conducting an escrow business
    (B) A broker dealing with his own transactions and charging a fee
    (C) A broker dealing with his own transactions and not charging a fee
    (D) A broker who is acting as an escrow agent for other brokers' transactions

93. An executory contract is a:
    (A) Contract with an executor of an estate
    (B) Contract that has been fully performed
    (C) Contract that is yet to be performed by one or both parties
    (D) Written contract that cannot be altered by oral agreement

94. What essential element is necessary between a broker and a principal when dealing with the title, right, or interest in real property:
    (A) Written contract of employment
    (B) Broker has the right to draw up a purchase offer
    (C) Broker has the right to accept a deposit
    (D) It must establish the rights of commission between the parties

95. A broker who is selling property on which he or she holds an option must inform the buyer that he or she is:
    (A) An optionor
    (B) A grantor
    (C) An agent
    (D) A principal

96. In a sales transaction, the broker acted as an agent for both the buyer and the seller and collected a commission from each. He failed to disclose to either that he was receiving a commission from the other party. In this case, after the close of escrow, which of the following could happen?
    (A) The broker could be disciplined by the Department of Real Estate
    (B) The broker could be denied any commission
    (C) The buyer could rescind the purchase
    (D) Any of the above

97. Smith signed an offer to buy Brown's property and gave it to the Broker. The broker took it to Brown who signed Smith's offer, giving an unqualified acceptance of it. Before the broker could deliver the accepted offer back to Smith, Smith died of a heart attack. Which of the following is correct?
    (A) Smith's death worked a revocation of the offer
    (B) The offer and unqualified acceptance constitute a valid contract
    (C) Delivery of the offer to the administrator binds Smith's heirs
    (D) Offer is void since the deed could not be delivered to Smith

98. Broker Fenton has a property listed for $114,000 and submits an offer of $112,000 the next day. There is a three-day acceptance period. One day after the expiration of the acceptance period, the seller accepts the buyer's original offer of $112,000. The buyer decides that he no longer wants the property. In these circumstances the acceptance is:
   (A) Valid
   (B) Voidable
   (C) Enforceable because of the original offer
   (D) Not a contract

99. A seller sued a real estate broker for misrepresentation of a material fact that the broker had made to him during the sale transaction. In defending the suit, the broker was able to prove that the listing contract with the seller had been an oral agreement. Under these circumstances:
   (A) This is a valid defense based upon the Statute of Frauds
   (B) The Statute of Frauds is not a bar in any real estate transaction litigation
   (C) This defense is not a bar because it was not the issue
   (D) The broker is only liable for misrepresentation to buyers

100. A listing agreement in which the owner promises to pay a commission under all circumstances of sale, except if he sells the property himself, is known as:
   (A) An exclusive right to sell
   (B) An exclusive agency
   (C) A net listing
   (D) None of the above

101. A property is sold in accordance with the listing terms and conditions. After the transaction is in escrow, the seller decides that he doesn't wish to complete the transaction and refuses to complete the sale. Under the Statute of Limitations, the buyer must bring any action against the seller for failure to perform under the deposit receipt within:
   (A) 90 days
   (B) One year
   (C) Two years
   (D) Four years

102. A broker used the following phraseology in his listing contract: "In consideration of the execution of the foregoing, the undersigned broker agrees to use diligence in procuring a purchaser." This is best described as:
   (A) Superfluous in such contracts
   (B) A necessary item in the creation of a unilateral contract
   (C) A necessary element in the creation of a bilateral contract
   (D) An agreement to advertise the property

103. All of the following are essential elements of a simple contract except:
    (A) Proper writing
    (B) Competent parties
    (C) Legal object
    (D) Mutual assent

104. A licensed real estate salesperson takes a listing that does not authorize her to take a deposit. The salesperson finds a buyer, however, who gives her a personal check as a deposit with an offer on the property. With regard to the deposit, the salesperson's broker would be:
    (A) The agent of the seller
    (B) The agent of the buyer
    (C) The agent of the bank
    (D) Required to place the check in escrow

105. Since land is unique in character and often cannot be substituted for another parcel, the courts have made available the right to request specific performance. Which of the following could not request such action in a court?
    (A) The seller of a large tract of land
    (B) The seller of a single-family residence
    (C) The buyer of a single-family residence
    (D) A broker acting as an agent of the seller

106. Jones bought an original general on-sale liquor license for a business. After two years he or she could sell the license for:
    (A) $2,000
    (B) $4,000
    (C) $6,000
    (D) No limit

107. A real estate salesperson effective 1998, who advertises a property must provide in the advertisement:
    (A) The broker's name
    (B) The broker's name and address
    (C) At least the salesperson's name
    (D) Both (B) and (C)

108. The instrument used in hypothecating title to personal property is the:
    (A) Trust deed
    (B) Bill of sale
    (C) Security agreement
    (D) Financing statement

109. Which of the following has the largest area?
    (A) 4,067 sq. yds.
    (B) One acre
    (C) 41,167 sq. ft.
    (D) 1 sq. rod

110. A broker lists and negotiates the sale of a home for Mr. "B," a young married man. At the time of the sale the broker was not concerned with the client's age. After the deed had been signed and escrow closed, the title company informed the broker that the seller was under 18 years of age. The deed is:
     (A) Valid
     (B) Voidable
     (C) Outlawed
     (D) Illegal

111. An offer to buy becomes a binding purchase contract:
     (A) The instant the offer is accepted
     (B) When the offer is accepted and the acceptance is communicated to the offeree
     (C) When the offer is accepted and the acceptance is communicated to the offeror
     (D) Any of the above

112. Robert Smith signed an offer and gave the broker his personal check made payable to an escrow company as a deposit. He stipulated that the broker was to hold the check until the seller accepted his offer. The listing agreement specified that any deposit money must be a cashier's check made payable to the seller. Under these circumstances, the broker should:
     (A) Submit the offer and hold the check
     (B) Submit the offer and deposit the check in escrow
     (C) Hold the check but do not reveal to the seller that he has accepted the check until the seller accepts the offer
     (D) Refuse to accept a deposit that does not conform to the precise terms of the listing

113. When dealing with the public, a broker may not:
     (A) Receive a commission from both buyer and seller
     (B) Delegate any of broker's duties to other persons
     (C) Remain silent as to material facts concerning the property known only to the broker
     (D) All of the above

114. The Uniform Vendor and Purchaser Risk Act provides that if a property is destroyed by an earthquake, a contract buyer in possession is:
     (A) Relieved of obligation to make payments
     (B) Not relieved of obligation to make payments
     (C) Required to rebuild structure
     (D) Not affected by the law

115. Mr. and Mrs. Snyder have sold their home to the Binghams with an agreement of sale. From a financing standpoint, the Snyders' relationship to the Binghams is like a:
     (A) Renter to tenant
     (B) Beneficiary to trustor
     (C) Lessor to lessee
     (D) Grantor to grantee

116. Which of the following agreements would not be required to be in writing under the Statute of Frauds?
    (A) An agreement between a principal and agent to buy or sell real property
    (B) An agreement that would not be completed within one year
    (C) A partnership agreement to buy or sell property
    (D) An agreement to rent for more than one year

117. A client contacts you to take a listing. You look at his papers and discover that he is purchasing the property on a contract or sale. The contract contains no alienation clause and there are no restrictions in the contract of sale prohibiting resale or assignment. One of the following is the most nearly correct statement. Your client could:
    (A) Sell his interest in the property but only after first paying off the existing contract of sale
    (B) Properly give a grant deed to the property to the purchaser providing a recorded purchase money second trust deed is given to make payments due on original contract
    (C) Properly give a warranty deed to the property to the purchaser providing the deed recited "subject to the existing contract of sale"
    (D) Sell or assign his rights but not his duties without approval of the contract seller

118. Which of the following is the minimum amount of time that a broker must keep signed copies of listings, deposit receipts, etc.?
    (A) One year
    (B) Two years
    (C) Three years
    (D) Four years

119. A buyer purchased a single family dwelling in a subdivision using a land sales contract which provided for monthly payments and which prohibited prepayment. Two years later the buyer decided to pay off the balance of the contract, but the vendor refused to accept it. Which of the following is correct?
    (A) The buyer can make equal monthly interest payments but can pay nothing on the principal before the due date
    (B) The inclusion of this clause makes the contract void
    (C) The buyer can ignore the clause prohibiting prepayment and pay off the loan after two years
    (D) The buyer must abide by the terms of the land sales contract

120. In the matter of a broker's commission to be paid by a seller, which of the following is true?
    (A) Listing agreement signed only by seller is unenforceable
    (B) Seller and buyer may rescind sale thus relieving seller of obligation to pay the broker's commission
    (C) Action for broker's commission must be brought within four years of earning the commission
    (D) Broker's commission earned but not paid creates a lien on seller's property

121. Mr. Martin contacted broker Katz to list a property for sale for $200,000. Martin indicated to the broker that he needed a quick sale of the property. The broker contacted a prospective buyer and told him that Martin would sell the property for $180,000. The buyer made an offer in the amount of $180,000 that Mr. Martin did accept when the broker presented it to him. Under these conditions:
    (A) Agent violated the fiduciary relationship as he acted in excess of authority given him
    (B) Agent violated the fiduciary relationship but did no harm as the offer was accepted
    (C) Agent did not violate the fiduciary relationship as Katz was employed by Martin and acted under such authority
    (D) Agent did not violate the fiduciary relationship as the offer was accepted

122. A final, specific, and definite termination date is required by law on all agreements between seller and real estate agent except:
    (A) A written instrument giving one agent the right to sell property for a specified time but reserving the right of the owner to sell the property himself without paying a commission
    (B) A written agreement between owner and agent giving the agent the right to collect a commission if the property is sold by anyone during the term of his agreement
    (C) An agreement in writing wherein it is provided that an agent appointed in an exclusive capacity may retain as compensation for his services all sums received over and above a net price to the owner
    (D) A written authorization given by a property owner to a real estate agent wherein said agent is given the right along with other brokers to secure a purchaser

123. Which of the following must be specifically stated in a purchase option agreement?
    (A) A statement that the offer must remain open for one year
    (B) A statement to the effect that the agreement is irrevocable
    (C) A statement that the optionee has the right to purchase the subject property
    (D) A statement to the effect that the optionor can retain the price paid for the option

124. A prospective buyer pays $2,000 for a four-month option to purchase a $300,000 property. All of the following are true except:
    (A) A unilateral contract has been established
    (B) The optionee has acquired a legal interest in the property
    (C) The optionor's temporary surrender of the right to sell is valuable consideration
    (D) The agreement imposes no obligation on the optionee to purchase the property

125. A contract signed under duress would be:
    (A) Void
    (B) Unenforceable
    (C) Voidable
    (D) Illegal

126. A lessor is renting a furnished apartment from period to period. Under the Fair Housing Act, the lessor may do all of the following except:
    (A) Obtain credit checks on married couples
    (B) Check with former landlords for references
    (C) Require only single tenants to have a co-signor for the lease
    (D) Collect the first, second and last month's rent

141

127. Jones bought two lots for $18,000 each and divided them into three equal lots that he sold for $15,000 each. His percentage of profit was:
    (A) 15%
    (B) 20%
    (C) 25%
    (D) 40%

128. If a minority buyer comes into a broker's office and asks to see a specific listed home, the broker should refuse to show it to him under which of the following conditions?
    (A) When the agent sincerely believes it will produce panic selling
    (B) When the property is listed with a co-op broker
    (C) When the seller is out of town and has instructed the broker that his house is not to be shown in his absence
    (D) Never

129. The Federal Open Housing Law was enacted for the purpose of:
    (A) Equal but separate housing within the states
    (B) Providing fair housing for minority groups
    (C) Providing fair housing opportunity for all persons throughout the U.S.
    (D) Elimination of prejudice throughout the U.S.

130. When a real estate broker submitted an offer at the full listed price to the seller, the seller inquired as to the ethnic background of the buyer. Under these circumstances the broker should:
    (A) Refuse to answer the question since it violates the Rumford Act
    (B) Answer the seller's question since this is a material fact
    (C) Answer the question but caution the seller that the ethnic background of the buyer cannot be used as a basis for discrimination
    (D) Contact the buyer's broker and obtain permission to disclose this information

131. With regard to local building codes (for example in Los Angeles) vs. the Federal Uniform Building Code, which would prevail?
    (A) Local building codes always take precedence over the Federal Uniform Building Code
    (B) Federal codes always take precedence
    (C) The Federal Uniform Building Code applies only to general codes while local codes are more specific
    (D) Whichever has the higher standards of health and safety will prevail

132. The housing and construction industry in California is governed by three laws that include:
    (A) State Housing Law, Local Building Codes, Real Estate Law
    (B) Health and Safety Code, State Housing Law, Real Estate Law
    (C) Housing and Community Development, Real Estate Law, Health and Safety code
    (D) Contractor License Law, Local Building Codes, State Housing Act

133. An investor purchased a property at 20% less than the listed price and later sold the property for the original listed price. What was the percentage of profit based on his cost?
    (A) 10%
    (B) 20%
    (C) 25%
    (D) 40%

134. Broker Thomas negotiated a 25-year lease with an annual rent of $15,000. The agreement was that Broker Thomas would receive annually his or her commission based on the following schedule:

    —7% for the first year, 5% for the next 4 years, 3% for the next 15 years, and 1% for each year thereafter to the completion of the lease.

    —How much commission will Broker Thomas have received at the end of the 19th year?
    (A) $ 9,350
    (B) $ 9,856
    (C) $10,350
    (D) $10,650

135. Jones was paying $550 per month to the bank. After the bank deducted the interest, $43.85 was applied to the principal. If the outstanding loan balance was $56,500, what was the rate of interest on Jones' loan?
    (A) 8 3/4%
    (B) 9 1/2%
    (C) 10 3/4%
    (D) 11 1/2%

136. Brown hired a broker to find a warehouse for lease. Green hired the same broker to find a lessee for a warehouse. Each agreed to pay a commission. The broker negotiated a lease between Brown and Green. Brown knew the broker was representing Green, but Green did not know the broker was representing Brown. Which of the following is correct?
    (A) Neither is liable for a commission
    (B) Brown is liable for the commission
    (C) Green is liable for the commission
    (D) Both Brown and Green are liable for commissions

137. A customer borrowed $1,968 for 3 years, 10 months and 20 days at 8 1/2% interest per annum. What is the amount of interest paid to the lender?
    (A) $399
    (B) $501
    (C) $650
    (D) $739

138. A bank made a loan and charged a 4-point loan fee. Later, the bank sold the note at a 3 1/2 point discount and received a check for $69,580. What was most nearly the face amount of the loan?
    (A) $70,000
    (B) $72,100
    (C) $73,000
    (D) $74,500

143

139. The S 1/2 of the NW 1/4 of the NE 1/4 of Section 11 was listed for sale at $350 per acre with the broker to get a 10% commission. Broker brought an offer of $6,100 for the property. The owner said he would accept if the buyer would pay the broker's commission based upon 10% of the offered amount. If the buyer were to agree, the difference between the original price and the amount as paid by the buyer would be:
   (A) $290
   (B) $295
   (C) $670
   (D) $900

140. Mr. Gordon bought $9,300 worth of stock-in-trade and sold it for 33 1/3% more than he paid for it but lost 15% of the selling price in bad debts. The entire profit on the investment was:
   (A) Nothing
   (B) 18 2/3%
   (C) $1,240
   (D) $3,100

141. A Fictitious Business Name Statement must be renewed and filed with the County Clerk in the County where the business is located and operated:
   (A) Never, unless abandoned
   (B) Every five (5) years, by December 31st of said year
   (C) By June 30th
   (D) One (1) year from original filing

142. The maximum amount of commission and loan costs that may be charged for a second trust deed of $4,000 for a 4-year term is:
   (A) $400
   (B) $550
   (C) $990
   (D) $850

143. The written employment agreement required between a broker and a salesperson must be retained:
   (A) By the broker for 3 years from the date of execution
   (B) By the salesperson for three years from the date of execution
   (C) Both (A) and (B)
   (D) By both for a reasonable length of time from the termination date

144. Broker refers all his clients and customers to the West Hills Title Insurance Company. The title company gives the broker a $10 fee for each referral. This practice is:
   (A) Permissible
   (B) Acceptable if the seller is paying for the policy and agrees
   (C) Acceptable if both buyer and seller are aware that broker is receiving a fee and agree
   (D) Forbidden

145. A one-acre parcel is divided into four equal rectangular lots parallel to each other and each 240 feet in depth. What is the approximate width of each lot?
   (A) 280.0'
   (B) 181.5'
   (C) 87.8'
   (D) 45.4'

144

146.   A broker told a customer that if he purchased a lot "it was a gold mine," and that it could be sold for four times what he paid for it by the end of two years. The customer bought the lot but did not attempt to sell it for four years. At that time, he discovered that the broker who had sold him the lot was now selling similar lots for less than the original price of his lot. What course of action could be taken against the broker?
(A)   Civil and disciplinary action could be taken against the broker
(B)   The broker was only "puffing," a common practice in selling real estate, and could not be held liable to the buyer; however the broker could be disciplined by the Department of Real Estate
(C)   Nothing could be done about such oral statements, as the real estate market is speculative and always involves some risks for the purchaser
(D)   Nothing, as the Statute of Limitations has expired

147.   A buyer of a business opportunity would obtain a Certificate of Clearance from which of the following?
(A)   State Board of Equalization
(B)   Secretary of State
(C)   Franchise Tax Board
(D)   County Tax Assessor

148.   Which of the following is prima facie evidence of deceptive or misleading advertising in the sale of real estate?
(A)   The misspelling of the subdivision's name
(B)   The omission of the purchase price or financial terms
(C)   Any guaranteed yield or return on a promissory note that does not agree with the advertised interest rate
(D)   A poorly drawn map that would make it difficult to find the location of the subdivision

149.   Johnson, who owns a ranch, gave Broker Otis an exclusive listing to sell the property. Johnson also advanced Otis $100 to advertise the sale of this ranch in a brochure published by Otis. The real estate law requires that brokers must account for such funds by complying with which of the following?
(A)   Place the $100 in the broker's trust account in order that the money may be returned to the seller if the property is not sold
(B)   Place this advance fee in the broker's personal office account and spend it only for advertising the property
(C)   Place the $100 in the broker's trust account, expend from the trust account only for advertising the property, and provide a report to the seller that will itemize all expenditures made
(D)   Place the $100 in the broker's trust account in case the seller defaults

150.   A developer owns three-quarters of an acre that is rectangular in shape and 110' in depth. He paid $1,400 for an adjacent parcel of the same depth but which is two-thirds the area of the first parcel. He then subdivides the combined parcels into lots that are eighty-two and one-half feet across their frontages. After selling these lots for $750 each, he realizes a 50% profit on the purchase price of his original parcels. What was the man's original cost of the three-quarter acre parcel?

(A) $1,600
(B) $2,500
(C) $3,000
(D) $3,100

Exam 11 - Screening Exam B

The 2nd screening exam can be your final test before you take the state exam.
° Take the entire exam at one time
° Do not mark the book. Use the pullout exam answer sheets at the back of this book.
° You have 3 hours and 15 minutes
° Calculate your score (example: # correct 105 divided by 150)
° Take the state test only if you scored 80% or higher for sales, 85% for broker
° Study the explanations of those you missed
° Don't memorize, Learn
° Write down your score and the date, wait 2–3 days, repeat as necessary

1. Mr. Able obtained a loan to build an apartment building. (1) He planned to charge a higher deposit to single males and, (2) His only source of advertising was referral from his tenants, predominantly white, to refer their friends as prospective tenants. With reference to Fair Housing Laws, Mr. Able's actions would be correct in which of the following choices?
   (A) 1 only
   (B) 2 only
   (C) Both 1 and 2
   (D) Neither 1 nor 2

2. When there is a gradual build-up of land as the result of action of water, it is termed:
   (A) Avulsion
   (B) Accretion
   (C) Dereliction
   (D) Erosion

3. A broker negotiated a loan for a client. The beneficiary did not specifically instruct the broker to record. The broker is obligated to record:
   (A) Within 10 days of date funds are disbursed
   (B) Before funds are disbursed
   (C) Immediately after funds are disbursed
   (D) At same time funds are disbursed

4. A lease based on gross income of the lessee is a:
   (A) Gross lease
   (B) Net lease
   (C) Percentage lease
   (D) Ground lease

5. Which instrument requires a list of inventory of buildings on real property to be sold, conveyed, or insured?
   (A) Land contract
   (B) Grant deed
   (C) ALTA
   (D) None of the above

6. In real estate, the word "tenancy" means:
    (A) Two or more people joined in an enterprise
    (B) Method or mode of holding title by lessees or owners
    (C) A tenacious person
    (D) A device

7. Personal property presents certain problems to a broker. It becomes difficult to ascertain its ownership because it can:
    (A) Become real property
    (B) Be alienated
    (C) Be hypothecated
    (D) All of the above

8. Under most normal competitive conditions, which of the following would be most likely to influence vacancy factors in apartment buildings?
    (A) Availability of housing units
    (B) Size and number of units
    (C) Rent schedule
    (D) Cost of construction funds

9. The distinguishing characteristic of real property as opposed to personal property is:
    (A) Long-term asset
    (B) High cost of acquisition
    (C) Can be depreciated over useful life
    (D) Immovable

10. When transferring fee simple title to real property that has been financed by a first deed of trust, you must first:
    (A) Receive permission from the beneficiary
    (B) Pay the beneficiary in full
    (C) Have the grantor sign the deed
    (D) None of the above

11. "A" grants an estate to "B" for the life of "X." "B" dies. The estate:
    (A) Ceases to exist
    (B) Reverts to the original owner
    (C) Vests in "X" in trust until "A" dies
    (D) Passes to the heirs or devisees of "B"

12. A lease for a period of years which is held by the lessor is an example of:
    (A) Real property
    (B) Personal property
    (C) Freehold estate
    (D) None of the above

13. When a tenant is delinquent in his rent under a written lease, the landlord may evict the tenant by:
(A) Giving a written three-day notice
(B) Filing a notice of default
(C) Giving a thirty-day notice
(D) Bringing a court action

14. A lessee assigns all of the leasehold interest. The receiver becomes:
(A) Landlord
(B) Assignor
(C) Subleases
(D) Tenant

15. Jones was paying $550 per month to the bank. After the bank deducted interest, $43.85 was applied to the principal. If the outstanding loan balance was $56,500, what was the rate of interest on Jones' loan?
(A) 8 3/4%
(B) 9 1/2%
(C) 10 3/4%
(D) 11 1/2%

16. If a person paid $220 interest on an $8,000 loan for 90 days, the interest rate was:
(A) 9%
(B) 10%
(C) 11%
(D) 12%

17. A deed made and delivered, but not recorded, is:
(A) Invalid as between the parties and valid as to third parties with constructive notice
(B) Valid as between the parties and valid as to subsequent recorded interests
(C) Valid as between the parties and invalid as to subsequent recorded interests without notice
(D) Invalid as between the parties

18. A quitclaim deed releases present claim, rights, and title of the:
(A) Grantor
(B) Grantee
(C) Servient tenement
(D) Property

19. All of the following are required for adverse possession except:
(A) Open and notorious use
(B) Confrontation with the owner
(C) Hostile to the true owner's title
(D) It must be under a claim of right or color of title

20. A broker and a buyer went to Western Hills Title Company. The buyer made out a $1,000 deposit check to Western Hills Title Company. What record, if any, does the broker have to keep of this deposit?
(A) Make an entry in his journal of the entry and exit
(B) Keep separate records for each beneficiary
(C) Not make any record of this in his trust account
(D) Make a record in his trust account but not his general ledger

149

21. A brother and sister owned property in joint tenancy. All his other affairs were separate. The brother died penniless, leaving many unsecured debts. The creditor could:
    (A) Attach the property that was owned in joint tenancy
    (B) Place a lien against the sister's property
    (C) Obtain no satisfaction since the property is owned by the sister
    (D) Appeal to the probate court, which would be able to pay creditors out of the sale of the sister's property

22. Which of the following is a requirement of joint tenancy?
    (A) Husband and wife relationship
    (B) The words "taken in joint tenancy" next to the names of the joint tenants
    (C) All parties have equal interests
    (D) All of the above

23. Businesses operating in California can take the form of an individual proprietorship, partnership or corporation. Each form has its advantages and disadvantages. One of the advantages of operating as a general partnership is that:
    (A) Management of the business can be left to the other partner with little concern or care
    (B) Each partner has the use of the assets of the other partners
    (C) The personal assets of a partner cannot be touched by creditors of the business
    (D) There is less responsibility and more time can be spent away from the business

24. Mr. Jones owned two pieces of property and sold the front property to Mr. Smith, reserving an easement in the deed for access to the rear property. Jones was gone for 31 years. When he returned, Smith claimed Jones no longer had an easement because of nonuse. The easement is:
    (A) Valid because easements created by deed do not terminate
    (B) Invalid because an owner cannot grant himself an easement
    (C) Invalid because of nonuse for over twenty years
    (D) Invalid because of nonuse for over thirty years

25. When standard coverage is extended by the coverage of an ALTA policy, the insurer is liable for all of the following except:
    (A) Liens of record
    (B) Unrecorded easements
    (C) Zoning restrictions
    (D) Unrecorded mechanic's liens

26. A buyer of a piece of property fails to examine public records on the property. The buyer is considered to have:
    (A) Actual notice
    (B) Constructive notice
    (C) Assumed notice
    (D) Conditional notice

27. An ALTA extended coverage policy of title insurance would:
    (A) Cover encroachments after the date of issuance
    (B) Be limited to stated conditions and title as of the date of issuance
    (C) Protect a lessee who moved onto the property after the date of issuance of title insurance
    (D) Cover easements created during the term of the policy

28. If a person wanted to transfer equitable title and retain legal title, he or she would use which of the following?
   (A) Mortgage
   (B) Grant Deed
   (C) Land Contract
   (D) Security Agreement

29. When a railroad needs specific land and the owner objects, the railroad may exercise the right of:
   (A) Eminent domain
   (B) Caveat emptor
   (C) Injunction
   (D) Writ of Replevin

30. The purchase price of a property amounted to $50,000 with the buyer assuming an existing $30,000 loan. If the documentary transfer tax is .55¢ for each $500 or fraction thereof, what was the tax paid on the transaction?
   (A) $55.00
   (B) $44.00
   (C) $33.00
   (D) $22.00

31. With regard to general and specific liens, which of the following groups of words do not contain any general liens?
   (A) Mortgage, attachment, judgment, corporation tax lien
   (B) Attachment, mechanic's lien, mortgage, taxes
   (C) Inheritance taxes, mortgages, assessment, mechanic's lien
   (D) Judgment, trust deed, attachment, taxes

32. Andrew purchased Bliss's ranch on May 1, 2001. The real property taxes for 2000-2001 are:
   (A) Added to the purchase price for Andrew
   (B) A personal obligation of Andrew
   (C) A personal obligation of Bliss
   (D) A lien on the ranch

33. When a trust deed is foreclosed in judicial foreclosure and the trustor fails to exercise his or her right to redeem, possession during the period of redemption would be held by the:
   (A) Trustor
   (B) Trustee
   (C) Mortgagor
   (D) Beneficiary

34. Mr. and Mrs. Crest purchased a home two years ago, financing it with a long term first trust deed and note. They encountered some financial difficulty and were unable to make their payment for two consecutive months. As a result, the beneficiary initiated foreclosure proceedings and the Crests received a copy of the Notice of Default that had been recorded. Their best course of action at this time is to exercise their right of:
   (A) Redemption
   (B) Reinstatement
   (C) Loan moratorium
   (D) Refinancing

35. Under a power of sale clause, the trustee has 3 months from recording a Notice of Default before:
    (A) Taking possession
    (B) Foreclosure is final
    (C) Deed of reconveyance is made to the beneficiary
    (D) Publication of sale

36. An investor bought a second trust deed with a face value of $1,500 on which a 20% discount was allowed. Payments of $131 per month including 9% interest were received for 1 year. What was the percentage of return on the investment?
    (A) 24 3/4%
    (B) 29%
    (C) 31%
    (D) 36 1/4%

37. A minority prospect came to you and requested to see a specific house in a minority neighborhood. You can lawfully assume the prospect is:
    (A) Interested in a house with a particular type of architectural style
    (B) Interested in a house in a minority neighborhood
    (C) Trying to test you
    (D) Unable to qualify for VA of FHA housing and you should refuse to show prospect any houses

38. A real estate licensee is canvassing an area in order to secure listings for an office. The agent tells the prospective sellers that minority groups are moving into the area and it would be advantageous to sell at this time. If the licensee canvasses in this manner:
    (A) Agent would be disciplined by the Real Estate Commissioner if he or she did not say that prices were going to decrease
    (B) Agent would not be disciplined by the Real Estate Commissioner if the broker had instructed him or her to canvass in this manner
    (C) Agent would not be disciplined by the Real Estate Commissioner if the prospective sellers were members of a minority group
    (D) Agent would be disciplined by the Real Estate Commissioner for canvassing in this manner

39. The Federal Open Housing Law contains provisions to prevent discrimination due to race, color, religion, sex, or national origin. A violation of this law would be considered:
    (A) Against public policy
    (B) Unlawful
    (C) Illegal
    (D) All of the above

40. According to Title VIII of the Civil Rights Act of 1968 and an 1866 law enacted by the Congress, a person discriminated against in the purchase of a home because of race could go into court and the court could do all of the following except:
    (A) Order specific performance
    (B) Award actual damages and punitive damages to prevent recurrence
    (C) Provide financial relief for the humiliation and embarrassment
    (D) Suspend or revoke the license of the broker involved

41. A broker was renting only to member of the Caucasian race. Under the Unruh Civil Rights Act, he or she would be subject to which of the following?
    (A) Liable to pay the aggrieved person $250 in penalties
    (B) Held liable for actual damages incurred by the aggrieved party
    (C) Subject to suspension or revocation of his real estate license
    (D) Any of the above

42. Who benefits most from a subordination clause in a trust deed?
    (A) Trustee
    (B) Trustor
    (C) Beneficiary
    (D) None of the above

43. A rectangular parcel of land which measures 1780' x 1780' contains approximately how many acres?
    (A) 20
    (B) 40
    (C) 60
    (D) 73

44. A subordination clause in a trust deed:
    (A) Permits the obligation to be paid off before the end of the term of the loan
    (B) Prohibits the trustor from obtaining another loan before the original loan is paid off
    (C) Places the loan in an inferior position in regard to other liens and encumbrances on the property
    (D) Allows readjustment and rescheduling of the terms as stated in the trust deed

45. In setting up a release schedule under a blanket encumbrance, the beneficiary will usually require a disproportionate amount of money to release a particular lot:
    (A) To have better security on the remaining lots
    (B) Because the best lots usually sell first
    (C) To protect the investment as individual lots are sold
    (D) All of the above

46. Under the 1911 Street Improvement Act, funds may be raised by the local government, benefiting a subdivider, for all the following purposes except:
    (A) Purchase of land for development
    (B) Payment for streets, walks, and curbs
    (C) Payment for drainage system
    (D) Payment for sewers and water mains

47. All of the following are true regarding an appurtenant easement except:
    (A) There must be at least two tracts of land under separate ownership
    (B) The dominate tenement must abut the servient tenement at the border
    (C) The easement would run with the land
    (D) The dominant tenement would benefit and the servient tenement would be burdened

48. A deed to an unlocated easement is:
(A) Void for lack of certainty
(B) Valid
(C) Invalid
(D) Void

49. An easement:
(A) Is a general lien on real property
(B) Is a specific lien on real property
(C) Is an encumbrance on real property
(D) Is an equitable restriction on real property

50. A fire insurance policy began March 1, 20XX and cost $316.80 for 3 years of coverage. The insured cancelled the policy as of November 16 of the same year. What is the amount of the unused policy?
(A) $ 74.80
(B) $121.00
(C) $242.00
(D) $316.80

51. In ridding an area of nonconforming uses, rezoning ordinances may require that certain conditions be met. These would include all of the following except:
(A) Prohibition of rebuilding
(B) Prohibition of expansion
(C) Retroactive zoning ordinances
(D) Allowing a reasonable time (amortized period) within which the abuses may be eliminated

52. The most common way for local planners to designate zoning for multiple residential units is:
(A) A-3
(B) C-3
(C) M-3
(D) R-3

53. The final balances on the seller's and buyer's closing statements:
(A) Must be the same
(B) Can never be the same
(C) May be the same
(D) Must be different

54. A licensee who has negotiated the sale of a mobilehome would not be subject to discipline by the Commissioner of Real Estate if he or she did which of the following?
(A) Sent a check to the Department of Housing and Community Development drawn on an account which has insufficient funds
(B) Failed to deliver the certificate of registration to the Department of Motor Vehicles
(C) Advertised a mobilehome as being new
(D) Sold a mobilehome which is greater than 8 feet in width and 32 feet in length

55. Whatever the purpose of a land survey, the resultant description should contain:
(A) A definite point of beginning and definite parcel corners
(B) A specific length and direction of the sides of the property
(C) The area in accepted units of measure contained within the described boundaries
(D) All of the above

56. Mr. and Mrs. Jenkins own a home worth $33,000 on which there is a $19,000 loan. Mrs. Jenkins alone filed a Declaration of Homestead. If there were a judgment lien filed against them:
    (A) The home could be sold to satisfy the judgment
    (B) The home would not be sold because there is insufficient equity over and above the exemption and the secured lien to satisfy the creditor
    (C) The homestead is invalid since only Mrs. Jenkins filed it
    (D) The exemption would be for $10,000 since Mrs. Jenkins filed it without her husband's signature

57. The S ½ of the NW ¼ of the NE ¼ of Section 11 was listed for sale at $350 per acre with the broker to get a 10% commission. Broker brought in an offer of $6,100 for the property. The owner said he would accept it if the buyer would pay the Broker's commission based upon 10% of the offered amount. If the buyer were to agree, the difference between the original price and the amount as paid by the buyer would be:
    (A) $290
    (B) $295
    (C) $670
    (D) $900

58. Condominium projects are expected to grow in demand in the future primarily because of which of the following factors:
    (A) Increased real property taxes
    (B) Land value
    (C) Comfort of unit owners
    (D) Demand for sociability

59. In the absence of expressed provisions in the deed restrictions and plans, which of the following is a part of a condominium unit?
    (A) Bearing walls
    (B) Central heating system
    (C) Elevator
    (D) None of the above

60. Real property taxes on a condominium:
    (A) Are billed to the individual unit owners
    (B) Are billed to the entire project and prorated by the project manager
    (C) Are a lien on the individual unit owner, but not on the individual unit
    (D) Do not include the value of common areas in assessment

61. A person borrowed $1,968 for 3 years, 10 months and 20 days at 8½ % interest per annum. What is the amount of interest paid to the lender?
    (A) $399
    (B) $501
    (C) $650
    (D) $739

62. When an existing contract is replaced by an entirely new contract, this is an act of:
    (A) Subrogation
    (B) Rescission
    (C) Novation
    (D) Hypothecation

155

63. Which of the following is of importance in filing a mechanic's lien?
    (A) Notice of Non-responsibility
    (B) Notice of Completion
    (C) Notice of Cessation of Labor
    (D) Any of the above

64. The written employment agreement, required by the Commissioner's Regulations, between an employing broker and salesperson is an example of:
    (A) Implied contract
    (B) Ratification
    (C) Bilateral executory contract
    (D) Unilateral contract

65. Harris, an unlicensed person, wanted to purchase 300 acres of land for $85,000 from Stevens, which he or she intended to subdivide in the future. Harris did not have the money for the purchase and convinced a friend, Williams, to purchase the property, and Harris immediately entered into a land sales contract with Williams to purchase the property for $98,000. With respect to the above statements, which of the following is correct?
    (A) The original transaction is valid but the subsequent sale is invalid
    (B) Both transactions would be considered unenforceable
    (C) The second transaction is illegal
    (D) The original purchase and subsequent sale are both valid

66. An executed contract is a contract:
    (A) Which has been signed
    (B) Under the jurisdiction of the probate court
    (C) Signed, notarized and recorded
    (D) To be rewritten

67. A person who has been judicially declared incompetent and who was bequeathed three properties by his brother:
    (A) Cannot receive title to real property because of his incompetency
    (B) Cannot receive title to real property but can receive title to personal property
    (C) Can accept title to real property given to him in a will
    (D) Can accept title only if it is placed with a trustee

68. A broker who is selling property on which he or she holds an option must inform the buyer that he is:
    (A) An optionor
    (B) A grantor
    (C) An agent
    (D) A principal

69. The maximum amount of commission and loan costs that may be charged for a second trust deed of $4,000 for a 4-year term is:
    (A) $550
    (B) $725
    (C) $990
    (D) $850

70. "A" led "C" to believe that he had the authority to act for "B." "B" went along with "A." The agency created was by:
    (A) Expressed contract
    (B) Ratification
    (C) Estoppel
    (D) Ostensible

71. For purposes of federal income tax, the taxpayer would be able to deduct which of the following for a personal residence?
    (A) Mortgage interest payments, prepayment penalty, and real estate taxes
    (B) Payment of broker's commission, late charges, mortgage interest
    (C) Mortgage payment, capital improvement, real estate tax
    (D) Mortgage payment, premium payments on a fire insurance policy, real estate taxes

72. A listing agreement in which the owner promises to pay a commission under all circumstances of sale, except if he or she sells the property himself, is known as:
    (A) An exclusive right to sell
    (B) An exclusive agency
    (C) A net listing
    (D) None of the above

73. In November, a storm caused damage in Able's house due to a leaky tile roof. In April, Able listed the house with broker Baker. Broker Baker showed the house to Smith, but did not mention the leaky roof, although Able had mentioned it. After close of escrow, Smith sustained damage to the interior of the house due to this leaky roof. Under these circumstances, buyer Smith:
    (A) Had no recourse since escrow had closed
    (B) Had no recourse under the doctrine of *"caveat emptor"*
    (C) Could take legal action against broker Baker but not against Able
    (D) Could take legal action against Able and if successful, Able could most likely recover the loss from broker Baker

74. Which of the following decides the amount of commission received from the sale of property of a deceased person?
    (A) Real Estate Commissioner
    (B) Administrator or executor of the estate
    (C) Real Estate board
    (D) Court order

75. Broker Fenton has a property listed for $11,400 and submits an offer of $11,000 the next day, with a three-day acceptance period. The seller makes a counter offer of $11,200. One day after the acceptance period, the seller accepts the buyer's original offer of $11,000. The buyer decided that he no longer wants the property. In these circumstances the acceptance is:
    (A) Valid
    (B) Voidable
    (C) Enforceable because of the original offer
    (D) Not a contract

76.   A salesperson wrote up an offer to purchase a home and took a "pay to bearer" note from the buyer as a deposit with the offer in the amount of $1,000. When his broker saw the "pay to bearer" note, she would be most likely to tell the salesperson that:
(A)   The seller's permission must be obtained before a note of this type could be accepted as a deposit
(B)   The note cannot be accepted because the deposit must be cash, personal check, or cashier's check
(C)   The seller must be told of the note before he agrees to accept the offer to purchase
(D)   In real estate transactions a "pay to bearer" note is the same as cash

77.   Under California law, it is necessary to give notice to terminate which of the following?
(A)   Estate for years
(B)   Estate at sufferance
(C)   Estate at will
(D)   None of the above

78.   All of the following are ways by which an offer to purchase real estate would be terminated except:
(A)   Failure to accept the offer within a prescribed period of time
(B)   Failure to communicate revocation of the offer before the other party communicates his acceptance
(C)   Conditional acceptance of offer by offeree
(D)   Death or incompetency of either offeror and offeree without notice thereof

79.   A licensee who is guilty of "conversion" is one who is:
(A)   Misrepresenting
(B)   Commingling
(C)   Misappropriating the funds of clients
(D)   Failing to make full disclosure

80.   An individual is appointed by an insurance company to procure first deed of trust loans and is compensated on a commission basis by the lending institution for each loan he procures. This requires:
(A)   An active real estate broker's license
(B)   A real property securities dealer license
(C)   A $5,000 surety bond
(D)   None of the above

81.   A Mortgage Loan Disclosure Statement (Broker's Loan Statement) is required by law to be retained by the broker for:
(A)   2 years
(B)   3 years
(C)   4 years
(D)   5 years

82.   Which of the following are considered artificial monuments?
(A)   Canals and streets
(B)   Streets and trees
(C)   Trees and fences
(D)   Fences and rock

83. If interest is paid at a rate of $60 a month and the rate of interest if 8% per annum, the principal amount of the loan is:
    (A) $4,000
    (B) $7,000
    (C) $9,000
    (D) $12,000

84. Interest paid on original principal and also on the accrued and unpaid interest that has accumulated is:
    (A) Simple interest
    (B) Compound interest
    (C) Multiple interest
    (D) Accumulative interest

85. The lenders that invest a major portion of their assets in long-term real estate loans, do not like to service their own loans, like large loans on newer high-priced homes as well as large loans on commercial property would be:
    (A) Commercial banks
    (B) Savings and loan associations
    (C) Insurance companies
    (D) Mutual mortgage companies

86. In a tight money market and utilizing VA financing, which of the following statements is correct?
    (A) Seller would pay discounts at a higher rate
    (B) Seller would pay higher loan origination fee
    (C) Buyer would pay discounts at a higher rate
    (D) Buyer would pay higher loan origination fee

87. An individual is purchasing a parcel of real property. The provisions of the contract require the seller to convey title to the property when the buyer pays the full amount of the contract to the seller. When the buyer has fulfilled his part of the contract and requests the seller to convey title, the seller refuses to fulfill his contractual obligation. Under these circumstances the buyer is said to have made a:
    (A) Tender
    (B) Demand
    (C) Covenant
    (D) Breach

88. Points are not charged on which of the following types of home loans?
    (A) Federal Housing Administration
    (B) Veterans Administration
    (C) California Department of Veterans Affairs
    (D) None of these

89. A home is being sold for $80,000 and has been appraised for $78,500. If the lender is willing to lend the maximum permitted by the Veteran's Administration, the GI buyer is required to put up which of the following amounts in cash?
    (A) $2,500
    (B) $2,000
    (C) $2,050
    (D) $1,500

159

90. When applied as a deduction from gross income, the vacancy factor is known to:
    (A) Be constant
    (B) Generally discourage prospective purchasers
    (C) Vary both in locality and from time to time
    (D) Be impossible for the appraiser to estimate with any accuracy

91. Broker Thomas negotiated a 25-year lease with an annual rent of $15,000. The agreement was that Broker Thomas would receive annually his commission based on the following schedule: 7% for the first year, 5% for the next 4 years, 3% for the next 15 years, and 1% for each year thereafter to the completion of the lease. How much commission will Broker Thomas receive at the end of the 19th year?
    (A) $ 9,350
    (B) $ 9,850
    (C) $10,350
    (D) $10,650

92. A home sold for $37,000 with a fair market value of $35,000. The seller took a purchase money second trust deed for $25,000 and sold it "without recourse" at a discount of $23,500. The buyer defaulted before the first payment was made. The holder of the second trust deed can do which of the following?
    (A) Foreclose for $23,500
    (B) Look to the seller since the "without recourse" has no effect
    (C) Look to the seller since the note was usurious
    (D) Foreclose for $25,000

93. A buyer seeking an FHA loan would least likely do which of the following?
    (A) Find a lender willing to give him the loan
    (B) Go to the nearest FHA office for an appraisal
    (C) Agree to pay mutual mortgage insurance
    (D) Agree to make amortized payments

94. A bank will usually make a conventional loan and charge a higher interest rate than the interest rate charged on an FHA loan on the same property. What would be the determining factor in choosing to make an FHA loan instead of a conventional loan?
    (A) Higher return
    (B) Degree of risk
    (C) Needs of borrower for lower interest
    (D) Number of properties sold by seller

95. A man listed a property for $76,000 and was willing to take back a trust deed and note for $10,000. FHA appraised the property for $70,000 and the broker secured a buyer who wanted to secure an FHA loan for $70,000, pay $4,000 cash and execute a second trust deed and note in favor of the seller. The broker should:
    (A) Write up the offer subject to FHA loan and second trust deed
    (B) Write up the offer "subject to better financing"
    (C) Write up the offer subject to $70,000 FHA loan and a personal loan for $6,000
    (D) Refuse to accept the offer

96. According to the Federal Reserve System Regulation Z, which of the following would be the proper usage in an advertisement relating to housing?
    (A) Assume a 7% mortgage
    (B) Take over a 7% mortgage
    (C) Assume a 7% annual percentage rate mortgage
    (D) Any of the above

97. When the Federal Reserve Board raises the discount rate to their borrowers, it has what effect on the money market?
    (A) Makes money more available
    (B) Makes money less available
    (C) Has no effect
    (D) Makes more marginal loans available

98. Which of the following best defines adjusted basis of a property for income tax purposes?
    (A) Acquisition cost
    (B) Acquisition cost plus capital improvements
    (C) Acquisition cost plus capital improvements minus depreciation
    (D) Acquisition cost plus capital improvements plus depreciation

99. Which single factor would least directly influence the level of movement of mortgage rates?
    (A) Inflation
    (B) Unemployment
    (C) Tight money
    (D) Demand for funds

100. To prevent investment erosion through inflation, an investor would place his funds in:
    (A) Mortgages and trust deeds
    (B) Equities
    (C) Savings accounts
    (D) Government bonds

101. A woman purchases a home for $80,000 and executes a note for $78,000 secured by a first trust deed. The balance she pays in cash. Subsequently, a period of slow economic inflation sets in. This would benefit:
    (A) Beneficiary
    (B) Trustor
    (C) Trustee
    (D) Neither beneficiary nor trustor

102. The Real Estate Settlement Procedures Act lists services a lender may charge for as settlement connected costs. Accordingly, as appropriate, the buyer and seller may be charged for all of the following except:
    (A) Credit reports
    (B) Loan documents
    (C) Appraisals
    (D) Uniform disclosure/settlement statements

103. Of the four appraisal terms listed below, which one has the least relation to the others?
    (A) Sales
    (B) Comparative
    (C) Comparable
    (D) Summation

104. Broker Wilson sells a house, and a loan for the buyer is secured through a savings and loan. Wilson carefully explains all loan costs to the buyer. According to the Real Estate Settlement Procedures Act (RESPA), which of the following is true?
    (A) Broker Wilson would not have to provide an estimate of settlement costs to the buyer because he had explained all costs
    (B) Broker Wilson must provide the buyer with an estimate of settlement costs within one week
    (C) The lender must provide an estimate of settlement costs to the buyer immediately
    (D) The lender must provide the buyer with an estimate of settlement costs within 3 days

105. Under the Real Estate Settlement Procedures Act (RESPA) lenders are required to give borrowers:
    (A) A Bill of Sale
    (B) A good faith estimate
    (C) The amount of mortgage interest
    (D) An invoice not exceeding $10.00 for the special information booklet

106. The amount of investment required to earn $75 per month at 5% per annum is:
    (A) $ 6,000
    (B) $18,000
    (C) $20,000
    (D) $24,000

107. What was the primary purpose of the Real Estate Settlement Procedures Act?
    (A) Standardize settlement procedures throughout the country
    (B) Set settlement costs on all real estate transactions
    (C) Set settlement costs on 1- to 4-unit owner-occupied dwellings
    (D) Give the buyer an opportunity to shop around for settlement services

108. A commercial property no longer has a commercial use because it exists in an area where zoning has been changed to industrial. Since this creates a hardship, which of the following could be a remedy?
    (A) Spot zoning
    (B) Conditional Use Permit
    (C) Variance
    (D) Any of the above

109. Which of the following is a unique feature of a VA loan as compared to conventional loans?
    (A) VA downpayment is 3% of the purchase price
    (B) VA downpayment is determined by the Certificate of Reasonable Value
    (C) VA downpayment is 5% of the appraised value
    (D) A VA loan requires no downpayment

110. A broker is given a listing on a house. The owner needs to net $37,000 after she pays a 4% commission on the sales price, which is to include $600 in closing costs. The sales price has to be at least how much?
    (A) $37,000
    (B) $38,541
    (C) $38,141
    (D) $39,167

111. In a sales transaction, an agent is paid by both parties but did not reveal dual agency. What could happen in these circumstances?
    (A) The agent would be subject to discipline by the Real Estate Commissioner
    (B) The sale could be rescinded
    (C) The agent may not be able to enforce payment of his commission
    (D) All of the above

112. State enabling legislation gives cities and counties various controls over real property. The enabling legislation gives to cities and counties all but which of the following:
    (A) Subdivision and land use regulations
    (B) Local planning and zoning ordinances
    (C) Lien and attachment laws
    (D) Rent control and city codes

113. The state fiscal year falls between the dates:
    (A) December 31 to January 1, midnight
    (B) January 1 to December 31
    (C) July 1 to June 30, midnight
    (D) June 30 to July 1

114. For federal income tax purposes, a taxpayer could adjust the cost basis of the personal residence on income tax records for which of the following items?
    (A) Depreciation
    (B) Interest on a loan
    (C) Fire insurance premiums paid
    (D) The addition of a concrete patio

115. A man owns property free and clear valued at $320,000 with a book value of $220,000. If he exchanges for another property, also free and clear valued at $365,000 and pays no boot, the book value on the second property will be:
    (A) $365,000
    (B) $220,000
    (C) $585,000
    (D) Cannot be computed with the facts given

116. Which of the following is not a method for providing for depreciation?
    (A) Straight-line
    (B) Sinking fund
    (C) Obsolescence
    (D) Sum-of-the-years' digits

117. Most real estate syndicates in California are:
    (A) Corporations
    (B) Limited partnerships
    (C) Joint ventures
    (D) Real estate investment trusts

118. A portfolio risk manager (financial manager) would be most concerned with:
    (A) Diversification
    (B) Liquidity
    (C) Reserves
    (D) Any of the above

119. Without being licensed by the Corporations Commissioner as an escrow company, a real estate broker may:
    (A) Handle escrows for all brokers in an area where there is no established escrow company
    (B) Handle escrows in connection with real estate transactions in which broker acted as an agent
    (C) Handle only those escrows pertaining to property which broker owns or has an interest
    (D) Never act as an escrow agent

120. An escrow agent is exempt from licensing requirements of the Corporations Commissioner in all but which of the following?
    (A) An attorney-at-law who is not actively conducting an escrow business
    (B) A broker who is acting as an escrow agent for other brokers transactions
    (C) A broker dealing with his or her own transactions and charging a fee
    (D) A broker dealing with his or her own transactions and not charging a fee

121. An escrow closing statement that refers to "recurring costs" would be describing:
    (A) Deed transfer taxes
    (B) Title insurance
    (C) Impound items
    (D) Escrow charges

122. In the event there is no provision in the escrow instructions with regard to a termination date, the parties to the escrow have:
    (A) 10 days
    (B) 30 days
    (C) 60 days
    (D) A reasonable time

123. A broker was to receive a 6% commission from the sale of a property. His or her salesperson was to receive 45% of the 6% commission. The salesperson received $8,100. What was the selling price of the property?
    (A) $ 40,000
    (B) $135,000
    (C) $300,000
    (D) $435,000

124. Real property taxes for the 2000-2001 fiscal year become a lien on:
    (A) January 1, 2000
    (B) November 1, 2000
    (C) December 10, 2000
    (D) February 10, 2001

125. Which of the following would have the least effect on property taxes in a community?
    (A) Number of commercial buildings and high priced homes
    (B) Compactness of the community
    (C) Zoning and private restrictions
    (D) Homestead exemptions

126. On or before June 30 each year, property in which owners are delinquent in their taxes is declared in default. This date is important because:
    (A) The occupant of the property must vacate the premises within 90 days
    (B) Interest on the delinquent taxes will begin from December 10th
    (C) The sale on or before June 30th starts the five-year period of redemption
    (D) All of the above

127. Which of the following has the responsibility for determining property values for real property tax purposes?
    (A) Board of Supervisors
    (B) Board of Equalization
    (C) Assessor's Office
    (D) Tax Commissioner

128. The second installment of real property taxes would become due and delinquent on which of the following dates?
    (A) November 1 and February 1
    (B) February 1 and April 10
    (C) December 10 and February 1
    (D) December 10 and April 10

129. Which of the following is not a type of soil or soil condition?
    (A) Alkaline
    (B) Expansive
    (C) Adobe
    (D) Deciduous

130. A man was going to build a home on a 50' by 150' lot and wanted it to fit in relation to its surroundings. This placement would be known as:
    (A) Orientation
    (B) Elevation
    (C) Plottage
    (D) Topography

131. "Soil pipe" relates to:
    (A) Sewer pipe
    (B) Hot water line
    (C) Irrigation pipe
    (D) Gas line

132.   An increase in the appraised value of property that is considered an unearned increment would most probably result from:
(A)   Increase in population
(B)   Capital improvements
(C)   Management expense
(D)   Increase in amenities

133.   In appraisal, the following are recognized methods for the valuation of land except:
(A)   Comparative method
(B)   Economic method
(C)   Abstract method
(D)   Development method

134.   An investment property is appraised at $400,000 based on a net income of $36,000 and a 9% capitalization rate. The value of the property based on a 12% capitalization rate would be:
(A) $250,000
(B) $300,000
(C) $450,000
(D) $423,000

135.   Which of the following groups of characteristics best defines the value of property?
(A)   Transferability, cost, utility, scarcity
(B)   Utility, scarcity, cost, demand
(C)   Transferability, utility, scarcity, demand
(D)   Utility, cost, demand, transferability

136.   In arriving at his estimate of value based on selling prices, the appraiser is most interested in the date the:
(A)   Buyer and seller agreed on the price
(B)   Deed was recorded
(C)   Sale went into escrow
(D)   Deed was signed

137.   The economic life of improved property is which of the following in relation to the physical life of the property?
(A)   Greater
(B)   Lesser
(C)   The same
(D)   Depends on the type of improvement

138.   In determining the value of income producing property, an appraiser may use which of the following appraisal techniques?
(A)   Land residual technique
(B)   Building residual technique
(C)   Property residual technique
(D)   All of the above

139.   A voidable contract is:
(A)   Unenforceable
(B)   Illegal
(C)   Enforceable
(D)   Valid until some action is taken to void it

140. When property tax increases and all other items remain the same, an income property:
    (A) Decreases in value by the amount of the taxes
    (B) Decreases in value by more than the amount of the taxes
    (C) Increases in value by the amount of the taxes
    (D) Increases in value by more than the amount of the taxes

141. With regard to appraisal techniques, all of the following are correct except:
    (A) The cost approach is difficult to use due to the great amount of knowledge needed regarding the current economic factors involved
    (B) The cost approach is most effective on new buildings
    (C) The cost approach should be used on single-use properties
    (D) The cost approach sets the lower limit of value

142. If an appraiser was appraising a residence built in 1910, which of the following would he use?
    (A) Cost of living index 1910
    (B) Original cost of materials in 1910
    (C) Original cost adjusted to today's cost of living index
    (D) Today's cost of reproduction

143. The terms "quantity survey," "unit-in-place," "square foot and cubic foot" are all methods of arriving at value estimate that are used in the:
    (A) Cost approach
    (B) Income approach
    (C) Market data approach
    (D) Sinking fund approach

144. Which of the following approaches to a value estimate tends to set the upper limit of value?
    (A) Market comparison
    (B) Replacement cost
    (C) Income
    (D) Comparative sales

145. Which of the following statements would be true with regard to bearing walls of a building?
    (A) Can be built at any angle to doors or windows
    (B) Are usually built sturdier than other walls
    (C) Are seldom moved during remodeling
    (D) Any of the above

146. Conduit in a new building would be installed by which of the following?
    (A) Carpenter
    (B) Electrician
    (C) Plumber
    (D) Roofers

147. The highest member of the frame in a conventionally constructed home is the:
    (A) Rafter
    (B) Collar beam
    (C) Girder
    (D) Ridge board

148. An appraiser received a $100 fee from Jones for appraising Brown's property. The appraiser may discuss the details of the appraisal with:
    (A) Jones
    (B) Brown
    (C) Anyone
    (D) No one

149. Appraisers have the most difficulty in determining the value of:
    (A) Replacement cost new
    (B) Basic cost data
    (C) Accrued depreciation
    (D) Capitalized income

150. An appraiser would consider all of the following as contributing to the stability of a neighborhood except:
    (A) Homogeneity of buildings, people, and uses
    (B) Many families with children going to school
    (C) Increased density and rapid turnover of population
    Residence in the path of urban directional growth

Exam Answers Section

Exam 1 Answers - Definitions

1. (D)   To alienate means to make the title leave the owner by conveying the title to another.

2. (C)   Amortization is (1) the liquidation of a financial obligation on an installment basis or (2) recovery of cost or value over a period of time.

3. (A)   Assignment of leasehold means the entire interest is transferred and includes the remaining term and the entire premises. Subleasing is transferring part of the premises or less than the entire term.

4. (B)   An exchange of promises creates a bilateral contract. Since a listing is for a period of time, the contract is executory during the listing term.

5. (A)   A blind ad is advertising by a licensee who does not disclose in the ad that the property is offered through an agent rather than by the principal.

6. (D)   Capitalization of (net) income is an appraisal approach in which net income is projected to a future date and discounted to today's rates to attract investors.

7. (C)   A commercial acre is the remainder of an acre of newly subdivided land after deduction of areas devoted to streets, sidewalks, curbs and the like.

8. (C)   The company dollar is money earned for the company and spent by the company. The money earned by a real estate company is the money retained by the company after commissions have been paid. From the company dollar, operating expenses will have to be paid before a profit can be realized.

9. (D)   A default constitutes a failure to perform either (a) a duty or (b) an obligation. In order to protect their security, most deeds of trust contain agreements between the mortgagor and mortgagee, which, if breached, constitute default. Among these agreements are (a) not to be delinquent in payment, (b) not to fail to maintain the property. Careful: If the question asks for the most common cause of default then choose "Is delinquent in monthly payments."

10. (D)   Deciduous is the term used to identify the type of tree that sheds its leaves annually. The other three choices refer to types of soil.

11. (C)   Davidson has a personal right to use Parkins' property (servient tenement) and which is not attached to any land. Since there is no dominant tenement, it is an easement in gross.

12. (D)   An encumbrance is anything that affects or limits the fee simple title to real property.

13. (B)   The owner who reserves the right to sell the property himself has signed an exclusive agency listing. This means if any other person sells the property the listing broker is entitled to a commission.

14. (C)   An administrator is appointed by the court when the deceased has died without a will. Executor, devise and testator refer to a will.

15. (C) A franchise agreement is set forth in the Franchise Investment Law as:

"A contract between two or more persons where one grants the other the right to sell, offer to sell, or exchange goods or services under a marketing plan designed by a grantor."

16. (A) The frontage is a term used to describe or identify that part of a parcel of land or an improvement on the land that faces a street.

17. (A) Freehold Estates are either
        (1)   fee simple estates or
        (2)   life estates.

Less than freehold estates are either
        (1)   estates for years
        (2)   periodic tenancies
        (3)   estates at will, or
        (4)   estates at sufferance.

18. (C) Percolation is the filtering process that occurs when water seeps through the ground. Water will percolate easily through a porous soil.

19. (D) A *hard money* loan is a loan of cash, as opposed to the extension of credit by a seller. It is a loan in which the lender makes out a check to escrow or to the borrower and transfers funds to the borrower. The purpose of the loan does not influence the hard money aspects.

20. (A) Holder in due course: One who has taken a note, check or bill of exchange in due course:

(1) Before it was overdue

(2) In good faith and for value

(3) Without knowledge that it has been previously dishonored and without notice of any defect at the time it was negotiated.

21. (B) An injunction is a court order restraining or requiring performance by a party (such as performing acts required by property covenants or refraining from acts restricted by such covenant).

22. (B) If noise from low-flying aircraft damages the owner in the use of his land, this may be a "taking" of property, for which compensation must be paid by the government. This remedy is called inverse condemnation because it is started by an owner who is seeking compensation from an agency that caused the situation.

23. (B) Choice (B) completes the sentence in the question. The two parts constitute a quotation from section 2985 of the *Civil Code* that defines a land contract.

24. (C) A lien usually makes specific property security for the debt or discharge of an obligation.

25. (A) A license is a personal, revocable, and unassignable permission given to another, thus is distinguished from an easement.

26. (D) Market price is the price actually paid for the property.

27. (D) This change in zoning would cause the existing apartment building to become a nonconforming use. Whenever zoning laws are changed and made applicable to improved city areas, a *variance* is sometimes granted to the owner to continue the existing use until the structure has reached the end of its economic life or is abandoned. The structure may be maintained but enlarging or rebuilding is generally disallowed.

28. (B) An option is defined as a contract under which the optionor (owner) promises to hold open for a specified time an offer to sell or lease property to the optionee. The optionee is not obligated to purchase. The $10 paid is the consideration given for the contract to keep an offer open.

29. (D) A pledge consists of transferring to the lender the possession of personal property (in this case the note) as security for the loan.

30. (B) Plottage increment is the resultant increase in value over the same number of parcels under separate ownership. *Assemblage* is the *act* of combing one or more contiguous lots under single ownership resulting in improved usability.

31. (D) A cloud on title may be removed by a quitclaim deed from the person creating the cloud. However, if a quitclaim deed cannot be obtained, one must institute a quite-title action to remove the cloud.

32. (B) Ratification is the adoption or approval of an act performed on behalf of a person without previous authorization. When B went along with A, he ratified A's authority to act on B's behalf. The difference between ratification and *estoppel* is that ratification results from an *action* by the principal, where as an estoppel results from a *failure* of the principal *to act*.

33. (C) The term recurring costs describes the expenses that the buyer can expect year after year. These include property taxes and fire insurance that are frequently impounded by the lender.

34. (D) Rescind means to annul the contract and restore the parties to the same position they held before they entered into the contract.

35. (D) The ridge board is placed at the peak of the roof.

36. (D) The owner who sells their interest is conveying the fee title (a freehold estate) to the buyer. When the seller becomes a lessee of the former property, through a leaseback arrangement, the seller has converted the former freehold (fee) estate to a less-than-freehold estate (a lease).

37. (B) Soil pipe is heavy cast iron or clay pipe used as sewer pipe.

38. (A) A standby loan commitment is a commitment to issue a permanent loan after completion of construction.

39. (B) Surrender is a mutual agreement between the landlord and tenant to terminate a lease. *Recission* is a mutual agreement to release each other from any contract *before performance*, under which the parties must restore each other to their former positions.

40. (C) A construction loan is an interim loan that is in effect during the construction period. Once the building is completed, the long-term financing or take-out loan is negotiated.

41. (B) Tenancy is a method or mode of holding ownership by lessees, (example, a tenant in common or a joint tenant).

42. (C) A turnkey project means a completed construction package ready for occupancy. The last step is to turn over the keys to the buyer.

43. (C) Undivided interest means that all owners have the unlimited use of every portion of the property. Tenancy in common does not have the unities of time, title or interest. It only has the unity of possession.

44. (B) Valuation is the process of estimating market value, investment value, insurable value, or other properly defined value of an identified interest(s) in a specific parcel(s) of real estate as of a given date. Valuation seeks an answer in dollars. *Evaluation* is a study of the nature, quality, or utility, of a parcel of real estate as to its suitability for a particular investor or use.

45. (B) A Writ of Execution is an order from the court to an officer, such as a sheriff, directing a sale of property to satisfy a judgment. Procedures are similar to that of mortgage foreclosure.

46. (A) Amenities are the features of a property and the surrounding areas that add to its value or desirability.

47. (A) An anchor tenant is the key tenant in a commercial development. The developer looks for a "blue chip" firm, such as J.C. Penny or Montgomery Ward. This gives the lender confidence in the expectation that the development will pay its own way.

48. (D) An annuity is a series of assured equal or nearly equal payments to be made over a period of time, or it may be a lump-sum payment to be made in the future. The installment payments due to the landlord under a lease are an annuity; so are the installment payments due to the lender.

49. (B) An attachment is a legal seizure *prior* to a court action. The instrument employed is a Writ of Attachment. A *lis pendens* effectively puts a "hold" on property, but it is not a seizure.

50. (C) "Equity financing" is the opposite of "debt financing." It means buying a property with the purchaser's own money (equity) rather than financing the purchase with borrowed money. Don't confuse this with an "equity loan" which is money borrowed against the owner's equity.

51. (C) A Power of Attorney is a written instrument giving authority to an agent, called an attorney in fact. Don't confuse with attorney at law.

52. (A) Blanket mortgage is a loan on real property that covers more than one parcel of land.

    Package mortgage is a loan on both real property and personal property.

    Purchase Money Mortgage is a security device that is (1) given by a purchaser to a seller, or (2) by a purchaser to a lender, for all or part of the purchase price and the security is the property purchased.

53. (C) Capitalization of net income is an appraisal method that bases the present market value of the property on the anticipated future benefits of ownership in dollars, discounted to a present worth at a rate that is attracting purchase capital to similar investments.

54. (D) Cash flow refers to the money the investor has at the end of the year after deducting all out-of-pocket expenses from gross income. Do not confuse with "net spendable," which is computed by deducting income tax from cash flow.

173

55. (D) Chattel real is personal property created by a lease, thus carrying a possessory right in real estate.

56. (C) Cul-de-sac (a French expression) literally means "bottom of the bag," and is used frequently in referring to a dead-end street.

57. (C) One meaning of the word demise as used in real estate, is to convey or transfer the possession and use of real property under the terms of a lease.

58. (B) Duress is defined as unlawful constraint exercised upon a person who is forced to do some act, such as sign a contract, against his will.

59. (D) An easement is the right to use another's property without payment. Although it is an interest in real property, it is not an estate—not a "possessory" interest.

60. (C) Economic rent is defined as the rent expectancy if the property were available at the time of its estimation or, as in choice (C), rents being paid for comparable space in the real estate market. Choices (A), and (D) relate to *contract rent.*

61. (B) Escheat is the reverting of property to the state when heirs capable of inheriting are lacking; for example, a person dies intestate (without a will) or the individual has no heirs to receive the property through intestate succession.

62. (C) Et ux, a Latin abbreviation for *Et Uxor,* means "and wife."

63. (C) An estate for years is an interest in lands by virtue of a contract (lease) for the possession of them for a definite and limited period of time. The term may be for any specified period of time, even for a certain number of years, months, weeks, or days.

64. (B) Fee simple estate is the greatest interest that one can have in real property. It is an estate that is unqualified, of indefinite duration, freely transferable and inheritable. However, a fee estate *can* be encumbered.

65. (D) Flashing is sheet metal (or sometimes composition material) that is used to protect, cover, and deflect water from joints or angles, such as roof valleys, or above window and door openings.

66. (C) A foundation plan shows the details of the foundation that includes footings, piers, and subflooring.

67. (D) A hip roof has four sloping sides. A *gambrel* has two sides, and each side has two slopes.

68. (C) The terms *ingress* and *egress* refer to the right of the easement holder to cross over the property of another to enter or exit from his property: an easement.

69. (C) Alienate means to transfer the title to real property from one person to another. To involuntarily alienate could occur by the operation of law as in the case of foreclosure due to non-payment of taxes or other lawful debts.

70. (A) Joint tenancy's most distinguishing characteristic is its "right of survivorship." An equal and undivided interest is one of the four unities required in joint tenancy.

71. (C) Jointly means the creditor can look to all the signers as a group; severally means he or she can look to any one signer for the entire amount due. Co-signers on a note are jointly and severally liable.

72. (A) Laches means delay or negligence in asserting one's legal rights.

73. (C) A legatee is the receiver of a legacy that is a willed gift of *personal property*. A *devisee* is the receiver of a devise that is a willed gift of *real property*.

74. (C) The basic idea of leverage is to use other people's money to finance purchases to realize greater return on your investment. The "increase" is called *appreciation*.

75. (C) Liquidity is the ability to convert assets into cash at a price close to true value. Stocks that are traded publicly are a relatively liquid investment. Real estate is considered to be a longer-term investment, as it is not highly liquid.

76. (C) Lis Pendens ("suit pending") is a notice filed or recorded for the purpose of warning all persons that the title or right to the possession of certain real property is in litigation. It is recorded to give constructive notice of pending litigation.

77. (D) Megalopolis is a very large, thickly populated region centering in a metropolis (city) or embracing several metropolises (cities).

78. (A) A lock-in clause is a clause that may appear in a note or land contract that prohibits the payor from paying off the indebtedness before the date set forth in the contract.

79. (D) The word nominal stems from the word "name" and is the rate named in the note.

80. (C) Off-site improvements are those that add to the usefulness (utility) of the site but are not located directly on it. Examples are streets, curbs, drainage, sidewalks, lighting, and so forth.

81. (B) An open-end mortgage is one containing a clause that permits the mortgagor to borrow additional money after the loan has been reduced without rewriting the mortgage.

82. (D) An option is a binding agreement to "keep an offer open" for a specific period of time.

83. (C) Pitch is the slope or inclination of the roof. Example: "5-in-12 pitch" means that for every 12 inches of horizontal distance, the roof slope rises 5 inches.

84. (C) Potable means suitable for drinking and would refer to water.

85. (C) Privity refers to the mutual interest in the same property. Under a lease contract, the lessor and lessee are said to have a mutual interest in the same property by contract.

86. (B) Purchase money mortgage applies to any money used to purchase the ownership of property, either from credit extended by the seller ("soft money") or a cash loan from a lender ("hard money").

87. (B) Reconciliation is the balancing of the broker's trust account record with the balance as indicated on the bank statement.

88. (C) Redevelopment is a term associated with clearing and rebuilding of a slum or blighted area.

89. (A) Rehabilitation is restoring without changes in floor plan or style.

90. (C) A reversionary interest is one in which the possession of the property returns by operation of law to the grantor or lessor. It exists when the estate conveyed is less than fee simple—for example, a life estate or leasehold estate.

91. (B) A rider is an addition or amendment to the original contract.

92. (D) Riparian rights deal with flowing water in a river, stream, or watercourse (a fixed or defined channel). Littoral are rights associated with a body of water such as the sea, or other tidal water (ocean), and lakes.

93. (C) A seasoned loan is one that has been on the books for a time and the payment record of the borrower is a known quantity.

94. (B) A take-out loan literally takes the construction lender out of the financing picture and their construction loan is replaced with a long-term conventional loan.

95. (D) A tenancy in common is created when two or more persons own undivided interests in a property *without* the right of survivorship.

96. (A) Tender is an offer to perform, not actual performance. If the offer is refused, it places the other party in default and permits the party making the tender to exercise remedies for breach of contract.

97. (A) A title plant is a collection of records in the title company's office. These records are developed from information recorded at the county recorder's office.

98. (D) A walk-up is an apartment building that does not have an elevator. It is a term common in the east but not in California.

99. (A) Acquisition is the act of acquiring; "alienation" is the act of transferring or conveying title.

100. (B) Personal property is all property that is not real property. A *fixture* is real property and should not be confused with the term "trade fixtures" which are personal property.

Exam 2 Answers - Preliminary Evaluation

Real Property and Laws Relating to Ownership

1. (B) "Time of annexation" is not a test of whether an item is a fixture of real property or personal property but the following are:

Method of attachment	Choice (a)
Adaptability	
Relationship between the parties	Choice (c)
Intention of the parties	Choice (d)
Agreement of the parties	

    MARIA

2. (A) As between buyer and seller, strict interpretation of "real property" is given if there is no specific agreement otherwise. Until the corn is sold, harvested or mortgaged, it is real property on the land of a seller who cultivated it. (On leased land, lessee has the right to the crop). Growing crops are part of the second category of real property: things attached to land.

3. (D) Fee simple absolute estate: both of the choices (A) and (D) apply; however, choice (D) best describes the absolute estate.

4. (C) A fee simple estate is of indefinite duration and the owner can dispose of it in life by sale or gift or, upon death, by will or intestate succession. However, it is possible to own property in fee simple and still have many encumbrances on it.

5. (A) The subdivision Map Act is concerned with the physical aspects of the subdivision.

6. (D) Easements pass automatically upon transfer of the dominant tenement. Choice (A) is incorrect as the dominant tenement is benefited not burdened by the easement. Choice (B) is incorrect as an easement can include, besides rights-of-way, the right of receiving air, light, or heat, the right of using a wall as a party wall or the right of flooding land, among other things. Choice (C) is incorrect as an easement is an encumbrance but not a lien.

7. (A) Deed restrictions, as a rule, are initiated for the protection of property owners. They are reasonable limitations on ownership to safeguard property values. An owner is very unlikely to place restrictions on a property that would make the property unmarketable. Zoning is a legally imposed restriction on the use of the site. A site's highest and best use may not necessarily be any of the uses designated by a zoning ordinance, thereby causing the property to be more unmarketable than in the case of private deed restrictions.

8. (C) Assessment liens and real estate taxes will generally always take priority over any other type of lien. This is true even though the assessment liens may be created subsequent to a recorded lien.

9. (A) Riparian Rights refer to flowing water as in rivers or streams or in other watercourses (waters flowing in a fixed or defined channel). Riparian rights do not refer to oceans and seas or underground waters.

177

10. (A) While more facts might help, we can reason this one to choice (A) as follows: The payment was "made" meaning accepted, indicating an agreement to continue between lessor and lessee. It is more reasonable to "assume" a quarterly rent payment than some other period. Civil Code section 1945 and 1945.5 states:

"In the absence of contrary knowledge . . . the parties are presumed to have renewed the hiring on the same terms and for the same time, not exceeding one month when the rent is payable monthly, nor in any case one year."

Thus, a renewal "for the same time" in this case means three years, which is limited by the code to "one year." This eliminates choice (B) and choice (C). Choice (D) does not take into account the Code section limitation but choice (A) does.

11. (A) The Government Code of the State of California enables the legislative body of a city to "Regulate the construction, repair, or alteration of buildings pursuant to Health and Safety Code § 15153." Although the city may also ". . . establish building materials that might be used . . ." they cannot dictate ". . . the cost of the materials used" as indicated in the latter half of choice (B). In choice (C), ". . . size and height . . ." are functions of zoning (land use), not local building codes.

Transfer of Property

12. (C) A Change of Ownership Statement must be filed with the County Recorder or County Tax Assessor at the time of recording, or if the transfer is not recorded, within 45 days of the change of ownership.

13. (B) There are five (5) essentials for acquiring title by adverse possession: (1) Open and notorious occupation (residence not required) (2) Continuous use for 5 consecutive years (3) Held under "claim of right" or "color of title" (4) Payment of the taxes for 5 consecutive years (5) Hostile to true owner, that is, without any degree of permission. "A confrontation with the owner" is not a requirement.

14. (A) Except for deeds used in financing, such as a trust deed, all deeds have a grantor and a grantee, including a quitclaim deed. The grantor is the owner of whatever rights are to be conveyed.

15. (A) Recording is not a requirement for a valid deed.

To effectively convey title with a deed, there must be:

(1) Delivery with the intention to convey and

(2) Acceptance by grantee

16. (D)

(1.00 − Comm.)	x	GSP	=	$\overline{)\text{Net (Everything except comm.)}}$
(1.00 − .06)	x	?	=	$\overline{)\$37{,}187.10\ +\ 403.50}$
.94	x	?	=	$\overline{)\$37{,}590.60}$

$$.94\overline{)37{,}590.60} = \underline{\$39{,}990}$$

17. (B) While a fee simple defeasible and a life estate can be transferred by a grant deed, they must be specified. A lease transfers an estate for years. A fee simple (absolute) is one that is not qualified.

18. (B) The best protection to assure title to real property is afforded by means of a title insurance policy that insures against both "of" record and "off" record risks.

19. (D) Civil Code § 683 enables joint tenancies to be created by (1) simple will or transfer, (2) transfer from sole owner to himself or herself and others, (3) transfer from tenants in common or joint tenants to themselves or to themselves and others, (4) transfer from husband and wife (holding title as community property or otherwise) to themselves or to themselves and others, and (5) transfer to executors of an estate or trust.

20. (C) In order to transfer a fee simple title that is encumbered with a trust deed lien, it is not necessary to obtain permission from the beneficiary or to pay off the loan in full. The grantor is required only to sign and deliver a deed. However, if the existing trust deed contains an enforceable due-on-sale clause, the beneficiary may call the loan and require that it be paid off. He cannot prevent the sale.

21. (B) The "proration of prepaid taxes," will be a credit to the seller (and a debit to the buyer) since the buyer will be in title and benefit from that prepayment. "Proration of prepaid rents" will be a debit to the seller (and a credit to the buyer) since the seller will not be in title during the period for which the prepaid rents were paid. "Cash charge for recording buyer's deed," is a buyer's expense and therefore a debit to him only. Cash charge for a quitclaim deed will be a seller's expense and therefore a debit to him only.

Financing Real Estate

22. (B) "A partially-amortized loan" is not fully paid off in installments. On the due date, the balance is paid off in a lump sum called a "balloon payment" because it substantially exceeds any individual installment.

Choice (A) uses the term "amortized" loan that generally means "fully-amortized." This is a loan fully paid off by installments over its term.

23. (D)

Interest	=	Principal	x	(Rate x Time)
?	=	$2,500	x	(.09 x 3 years, 10 months and 20 days)
$225	=	$2,500	x	(.09 x 1 year)

3 years:	$225/yr	x	3 years			=	$675.00
10 Mos:	$225/yr / 12mos	=	$18.75/mo	x	10 mos	=	+187.50
20 days:	$18.75/mo / 30 days	=	$.625/day	x	20 days	=	+12.50

Total Interest for the Period   <u>$875.00</u>

24. (C) When a lender gets his principal back in full, he suffers no direct loss, even though he may not gain as much as expected in terms of future interest not paid. Inflation can result in a lender's being paid back with money of lower buying power. Recession and unemployment can result in borrower's going into default with loss to a lender.

25. (A) Regulation Z (of the Federal Truth-in-Lending Act) does not apply to:

    (a) Business, commercial, organization credit and agricultural credit (not withstanding any dollar amounts)
    (b) Credit over $25,000 not secured by real property or dwelling

    Regulation Z does apply to individuals and businesses who (a) offer or extend credit regularly which is (b) subject to finance charge or is (c) payable by a written agreement in more than four installments and is (d) primarily for personal, family or household purposes.

26. (C) The facts given involve purchasing a property on behalf of someone who may be unable to do so for himself and reselling to that person under a land contract. This is a common and acceptable method of acquiring property, without the vendee's having to qualify to borrow money from a lender. The vendor may benefit from capital gain installment sale treatment. The vendee gets the use of the property, time to pay off the credit extended by the vendor, and other benefits of ownership such as increasing equity, and income tax benefits.

27. (A) The California Department of Veterans Affairs requires each borrower under the Cal-Vet plan to apply for life and disability insurance.

28. (D) The mortgagor is the owner of the property who is borrowing the money and would therefore "sign the note." The mortgagee is the receiver of the note who lends the money or extends credit, as the seller.

29. (A) The buyer (vendee), under the terms of a conditional sales contract, receives an (1) "equitable" title together with (2) possession of the property. In addition the vendee receives the (3) right to acquire the fee title after all of the conditions of the contract have been met. At that time, the vendor grants him the fee title which includes the (1) "estate of inheritance" and the (2) "freehold estate" as indicated in choices (B) and (C).

180

30. (D) A subordination clause is a clause in a junior lien permitting retention of priority for prior liens or it may be used in a first deed of trust permitting it to be subordinated to subsequent liens.

31. (A) The secondary mortgage market is the marketplace for mortgagees holding existing mortgages. The purchasers of these existing loans would be other lenders or mortgagees.

32. (B) Choices (A), (C) and (D) would have an effect, but a conventional lender would be most concerned with the degree of risk involved in the loan.

33. (A) Charges which are not included as part of the finance charge are appraisal fee, credit report, notary, recording, title insurance, document preparation, property insurance and termite inspection, all of which are fees for services rather than fees for the use of money.

34. (A) The recording of the contract or taking possession of the property gives constructive notice and therefore creates a cloud on the title under the circumstances outlined. Unless the vendee could be found and persuaded to deliver a valid quitclaim deed to the vendor, a successful quiet title court action would be necessary to make the title marketable.

35. (C) FHA loans contain only very limited due-on-sale clauses and, after the first two years, can be readily assumed by anyone. In choices (A), (B), and (D), the loans do or may contain due-on-sale clauses which could mean that the loan is not assumable without specific approval of the lender and at a higher interest rate.

36. (B) "Inflation," "tight money," and "demand for funds" are all factors that directly influence interest rates. "Unemployment" has the least effect among the choices presented.

37. (B) The Certificate of Eligibility will state the amount of the guarantee entitlement that would only indirectly affect a lender's decision about the amount of the loan. The "Lender's requirement" (D), including the "Buyer's (Borrower's) paying capacity" (C) would directly limit the amount of a GI loan as would the "Certificate of Reasonable Value" (A).

38. (C) A "judicial foreclosure" means that the foreclosure was held in court. This is the typical procedure for a mortgage and an optional trust deed foreclosure procedure. In some circumstances, court-held foreclosures entitle the delinquent borrower to a maximum of one year in which to remain in possession and to redeem (equity of redemption).

Valuation/Appraisal of Real Property

39. (D) Expectation is not one of the elements of value. The four elements of value are:

   (1) Utility

   (2) (2) Scarcity

   (3) Demand

   (4) Transferability ("USDT")

40. (A) All building cost estimates should include both direct construction costs and indirect costs. Direct costs are those for material and labor, generally including the contractor's overhead and profit. However, "the most comprehensive method of cost estimating" is the "Quantity Survey Method."

41. (B) $.12\overline{)36,000}$ =   <u>$300,000</u>

          (R)   (I)   (V)

42. (C)   In some communities the trend in real estate taxes is a very important consideration. In cities with an increased trend of public expenditures for schools and municipal services, a heavy burden of taxation may adversely affect the level of real estate values. Under these circumstances, new construction may be discouraged in such an area.

43. (C)   First story: 46' x 80' x 16'   =   58,880 cu. ft.

                  x $1.60/cu. ft.   = $94,208

         Second story: 46' x 80' x 14'   =   51,520 cu. ft.

                  x $1.20/cu. ft.   =   <u>$61,824</u>

                                                   <u>$156,032</u>

44. (A)   Land is subject to the influence of its surroundings (C); no two pieces of land are the same (B); and land is permanent (D). Scarcity of land is an economic concept, not a physical characteristic. It is part of the law of supply and demand.

45. (A)   If prices to build are relatively low and rents are high, builders will expand the available space to meet demand.

46. (B)   The property will "decrease in value by more than the amount of the taxes" based on the reduced annual net income (Assume a $500 tax increase, and a 10% capitalization rate; loss of value would be $5,000).

47. (D)   The Principle of Contribution affirms that after a certain point of development is reached, additional expenditures do not produce an appropriate return on the added investment (that is, the return is less than the existing or desired overall investment). Therefore, the owner should base the decision to make extensive improvements on their proper contribution to the net income.

48. (C)   If there is an existing structure on the property, the appraiser will value the land for its highest and best use as if vacant, but must allow a reduction for the cost of removal of the structure.

49. (D)   Undesirable or unattractive nuisances outside a property would be economic obsolescence.

50. (D)   Taxes are more directly related to net income than to the capitalization rate. (Property tax is a legitimate expense to be deducted from the gross income when appraising.) Furthermore, "overall" capitalization rates provide for a return "on" (profit) and a return "of" (or depreciation of) the investment.

51. (B)   There are four basic procedures for the valuation of land: comparative, abstraction, development and land residual. The term "economic" is not used in designating a recognized method.

52. (C)   The term "accrual for depreciation" means to provide for future depreciation. This is done by setting aside funds or charging off against the future income an amount to eventually replace or recapture the investment in the improvements. This is usually provided for in the capitalization rate in the income approach. Accrued depreciation (past) is used in the cost approach.

53. (D) Comparable sales data for estimating the value of land would be used "whenever possible"; that is, when there are an adequate number of recent sales in a given area with which to compare.

Real Estate Practice

54. (C) Under the Statute of Frauds, not the commissioner's rules and regulations, a listing for the sale of real property must be in writing to be enforceable. However, the seller may agree to pay a commission on an oral listing.

55. (C) The buyer can revoke an offer anytime before the seller has communicated acceptance. Funds received by the broker prior to acceptance of the offer belong to the offeror and must be refunded if demanded.

56. (A) These three terms apply to newspaper advertising.

57. (D) Oral agreements between brokers to split commissions are enforceable, and civil action is the means of legal recovery. This is true regardless of the type of listing.

58. (D) Most investors in real estate demand a greater return than is customary with bonds or trust deeds because the risk of ownership is higher and the investment does not have the same degree of liquidity.

59. (C) Since the broker is not a party to the contract he cannot sue for specific performance.

60. (D) Tender is the act by which one "offers to perform" under a contract. It is not the actual performance.

61. (B) A bilateral contract is one in which the promise of one party is given in exchange for the promise of the other party. In exchange for the owner's promise to pay a commission, the broker promises "to use diligence . . ."

62. (B) The parties may agree to terminate an agency, choice (D). An agent may renounce it, choice (C). An agency is terminated by extinction of the subject matter, choice (A), but a principal's refusal of an offer to purchase does not terminate an agency agreement.

63. (A) An income property that will maintain its value does so by providing an increased income when inflation makes money worth less. The property thus keeps its exchange value compared to other properties and so protects against inflation.

64. (C) A franchise agreement is set forth in the Franchise Investment law as: A contract between two or more persons where one grants the other the right to sell, offer to sell, or exchange goods or services under a marketing plan designed by the grantor.

65. (B) Real estate brokers are not allowed to list mobilehomes that are "new"—which means those not registered with the DMV or HCD. An exception is allowed if the mobilehome is bought to be installed on a "regular" lot, or is so installed, and is handled as real property by a proper recordation with the County recorder. When a manufactured home is properly installed on a permanent foundation on the owner's lot, it becomes real property and is no longer a mobilehome. Choice (D) is too limiting since this question is about a mobilehome.

66. **(D)** Since the divorced woman is "emancipated" she need not seek court approval as suggested in choice (A). Choice (B) is incorrect because she is emancipated. Choice (C) implies she is not emancipated. Therefore, choice (D), indicating the Broker "Can proceed with the listing request" is correct.

67. **(B)** Handwriting takes precedence over printing. The handwritten part would indicate the portions of the printed contract that they wanted to change or emphasize. The parties may accidentally have overlooked printed matter and have failed to strike it out.

68. **(C)** An understanding of the terms "revoke" and "reject" is essential in these answers. An offeror revokes an offer, but an offeree can accept or *reject* an offer.

69. **(B)** Although an investor considers leverage an asset for income speculation, 100% equity will provide greater flexibility of personal income.

70. **(D)** The liquidity of an investment is the ease with which it can be immediately converted to cash. Compared to stocks and commodity investments, real estate is less liquid so its "turnover is slower than other investments."

71. **(B)** The option to purchase real estate is a written agreement in which the owner agrees that the buyer shall have the right to purchase the property at a fixed price within a certain time. A separate sales agreement is not necessary for the option to be binding.

72. **(B)** The acts of an agent, in transacting his principal's business, and which are within the scope of his authority, are the acts of his principal; therefore, the seller would be liable to the buyer for the loss.

73. **(A)** That an agent "gave part of his commission to the buyer" would be considered a "material fact." Because of the fiduciary relationship between the agent and his principal, the agent is required to fully disclosure all material facts to his principal. Choice (D) would not be correct unless the broker failed to disclose this material fact to his principal.

74. **(A)** The Statute of Frauds (Civil Code Section 1624) requires that a contract employing an agent to purchase or sell real estate, or to lease real estate for a longer period than one year, must be in writing.

75. **(A)** Even though instructed otherwise, the broker's fiduciary obligation to the principal requires that all offers be presented, unless clearly frivolous.

Tax Implications of Real Estate Ownership

76. **(D)** Depreciation reduces the original cost basis, thereby increasing the difference between the selling price and the new (or "adjusted") cost basis. That difference is a long-term capital gain on which the taxpayer will pay taxes. In this case, Smith's gain equaled the depreciation taken.

77. **(D)** Between March 1 and July 1, the County Tax Assessors compile a list showing the assessed value of all taxable property in the county (the tax rolls) as of March 1. This total is the "tax base." Using this, and the budget to run the county, the Board of Supervisors sets the tax rate needed to meet the budget, within the limits set by Proposition 13. The County Tax Collector applies the rate to each property's assessed value to determine that year's individual property tax.

78. (C) COMMERCIAL EXCHG. SITUATION FARM
    BLDG.

    | $85,000 | Exchange Value | $55,000) | $30,000 difference |
    | | Cash ("Boot") | $20,000) | in equities are |
    | | Note ("Boot") | $10,000) | balanced by two |
    | | | | forms of "Boot" |
    | | | | given to building |
    | | | | owner: (1) Cash & |
    | | | | (2) Equivalent of |
    | | | | cash (note). |

    | $85,000 | Balanced Equities | $85,000 |

    TAX CONSEQUENCES TO BUILDING OWNER

    | $85,000 | Exchange value received |
    | −65,000 | Adjusted basis |

    | $20,000 | Recognized gain (taxable now) since building owner (1) traded down and (2) received "Boot" |

    NOTE: (d) $30,000 "Boot" is not the correct amount because "Boot" is taxable only up to the extent of any recognized gain.

79. (B) In an exchange, if a party gives no "boot," his or her basis in the property acquired is the same as in the property traded away. Both parties keep the basis they each started with if no "boot" is given by either side.

80. (D) Only two items are deductible to the property owner.

    (1) Interest $202.00 per month

    (2) Real Estate Taxes $104.00 per month

    $306.00 per month x 12 months = $3,672.00/yr

81. (B) $500,000 building cost is the depreciable asset regardless of the amount financed.

82. (D) If "points" are paid to a lender solely for the use of the money borrowed (discount points) they may be deducted in full by the borrower as an interest expense. If they are paid for specific services of the lender, they are not deductible as interest. Choice (C) says that points are always deductible if paid for interest, but there are exceptions, such as points paid by a seller.

83. (B) Depreciated book value of one owner is never of concern to the next owner. A buyer always establishes his own new book value upon acquisition of the property.

Brokerage: Responsibilities and Functions of Salespersons
Broker's responsibility of Office Management

84. (C)   2.7% is salesperson's share (6% gross x 45% split)

$$2.7\% \ \times \ ?\text{S.P} \ = \ \overline{)\$8,100}$$

$$.027\overline{)\$8,100} \ = \ \underline{\$300,000}$$

85. (A)   4.5% Gross commission x 50% split between brokers = 2.25% net commission

2.25% net to salesperson's broker x 50% = 1.125% to salesperson

$162,500 sales price x 1.125% = $\underline{\$1,828.13 \text{ to salesperson}}$

86. (B)   In the event there is no "release clause" in a subdivision which is subject to a "blanket encumbrance," one alternative of the Real Estate Commissioner is to require an escrow for all or a part of the purchaser's money as indicated in Section 11032 (a) of the Business and Professions Code:

> "The entire sum of money paid or advanced by the purchaser (or lessee) of any such lot or parcel, or such portion thereof as the Commissioner shall determine is sufficient to protect the purchaser (or lessee), shall be deposited into an escrow depository acceptable to the Commissioner until . . ."

87. (B)   (1) $(1.00 - \text{Comm.}) \times$? GSP $= \ \overline{)\text{NET (EEC)}}$

           everything except commission

$(1.00 - .10)$ $\times$?GSP $= \ \overline{)1.40 \ \times \ \text{Cost}}$

$.90$ $\times$?GSP $= \ \overline{)1.40 \ \times \ \$17,424}$

$.90$ $\times$?GSP $= \ \overline{)\$24,393.60}$

$.90\overline{)\$24,393.60} \ = \ \$27,104$

(2)   Width $\times$ Length $= \ \overline{)\text{Area}}$

?W $\times$ 140 ft. $= \ \overline{)21,780}$

$140 \text{ ft}\overline{)21,780} \ = \ 155.6 \text{ ft.}$

(3) $\dfrac{\$27,104 \ AP}{155.6 \text{ fr. ft}} \ = \ \$174.19$ or closest choice $\underline{\$174/\text{fr.ft.}}$

186

88. (B)

Width	x	Length	=	$\overline{)\text{Area}}$
330 ft.	x	220 ft.	=	$\overline{)\text{72,600 sq. ft.}}$

$$\frac{72,600 \text{ sq. ft.}}{43,560 \text{ sq. ft./acre}} = 1.67 \text{ rounded or } 1\frac{2}{3} \text{ acres}$$

89. (C) All prospects are to be shown properties within their affordability range, without regard to racial make-up of neighborhoods. Doing otherwise exposes agents to the charge of "steering."

Choice (B) is a true statement describing a wrong practice by some agents and investors. Agent "scares" an owner into selling at a low price to agent's fellow-conspirator buyer. Agent gets a commission. Buyer turns around and resells at a higher price, usually to a minority buyer, and makes a profit. Agent gets a second commission. This is how the ". . . buyer is also the seller." It also exemplifies "panic-selling or peddling" and "block–busting."

90. (C) All offers should be submitted. The Real Estate Commissioner could discipline a broker for withholding material facts.

91. (D)

%	x	PAID	=	$\overline{)\text{MADE}}$
?	x	$75,000=		$\overline{)\$30,000}$

*$300,000 purchase price
$$\frac{\times \ .10}{\$30,000} \text{ increase}$$

$$\$75,000\,\overline{)\$30,000} = .40 = \underline{40\%}$$

92. (D) A planned development is a subdivision of 5 or more lots, including areas owned in common and could be residential, commercial or industrial. (Note: a condominium, although defined differently, could also be any of the above mentioned).

93. (C) $550 – $43.85 = $506.15 interest for the month

$506.15/month x	12 months	=	$6,073.80 annual rate

(R x T)	x	P	=	$\overline{)\text{I}}$
?	x	$56,500=		$\overline{)\$6,073.80}$

$$\$56,500\,\overline{)\$6,073.80} = .1075 = \underline{10.75\%}$$

94. (A) A minor lacks the capacity to appoint an agent under state law. A minor has the capacity to enter into contracts for necessaries. The party with whom he contracts runs the risk of having the minor disaffirm the contract before he reaches majority or within a reasonable time thereafter.

95. (D) Max. costs: 5% or $390, whichever is greater

Max. Comm.: Junior T.D.s of 2 years or more   (10%)

Total Costs and Commission

$390	Costs
$250	Comm.
$640	

187

96. (C) The $100 collected by the broker is an "advance fee" because it is used for advertising in a special brochure published by Otis, distinguished from advertising in some regular publication such as a newspaper. By law, in order to avoid possible misuse or errors, such advance fees must be treated as trust funds and handled as shown in choice (C).

97. (C) Blind advertising is never permitted. The name and address of the broker need not be mentioned in the advertisement, however at the minimum, the name of the salesperson must be included.

98. (D) The Real Estate Settlement Procedures Act (RESPA) forbids kickbacks, referral fees or any other unearned fees. Referral fees between real estate brokers are permissible but not between real estate agents and nonlicensees.

99. (C) A lessor may not discriminate based on marital status as would be the case in requiring only single tenants to have co-signors. For an unfurnished residential unit a landlord may require advance payment of the first month's rent plus a security deposit equal to two months' rent.

100. (D) Acting for more than one party in a transaction without the knowledge and consent of all parties thereto is a violation of California Real Estate Law and could therefore result in all the penalties recited.

Exam 3 Answers - Real Property and Laws Relating to Ownership

1. (A)   A license is defined as a personal revocable and nonassignable permission to enter upon the land of another, but without possessing any interest in the land.

2. (C)   A lien is a charge upon property for the payment of a debt. Of the choices listed only the mortgage is a money claim or lien.

3. (B)   The government's police power is the basis for zoning ordinances. The *taking* of private property is based on the government's rights of eminent domain. *Judgments* result from the power of the judicial branch of government. *Deed restrictions* are private restrictions.

4. (B)   If noise from low-flying aircraft damages the owner in the use of his or her land, this may be a "taking" of property, for which compensation must be paid by the government. This remedy is called "inverse condemnation" because it is started by an owner seeking compensation from the agency that caused the situation.

5. (C)   To achieve planning goals, local, state and federal government have the authority to regulate the use of private property provided such right is used only to promote the public health, safety and general welfare. Government also can negotiate to purchase private property for public use. The source of this authority is the police power of the state.

    Note: The three other powers inherent in the state are:

    (1)   Eminent Domain: taking (not purchase) of private property for a public use, with compensation

    (2)   Escheat: reversion of property to the state upon death of an owner without heirs

    (3)   Taxation

6. (A)   It is possible to own property in fee simple and still have many encumbrances on it. The three characteristics of a fee are: freely inheritable, freely transferable, and of indefinite duration.

7. (A)   The effective date of any mechanic's lien relates back to the date construction began on the project. This could include the delivery of construction materials to the site.

8. (A)   The effective date of any mechanic's lien relates back to the date construction began on the project.

9. (C)   Easements are appurtenant to the land and pass automatically upon transfer of dominant tenement. In choice (A), easements can include rights other than ingress (in) and egress (out), for example, the right to collect wood. In choice (B) the dominant tenement is not burdened by the easement. In the (D) choice, an easement appurtenant runs with the land.

10. (D)   An estate of inheritance, a fee simple absolute, is the highest form of ownership. A "defeasible" estate is defeatable under certain conditions.

11. (A)   Whereas mechanics liens are created by statute, judgment liens are created by court decisions. Both may take priority before the recording date (B). Neither is effective as a lien until recorded (C). Both are involuntary liens (D).

189

12. (D) Any lease for a definite period of time creates an estate for years, regardless of the period of time for which it was established.

13. (D) Intentional abandonment by the owner of the dominant tenement terminates an easement. Also, an easement created by adverse use for 5 continuous years (easement by prescription) can be lost by nonuse for 5 years.

14. (B) Since it is cumbersome to list all restrictions in each deed, the subdivider could set forth the restrictions in a recorded declaration, the provisions of which are incorporated in each conveyance by an appropriate reference.

15. (D) A recorded reconveyance deed releases the lien of the deed of trust from the records.

16. (D) Riparian rights refer to "the reasonable use of flowing water." Some examples are: rivers, streams or other "watercourses" (water flowing through a fixed or defined channel).

17. (C) A notice of lis pendens is a notice recorded for the purpose of warning all persons that the title or right to the possession of certain real property is in litigation, giving constructive notice to the world and thus preserving rights pending litigation. Property identified in a lis pendens would be difficult to sell. The doctrine of lis pendens makes an exception to the general rule that a person not a party to a court action is not affected by any judgment in that action (Choice A is false). A lis pendens is applicable only to lawsuits affecting the title or possession of real property (Choice B is false). A notice of withdrawal of pendency of an action may be recorded by the person who recorded the lis pendens (Choice D is false).

18. (D) Percolation tests are used to determine the ground's ability to pass fluids through the soil and remove impurities.

19. (A) Any lease for a definite period of time creates an estate for years, regardless of the period of time for which it was established.

20. (B) An injunction is a court order restraining or requiring performance by a party to a suit (such as performing acts required by property covenants or refraining from acts restricted by such covenants).

21. (C) While the exact words "taken in joint tenancy" are not required, the intent to establish a joint tenancy must be clearly expressed. All joint tenants must have equal interests.

22. (D) When personal property ("movable") becomes affixed to land it "becomes real property," for example, fence posts when installed. Personal property may "be conveyed," using a Bill of Sale, or "hypothecated," that is, used as security for a loan.

23. (D) Among nine elements of the Planning Commission's concerns are:

 (1) Circulation ("Highways and streets")

 (2) Land use ("Commercial and industrial districts")

 (3) "Seismic safety"

24. (B) Private restrictions are those created by an individual and not the government. These may be in the form of a written agreement or placed in a deed.

25. (D) A court may act fully on behalf of a minor who is a ward of that court. An unemancipated minor cannot enter into such a contract, and federal or state laws place certain restrictions on aliens and convicts in the purchase of land.

26. (D) The term in "severalty" in real estate means one or sole owner.

27. (C) The interest of a joint tenant terminates with death; the surviving tenants are the owners of the interest as joint tenants.

28. (C) Any mechanic's lien takes its priority as of the date work first started on that project as a whole. Removing an old building from a site is a part of the work required for the construction of a new building. In order for a trust deed to take priority over a mechanic's lien, the trust deed must be recorded before any work starts on the site.

29. (D) Among those able to exercise the power of Eminent Domain and take private property for a public use are: Government bodies (Federal, State, and local), improvement districts, public utilities, public education institutions, and similar public and semi-public bodies.

30. (C) A lien can be defined as a charge imposed upon specific property by which it is made security for the performance of an act, typically the payment of a debt.

31. (D) Appurtenant easements, covenants that are beneficial to the land, and stock in a mutual water company "run with the land" and pass to subsequent grantees.

32. (C) The governing authority of a city has the power to adopt ordinances for the preservation and protection of public health, safety, morals, or general welfare. The basic legal tool a city will use for a layout plan is zoning, an exercise of the police power of government.

33. (C) An interest held "in severalty" is one that has been severed from all others and is held all alone. An ownership in severalty is a sole ownership. A fee simple estate can be either absolute or defeasible. Therefore, choices (A) and (B) are incorrect answers.

34. (C) In most cases, laws (including zoning ordinances) cannot be enacted which are retroactive. In ridding an area of nonconforming uses of the land, the courts and zoning authorities, in order to satisfy the policy of gradual and eventual elimination of such nonconforming uses, employ the methods of: (A) prohibition of rebuilding (B) prohibition of expansion (and) (D) allowing a reasonable time (amortization period) within which the abuses may be eliminated.

35. (B) A general lien is directed against the individual debtor and attached to all of that person's real property in the county in which the abstract of judgment is recorded. The other choices all relate to specific properties.

36. (C) Davidson has a personal right to use Parkins' property (servient tenement) and which is not attached to any land. Since there is no dominant tenement, it is an easement in gross.

37. (A) This is an example of an exception made by a building inspector. The term "variance" applies to permission to use land for a purpose that does not strictly conform to a zoning restriction. If approved by a building inspector it is not an infraction.

38. (D) Generally, conflicts of law are decided with the health, safety, and general welfare of the people as the highest standard.

39. (D) Nearly all buyers accept title with some encumbrances, such as tax liens and public or private restrictions. Therefore all title insurance companies insure encumbered titles. All liens are encumbrances, but not all encumbrances are liens. Some specific liens are involuntary, e.g. property taxes.

40. (D) Spot zoning, conditional use permit, and variance are all remedies to the described situation. Either allows a change in the local zoning ordinances that permits a particular use not consistent with the area's zoning classification. Either remedy may be granted from the local zoning Board of Appeals for a small area provided: (1) undue hardship can be shown, and (2) the use permitted must still be consistent with the general plan of the area.

41. (D) Real property consists of that which is immovable by law.

42. (B) In every lease the law implies a covenant (promise) on the part of the lessor ("owner of the paramount title") to the "quiet enjoyment" and possession of the property by the lessee during the term of the lease. It is a warranty by the lessor against the lessor's own acts, not those of strangers (neighbors and the like).

43. (B) A characteristic of a joint tenancy is that it is a "single" estate, that is, the original joint tenants, or the surviving joint tenants, own the estate as though they were one person.

44. (C) The legislative bodies of states create lien and attachment laws. A state's enabling act gives legislative powers to the local governing authorities, such as city councils and county board of supervisors, to enact local ordinances.

45. (B) Judgment liens are recorded against the wishes of the judgment debtor and therefore are considered involuntary.

46. (D) A quitclaim deed releases any present interest held by the grantor. This would include the right to use the real property of another.

47. (C) A grantee of a deed or the beneficiary of a will is not required to have any capacity except the capacity to hold title. Therefore, a judicially declared incompetent person can receive title to both real and personal property.

48. (A) A lien is a charge upon property for the payment of a debt or obligation, and does not affect the physical nature or use of the property. Conditions, covenants and restrictions (often called "CC&R's") all provide for or limit the use of real property.

49. (C) A duly recorded Abstract of Judgment affects all the property of the debtor in the county where it is recorded. It may be recorded in any county or counties.

50. (B) An easement acquired by prescription is terminated by nonuse for a five-year period. Neither easements created by deed nor easements created by implication of law are terminated by nonuse.

51. (A) A minor can receive property through gift or inheritance, but because a minor is incapable of appointing an agent, such delegation of authority as appointing a power of attorney is void. Negotiating in real property with or for a minor is permitted through a court-appointed guardian if each transaction receives court approval.

52. (B) An easement that is "strictly personal in nature" would be an easement in gross—an easement attached to the person of the easement holder and not attached to any specific land. Thus, there is no dominant tenement—only the servient tenement that is burdened.

53. (C) Lessees are the holders of leasehold estates, all of which are less-than-freehold (those estates with limited time durations). Grantees of life estates have freehold estates, that is, of indefinite duration. Beneficiaries of trust deeds and holders of easements have interests in real property but not estates—not possessory interests.

54. (D) All of the examples in the choices can be considered to be within the category of public control.

55. (A) Of the four choices given in this question, only Choice (A) is real property. A stud is a vertical framing member of a wall to which horizontal boards are attached. They are the supporting elements in walls or partitions.

56. (D) The right of eminent domain is the right of government to take private property for public or quasi-public use, although the U.S. Constitution does require the payment of just compensation. The right of eminent domain is never a part of the bundle of rights comprising the private ownership of property. Choices (A), (B), and (C) enumerate rights that are at times included in that bundle of rights.

57. (A) No person can convey a greater interest in real property than that person holds. Since Able holds only a leasehold interest, he can encumber only that leasehold interest. Therefore, Able can grant an easement only for the term of the lease.

58. (C) Only joint tenancy interests have the right of survivorship. People can execute new deeds to themselves to change the mode of holding title.

59. (B) An *estate* in real property is a possessory interest. A deed of trust conveys only a security interest, not a possessory interest. Estates in remainder and in reversion are both future possessory interests. A leasehold estate is a present possessory interest.

60. (B) Police power is the right of the state to enact laws and enforce them for the order, safety, health, morals, and general welfare of the public. Zoning regulations are examples of the implementation of police power.

61. (D) The governing authority of a city or county has the power to adopt ordinances establishing zones within which structures must conform to size, setback, and location limitations.

62. (A) Personal property has the characteristics of being movable. Therefore, it has mobility. Choices (B) and (C) are characteristics of real property.

63. (D) Real property consists of land, that which is affixed to land or appurtenant to land, and that which is immovable by law.

64. (C) A lien usually makes specific property subject for the debt or discharge of an obligation.

65. (C) Utility company easements are considered encumbrances to property. Since it restricts the use of the property and has nothing to do with money, it is not a lien.

66. (B) A judgment lien is a general lien on all property of the debtor not otherwise exempt by law. A property tax lien, a mechanic's lien and a blanket mortgage are all specific liens.

67. (B) A lien placed by a mechanic, materialman, artisan, or laborer for the furnishing of work or material is termed a specific lien; such a lien burdens only the particular property upon which the construction occurred. Mechanic's liens are involuntary.

68. (C) At common law, an estate at will can be terminated at the will of either party without advance notice. The Civil Code of California, however, requires that any estate created by agreement, except an estate for years, requires advance notice to terminate. Therefore, an estate at will can be created only by operation of law in California.

69. (D) Deed restrictions are created by the grantor in the deed. For a new subdivision this would be the developer.

70. (B) Where there is a conflict between deed restrictions and zoning restriction, the more stringent of the two would apply.

71. (D) Under "common law," but not California law, none of these choices requires advance notice to terminate. A tenancy for a specific term (estate for years) ends at the expiration of the term without notice. A tenancy at sufferance is not entitled to a notice. At common law, an estate at will was terminated without notice. California statutory law requires notice to terminate an estate at will, but common law does not.

72. (A) Choice (A) is the false statement. The liability of a limited partner is the amount of his investment paid in or pledged. It may or may not go as high as the debts of the partnership.

73. (A) All restrictions on the use of property are encumbrances. Only money encumbrances are called liens.

74. (D) Restrictions on the use of property are encumbrances but are not liens. Taxes, trust deeds, and judgments are all examples of liens.

75. (D) The only unity required in tenancy in common interests is the unity of possession. This means that each interest is an undivided interest, a fractional interest in the property as a whole.

76. (D) All three of the choices given "run with the land." Covenants are encumbrances that remain on the land when the property is transferred. Choices (B) and (C) name real property rights that are transferred with the land when property is transferred.

77. (B) A bearing wall in a building is nearly always real property. Choices (A), (C), and (D) are all examples of personal property.

78. (D) More than one estate can exist, for example, when a lessor has a leased fee estate and a lessee has a less than freehold estate. Title can be transferred by patents, wills, accession or involuntary alienation. A life estate is a form of ownership, fee title. A lease creates a less than freehold estate.

79. (C) Stock in a mutual water company is a real property interest which is appurtenant to the land and which runs with land. When the ownership of the land is transferred, the ownership interest in the mutual water company is also transferred without any further documentation.

80. (D) Any person can request (initiate) the city or county government to make a zoning change.

194

Exam 4 Answers - Transfer of Property

1. (A)   A promissory note is the evidence of the debt and is secured by a deed of trust. The promissory note is not usually recorded but the deed of trust is. A notice of completion and a trustee's deed must be recorded. Conditional sales contracts are often recorded.

2. (C)   A Change of Ownership Statement must be filed with the County Recorder or County Tax Assessor at the time of recording, or if the transfer is not recorded, within 45 days of the change of ownership.

3. (B)   If two or more inspections exist, all reports must be disclosed. The results of a pest control inspection report, including the cost of corrective work, would be material facts to a buyer and must be disclosed.

4. (B)   There are five (5) essentials for acquiring title by adverse possession: (1) Open and notorious occupation (residence not required) (2) Continuous use for 5 consecutive years (3) Held under "claim of right" or "color of title" (4) Payment of the taxes for 5 consecutive years (5) Hostile to true owner, that is, without any degree of permission. "A confrontation with the owner" is not a requirement.

5. (B)   To be capable of contracting, a person must have reached "majority," (18 years), or be "emancipated" as defined by law. A "minor" cannot legally give a delegation of power or make a contract relating to real property or relating to personal property not within the minor's immediate possession and control.

6. (A)   Except for deeds used in financing, such as a trust deed, all deeds have a grantor and a grantee, including a quitclaim deed. The grantor is the owner of whatever rights are to be conveyed.

7. (A)   Most deeds have a grantor and a grantee. They are referred to as such, except in a trust deed, where the grantor is termed the trustor. Quitclaim deeds are executed by grantors to clear up conflicting claims or deficiencies in titles, in favor of grantees.

8. (D)   The contents of a pest control certification report would be material facts to owners, buyers, and often to real estate lenders.

9. (C)   In a deed of trust arrangement, the trustor is the owner-borrower who has placed bare legal title in trust with a third neutral party called the trustee. When the debt to the lender (beneficiary) is satisfied, the trustee reconveys the title back to the trustor by using a reconveyance deed.

10. (A)   Recording is not a requirement for a valid deed.

   To effectively convey title with a deed, there must be:
   (1)   Delivery with the intention to convey and
   (2)   Acceptance by grantee

11. (A)   The deed would be valid. A married person under 18 is an emancipated minor and has the legal capacity to deal in real property.

12. (D)   When a structural pest control report is a condition of a transfer or the financing of a transfer, the transferor, fee owner, or his agent, shall deliver a copy of the report to the transferee (buyer) as soon as practicable before transfer of title. (Civil Code Section 1099)

195

13. (C)   Facts appearing in a correct survey would be one of many risks covered by an ALTA policy not covered in a CLTA policy.

14. (B)   A bill of sale is used to convey title to personal property, not real property.

15. (D)   A deed made to a fictitious person, one that does not exist, is void. The other choices are acceptable.

16. (A)   In California title protection against future claims is totally through a policy of title insurance. Recording of a deed gives protection against past claims against title. The certificate of title and the abstract of title are ancient forerunners of the title insurance policy.

17. (A)   This quitclaim deed would be executed by the buyer.

18. (D)   While escrow procedures vary somewhat according to local custom, one of the steps that comes after preparing escrow instructions, ordering the title search and accepting the structural pest control reports, is for the escrow officer to call for the closing funds that are deposited into the escrow. The escrow could not (A) authorize work to be done, (B) change the broker's commission, or (C) tell the buyers where to obtain financing.

19. (C)   Since the will failed and Able left no heirs, the property would escheat to the state. Since the will was invalid, we cannot say that it was Able's intent to pass title to Baker.

20. (C)   A sublease is a transfer of less than the leasehold with the reversion in the sublessor and would create no form of title in the sublessee. A land contract transfers (1) possession, (2) "equitable" title, and (3) the right to acquire the fee title after all the conditions of the contract have been met. A mortgage does not convey any possessory interest.

21. (B)   Involuntary conversion means the destruction, theft, seizure, requisition, condemnation (through the power of Eminent Domain) or the sale or exchange under the threat or imminence of requisition or condemnation. The property is converted involuntarily into (1) other property or (2) money as the result of insurance proceeds or a condemnation award. The IRS has special rules relating to the recognition or non-recognition of the taxpayer's capital gains or losses in these situations.

22. (B)   A real estate broker who is not a party to the transaction would not be exempt from the Regulations of the Corporations Commissioner. A broker who is an agent for one of the parties to the transaction may handle the escrow without being licensed by the Corporations Commissioner whether the broker charges a fee or not. (Other exemptions include attorneys, banks, savings and loans, title companies and related entities).

23. (B)   This choice is clearly a correct statement, as there is no evidence that Tooly was "emancipated" when he deeded. However, there is some question regarding the improvements. Likely they could be removed by the organization if the property is returned to Tooly, so choice (D) is too restrictive in its wording.

24. (D)   With the assignment of a contract (such as a lease) the assignee takes the position that was held by the assignor. The assignor of the lease was the tenant; therefore the assignee becomes the tenant.

25. (C)   A bill of sale is a written instrument by which one person sells, assigns or transfers an interest in personal property to another.

26. (C)   Equitable title is the title held by the vendee under a land sales contract. In a trust deed, the trustee holds the legal title and the trustor "retains" equitable title.

27. (B) There are six essential elements to a valid deed. One essential element is a competent grantor. If the grantor has been declared by a court to be incompetent, then a deed is void at its inception. Choices (A) and (C) do not make a deed void at inception.

28. (B) $125,000   ÷ $500   =   250

     250   x   .55   =   137.50

     Closest: $138.00

29. (A) The date of the item (DI) is January 1. The close of escrow (COE) is February 1. Since the DI is short of COE, the seller owes for this one month. One month's taxes would be $100.

30. (B) Since the grantor was a minor, the deed is void ab initio, that is, "void at inception."

31. (B) This situation creates a cloud on title. Property acquired by a person before marriage remains his or her separate property unless commingled, in which case it becomes community property. Property acquired in the name of one spouse only while that person is married is presumed to be community property, although it is a rebuttable presumption. The second deed described here leaves a doubt about what Joan intended. If it was intended that it remain her separate property, the community property presumption would have to be rebutted.

32. (A) A tenant is an owner of an interest in real property and therefore is subject to eminent domain and condemnation proceedings. In every lease or rental agreement the landlord implies (by law) that his tenant will have the quiet possession and enjoyment of the premises during the tenancy. The landlord shall not unlawfully interfere with this covenant by "threatening expulsion" (C) or by excessive or unwarranted changes (D). In the event he does breach this covenant it may be deemed "constructive eviction" and the tenant would be justified in terminating the lease and abandoning the premise.

33. (B)   Time: C.O.E.: May 1

     D.I.:   July 1*
     2 months

     Money $1,380   ÷   12 months   = $115.00/mo
     $115.00   x   2 months   = $230.00

     * Date to which Item has been paid is Beyond Close of Escrow; therefore Buyer Owes "All of" May and "All of" June or 2 Mos.

34. (B) Since a fire insurance policy calls for some personal quality of the insured, it is a type of contract that cannot be assigned without the consent of the insurer. In the event a policy is assigned without their consent, no coverage extends to the assignee. It is not incumbent upon the insurance company to notify the assignee that they will not allow the assignment. Unless they agree to the assignment, no insurance is transferable.

35. (C) Either the seller or broker must ensure that the buyer receives a copy of the report showing the repairs accomplished and that the property is free of termites.

36. (D) Since the policy of title insurance affords protection against matters of record, the title company would search all public records, not only the County Recorder's Office.

37. (C) An employee or officer of a corporation may take an acknowledgment if such individual is not personally interested and does not execute the instrument as an officer of the corporation. Duties as a notary public or as an officer of the corporation are distinct.

38. (C) A prisoner is not automatically deprived of his civil rights (including his right to contract or deed his property) unless he has been sentenced to death or to life in prison.

39. (D) The escrow officer should return both reports to the broker because a licensee must disclose to any and all purchasers and sellers any knowledge he may have of any infestation on the premises.

40. (B) A subsequent document (such as escrow instructions) will prevail over an earlier document (the deposit receipt).

41. (D) The escrow holder is really only a stakeholder, not legally concerned with controversies between the parties, and is entitled to enjoin such parties in an action of interpleader to require them to litigate controversies between themselves.

42. (D) "Proration" is the process of apportioning of (1) expenses (such as insurance and taxes) or (2) benefits (such as prepaid rents) in a fair amount to each party. The buyer would have no obligation on the seller's non-secured loan.

43. (B) $90,750– $30,000= $60,750 equity transferred

    $500)$60,750 = 121.5 rounded up to 122

    122 x .55 = $67.10 closest choice: $67.00

44. (B) Interest payments are paid in "arrears," that is, the payments are made to the lender only for the period during which the borrower had full use of the funds. Therefore, when a loan is taken over by the buyer, lets say in the middle of the interest paying period, one half would be owed by the seller and the remaining one half by the buyer. Since the buyer will be obligated to pay the lender at the end of the scheduled payment period, and for the whole amount even though he owes only for one half of it, the debit made to the seller in escrow will therefore be credited to the buyer. Discount points on a new FHA loan would likely be a debit on the buyer's closing statement. Prepaid insurance premiums could be prorated and would be a debit to the buyer. Tax prorations could go either way.

45. (B) Recording gives constructive notice "to the world" of the contents of the recorded document, and anyone dealing with the property has constructive notice of any recorded claims of interest in the property even though the public records have not been inspected.

46. (B) An escrow may be terminated by mutual consent of the parties. An escrow may not be terminated unilaterally by:

    (A) Incapacity or death of either party; or (C) An attorney-in-fact acting for one of the parties; or (D) Revocation by the broker.

47. (B) Among the risks listed, a standard coverage policy of title insurance protects against only lack of capacity of persons conveying or holding interests in the property.

48.　(C)　The recording of a document affecting rights, title, or interest in real property gives constructive notice to the world of the contents of that document and thus constructive notice to the world of the existence of the rights or interests conveyed. If the document was valid, the recording is said to "perfect" the claim by establishing its priority. Actual notice is that knowledge which a specific person actually has or is implied by law to have. Actual notice is not given by recording.

49.　(D)　An unrecorded deed is considered void as against a subsequent good-faith purchaser who is without notice and who does record or take possession. The two methods of giving constructive notice of a claim of interest are (1) recording and (2) occupying the property. In choice D, the holder has done neither. In choice A, the certificate of title is indicative that the named holder is the owner of the record.

50.　(B)　The tax rate is .55 for each $500, or fraction thereof, of equity transferred.

$$\begin{array}{rl} \$100,000 & \text{purchase price} \\ \underline{-60,000} & \text{Loan} \\ \$\ 40,000 & \text{equity transferred} \end{array}$$

$$500\,\overline{)\$40,000} \quad 80 \times .55 = \underline{\$44}$$

51.　(B)　One of the essential elements of a valid deed is that the deed must adequately designate or name a grantee capable of holding title, but a deed to an actual person under a fictitious name (such as dba) is valid. If the grantee is misnamed in the deed, the error can be corrected by a second deed. If a grantee's name has changed, such as through marriage, to transfer title the grantor should refer to the former name. For example, a married woman who received title as Mary Doe could grant the property as "Mary Doe Smith, formerly Mary Doe."

52.　(C)　An employee or officer of a corporation may take an acknowledgment if such individual is not personally interested and does not execute the instrument as an officer of the corporation. An acknowledgment taken by a directly interested party is void.

53.　(A)　An emancipated minor has the legal capacity of an adult, for example to enter into contracts and to buy, sell, lease, encumber, exchange or transfer any interest in real or personal property. An escrow company would need to ascertain that the seller had capacity to act. A minor cannot appoint an agent such as an escrow agent.

54.　(C)　Title to real property can be acquired by accession—the addition to property through the efforts of man or by natural forces. Riparian and littoral rights are water rights that can be appurtenances to real property.

55.　(B)　Escheat is the reverting of property to the state when heirs capable of inheriting are lacking. Therefore, only the state has the right of escheat. Individuals can acquire interests in real property by (A) prescription, (C) succession, and (D) accession.

56.　(D)　Civil Code Section 1942 provides that a landlord must make repairs within a reasonable time after written or oral notice of dilapidations which make premises untenantable. Otherwise the tenant may "repair and deduct" or vacate the premises, owing no further rent.

57. (A) Documents which affect title or interests in real property are eligible to be recorded to obtain the protection that recording affords (constructive notice to the world of the contents of the document) but most are not required to be recorded to be effective. Choice (A) is a false statement and therefore the correct choice. It may be foolish not to record a deed of reconveyance, but recording is not required.

58. (B) A lender's insurance policy (an ALTA policy) insures the interests of that lender, or mortgagee. An owner's policy (a CLTA policy) insures the owner against risks of record and some off-record hazards such as forgery and lack of capacity. Only the ALTA policy extends coverage to water and mining rights (Choice C). An ALTA policy does extend coverage to off-record easements and rights of parties in possession, but not because the information is difficult to ascertain (Choice D).

59. (C) Generally, recording establishes the priority of a trust deed. "First to record is first in right." An exception would result from the existence of a subordination clause. Other exceptions may exist in relation to mechanics liens and judgment liens.

60. (C) Any lease or sub-lease conveys a possessory interest in real property without conveying actual ownership. A license (A), a mortgage (B), and an easement (D) are not *possessory* interests in real property.

61. (A) The stem of this question gives us a good definition of abstract of title. The part of the question that suggests *abstract of title* rather than *chain of title* is the phrase " . . . facts relied on as evidence of title . . . "

62. (B) A deed is a written instrument that conveys title to or an interest in real property.

63. (A) A landlord would not likely be found guilty of constructive eviction for failing to repair excessive wear and tear caused by the tenant. The three other circumstances would be classified as constructive eviction.

64. (C) When preceded by a 3-day notice "to quit or pay rent," the unlawful detainer is the proper procedure designed by law by which the lessor can have the tenant evicted.

65. (B) A survey and physical inspection of property is required in an extended coverage policy and would show correct survey lines and any encroachment.

66. (D) A grant deed carries a warranty to the purchaser; a land contract does not. The grant deed requires the signature of the grantor only; a land contract requires the signature of the vendor and the vendee. A grant deed does not require a designation of the price; a land contract does.

67. (A) Taxes, and interest in an assumption, are usually prorated in escrow. If the seller's insurance is taken over by the buyer, the seller will be credited proportionately (pro rata) for the portion of the premium the buyer is debited for. When the buyer gets new insurance, the seller's policy will be cancelled and the premium returned to the seller by the insurance company short-rated on a uniform schedule approved by the Insurance Commissioner.

68. (C) The escrow holder acts as the agent for both the seller and buyer, a dual agency. The holder would also be an independent contractor, but choice (C) is the more significant of the 2 choices and is the "best" answer.

69. (C) Escrow companies prorate on the basis of a 30-day month and 360-day year, unless instructed otherwise.

70. (D) The records of the Office of the County Recorder are public records, with access available to all persons.

71. (B) The best protection to assure title to real property is offered by means of a title insurance policy that insures against both "of" record and "off" record risks.

72. (C) A title search is an examination of matters disclosed by the public records, including the county recorder's office and such other sources as the county clerk, various tax agencies, federal court clerk, and the Secretary of State. The standard policy of title insurance, in addition to protecting against risks of record, protects against off-record hazards such as forgery, lack of capacity, non-delivery of a deed, or federal estate taxes, etc.

Exam 5 Answers - Financing Real Estate

1. (B) A "Beneficiary's Statement" (a.k.a.: "Bene" Statement) is a statement issued by a lender giving the remaining principal balance and other information concerning the loan. Escrow agents usually write for this statement when an owner wishes to sell, assume, or refinance property.

2. (D) A "compensating balance" is sometimes a requirement of a commercial bank that makes the borrower keep a certain amount of funds on deposit in the institution as a condition of the loan or line of credit. The compensating balance, through the "multiplier effect," can increase the lending capacity substantially more than by just the balance left on deposit. For this reason, a compensating balance adds to the quality of the loan and would warrant more favorable consideration by the lender.

3. (C) By tightening the reserve requirements, the Federal Reserve Bank can decrease the amount of money that is available for loans. This action would create a demand for more private loans in the form of second trust deeds.

4. (B) A trust deed foreclosed through court (judicial sale) follows the same proceedings as a mortgage foreclosure. In some cases, the borrower would have one year after the sale to redeem the property.

5. (C) The nominal interest rate is the rate indicated (named) in the note also known as the contract rate.

6. (A) Mortgage companies characteristically:

   (1) "Participate and supervise construction loans (and "take-out" loans)
   (2) "Solicit loans from anyone" (institutional or non-institutional lenders), represent them and also seek out borrowers for such loans
   (3) Sometimes have money of their own to lend
   (4) Accumulate loans ("warehousing") which can be sold in groups and which are readily saleable in the secondary money market
   (5) Service loans that are arranged by their correspondents

7. (D) The borrower would need to know the "schedule of payments" for his loan. FHA loans do not have "prepayment penalties, choice (A). Choice (B), "Secondary financing," is not normally permitted at the origination of the first loan. Choice (C), "Mortgage life insurance," is not a requirement of an FHA insured loan (although Mutual Mortgage Insurance is a requirement to protect the lender against default of the borrower).

8. (A) An assumption fee is the lender's charge for changing over and processing new records for a new owner who is assuming an existing loan.

9. (C) If market prices rise, then the property value appreciates and the borrower's equity rises. An increased equity increases the owner's interest in protecting the investment, making that borrower less likely to default on the loan.

10. (C) The "price" of money, commonly expressed as interest rates, is determined in the market, where the principle of supply and demand is the dominant factor.

11. (D) Choices (A), (B), and (C) do not offer a benefit to a seller using a land contract. There are probably no advantages since law changes in 1985.

12. (C) A conditional/installment sales contract transfers equitable title to the buyer but the seller keeps the legal title until the contract has been fulfilled.

13. (A) Institutional and private lenders usually charge a penalty fee if a conventional loan is paid in full prior to its maturity. A VA or FHA loan may be repaid in full at any time without penalty.

14. (A) The ultimate source of all mortgage money is savings. The proportion of the nation's surplus money that will enter the real estate market depends largely on conditions in the mortgage market that may be divided into supply and demand factors. Mortgage interest rates increase when mortgage money is in short supply relative to demand for this money. Higher interest rates in non-mortgage markets attract mortgage lenders away from mortgages to other types of investments and as a result financial institutions have fewer funds to make mortgage loans.

15. (A) Many lenders have established standards to evaluate a borrower's ability to repay. These standards are usually tied to the borrower's income. In addition to the ability to pay, the question of willingness to pay is a central point in credit analysis.

16. (C) A borrower does not apply directly to HUD or FHA for a mortgage loan. Instead, application is made for a mortgage insurance commitment to a HUD/FHA-approved mortgagee.

17. (B) A "due on sale" clause is a form of an acceleration clause found in some mortgages or trust deeds, authorizing the lender to call the loan when the property is conveyed. This clause eliminates the new buyer's assuming the mortgage unless the mortgagee permits the assumption, in which case the mortgagee could increase the interest rate and/or charge an assumption fee.

18. (B) Choices (C) and (D) are eliminated by the fact that no deed can be given because vendee does not have legal title. A vendee may assign his rights but not his obligations.

19. (D) Mortgages and trust deeds are the security for promissory notes. A land contract is also a security device by which the seller retains legal title as security for payment of the purchase price.

20. (D) If only the APR is given, no additional disclosures are required. Don't confuse that with the following rule:

    If any one of the following is given:
    1. Amount or percentage of any downpayment
    2. Number of payments or period of repayment
    3. Amount of any payment
    4. Amount of any finance charge

    Then, the ad must disclose:
    1. Amount or percentage of the downpayment
    2. Terms of repayment
    3. APR, and if the rate may be increased, that fact

203

21. (D) The unique feature of VA loans is that they generally require no down payment; conventional loans nearly always require a significant down payment. While the CRV may affect the downpayment in some circumstances, that fact is not the distinguishing characteristic this question seeks.

22. (D) An open-end mortgage is one that contains a clause that permits the mortgagor to borrow additional money after the loan has been reduced without rewriting the mortgage.

23. (D) There is no prepayment penalty on a Cal-Vet loan, effective 1998.

24. (B) Amortization tables are sometimes called "Table of Monthly Payments to Amortize a Loan." "They indicate the monthly payment needed for the periodic repayment of the principal amount of the loan plus the interest due for money loaned." (DRE Reference Book) The tables can also be used to determine interest rates, and term of repayment. However, the tables are constructed primarily to indicate monthly payment. Financial calculators have now replaced amortization tables for many licensees.

25. (B) Variable Interest Rate (VIR) or Variable Mortgage Rate (VMR) is an interest rate on a real estate loan that, by the terms of the note, varies upward or downward over the term of the loan depending on market conditions. The fluctuation is based on an "index," such as the Consumer Price Index (CPI). The most commonly used now is the Adjustable Rate Mortgage (ARM).

26. (C) RESPA states: Coverage is restricted to first mortgage loans secured by 1- to 4-family residential properties made by federally-regulated or insured lender.

27. (C) RESPA states: Coverage is restricted to first mortgage purchase money loans secured by 1- to 4-unit residential properties, made by federally regulated or insured lenders.

28. (B) When mortgage money is plentiful, lenders tend to drop interest rates to attract more borrowers (the Law of Supply and Demand).

29. (C) An "acceleration clause" is a clause in a trust deed or mortgage giving the lender the right to call all sums owing to him to be immediately due and payable upon the happening of a certain event. If the "certain event" is the conveyance by the original titleholder, it is termed an "alienation clause."

30. (C) Under the Truth in Lending law, "Buyer's points, time-price differential and Finder's fees" must be disclosed in the finance charge. Exempted charges on residential mortgage transactions include title insurance, document costs, recording and notary fees, credit investigations, and appraisal fees.

31. (A) The National Housing Act of 1934 created FHA. Choices (B), (C), and (D) are all secondary benefits plus establishing minimum standards of construction, not maximum.

32. (B) Answer (B) defines correctly the effective interest rate as the percentage of interest actually paid (or received by the investor) and may reflect periodic compounding. The effective rate may also include some non-recurring costs such as discount points and is similar to an Annual Percentage Rate (APR) as defined by Regulation Z. The nominal rate is the percentage of interest stated in the note

33. (D) An "assumption fee" is one of many fees that must be included in the finance charge to determine the annual percentage rate as part of a Truth-in-Lending Disclosure Statement. Among other fees not required are "appraisal fees, recording and document fees and title insurance fees." Such fees are shown on the Disclosure Statement, however.

34. (B) A mortgage evaluation takes into consideration the characteristics of the borrower, of the property, of the loan, and of the money market. A loan committee's commitment decision—to lend or not to lend, etc.—is based on the mortgage evaluation.

35. (C) Private Mortgage Guaranty Insurance (more commonly called Private Mortgage Insurance, or PMI) protection is available to lenders approved by a mortgage insurance company as additional security for "low downpayment" home loans. It guarantees the lender that should the borrower default in loan repayment, the insurer will reimburse the lender for the dollar loss suffered or for the insured amount - whichever is less.

36. (D) A "default" constitutes a failure to perform either (1) a duty or (2) an obligation. In order to protect their security, most deeds of trust contain agreements between the mortgagor and mortgagee, which, if breached constitutes a default. Among these agreements are (A) not to be delinquent in payments (B) not to use the property for other than its intended purpose and (C) not to fail to maintain the property. Careful: if the question asked, "The term default, in most mortgages most commonly means that the mortgagor": choose (A) is delinquent in monthly payments.

37. (D) To curb inflation, the Federal Reserve Board would raise the reserve requirements for its member banks and enter into the bond market in a selling capacity.

38. (D) Under RESPA, the lender must furnish a copy of a Special Information Booklet prescribed by HUD together with a good faith estimate of closing costs to every person from whom the lender receives a written application for a first mortgage loan. The lender shall supply the good faith estimate by delivering or placing it in the mail not later than three business days after the application is received.

39. (D) The borrower may waive the right to delivery of the completed Uniform Settlement Statement no later than at settlement. In such case, the completed Uniform Settlement Statement shall be mailed or delivered to the borrower and seller "as soon as practicable after settlement."

40. (B) RESPA requires the lender to furnish the borrower the following two items by delivering them or placing them in the mail not later than 3 business days after the application of the borrower is received:

 1. A "Special Information Booklet" prepared or approved by HUD which explains settlement costs; and,

 2. A "good faith estimate" of the settlement costs.

41. (D) "Kickbacks, unearned fees, and the seller designating the title insurance company" are all violations under RESPA. Buyers may, however, designate the lenders of their choice.

42. (D) "Title acquired by the mortgagor subsequent to the execution of the mortgage inures to the mortgagee as security for the debt in like manner as if acquired before the execution" (Civil Code § 2930). Also, the parties may agree to create a lien on property not yet acquired (Civil Code § 2883).

43. (D) If a Deed of Trust (or Mortgage) is executed in the act of and for the purpose of purchasing property that is the security, it is a "purchase money" deed of trust (or mortgage), regardless of whether the beneficiary (lender) is the seller or a third party.

44. (A) The right of rescission under the federal Truth-in-Lending Law never applies to purchase money loans. Therefore, the Jacksons do not have a right of rescission. The Truth-in-Lending Law applies only to loans for personal, family, or household purposes, never to business loans regardless of what collateral is put up. Therefore, the Londons have no right of rescission.

45. (D) Choices (A), (B), and (C) are all conditions that may result from a subordination clause. Choice (D) is incorrect because it does not create a hardship for the buyer but would assist him in obtaining a construction loan.

46. (B) A borrower would not prefer a straight loan for reason (B). Under a straight note, interest is charged on the face amount of the loan for the full term of the loan. The cost of a straight note therefore is higher than the cost of an installment loan that is paid off on a decreasing balance basis.

47. (B) Mortgage bankers who assemble loans and temporarily hold these portfolios until they can be sold to investors in the secondary mortgage market are said to be "warehousing" loans.

48. (C) If any financing terms are used in an advertisement promoting closed-end credit, then three specific disclosures must also be included. They are: (1) Amount or percentage of downpayment (2) the term of the repayment (3) The "Annual Percentage Rate," using the term spelled out in full, or the abbreviation APR.

49. (C) A purchase money lien in real property will take priority over all other liens created against the purchaser, subject to the operation of the recording laws (Civil Code Section 2898).

50. (D) A beneficiary of a trust deed has a lien on the real property, and the lien is a security interest in all of the land, fixtures, and appurtenances thereto. No changes of any kind that will change the real property or the priority of the lien can be made without the consent of the holder of the security interest.

51. (C) Insurance companies at times lend directly but most often invest funds through mortgage companies that are appointed as loan correspondents. Mortgage companies make loans in their respective cities and areas and, when completed, deliver these loans to the life insurance companies.

52. (C) The 3-day right of rescission that applies to some loans under the federal Truth-in-Lending law begins with the delivery of the disclosure statement or the signing of the promissory note, whichever occurs later.

53. (D) Choices (A), (B), and (C) are all legitimate reasons for the release schedule to be disproportionate in favor of the beneficiary.

54. (A) An alienation clause is a certain kind of acceleration clause which provides that the entire loan amount may be called due and payable in the event of sale, which circumstance would preclude a buyer's taking over the loan without the lender's consent.

55. (B) A "package mortgage" covers both real and personal property. Choice (A) is an "all-inclusive" deed of trust. Choice (C) is a "blanket" encumbrance and choice (D) is an "open-end" mortgage.

56. (C) "Jointly" means the creditor can look to all of the signers as a group; "severally" means the creditor can look to any one signer for the entire amount due. Co-signers on a note are "jointly and severally" liable.

57. (D) Since construction lenders require first priority, the previously recorded trust deed must have a clause that requires it to "relinquish priority" to a subsequent trust deed.

58. (A) If a note is negotiable, the insertion of an acceleration clause will not affect its negotiability. It could enhance its value to a holder in due course.

59. (D) The beneficiary obtains the power to declare the entire amount of an obligation due and payable upon default of the trustor by using an acceleration clause.

60. (B) A subordination clause benefits the trustor (borrower) by making it easier for the borrower to obtain additional financing using the title of the same property as security. The lender of a prior loan that includes such a clause agrees to relinquish the priority of his trust deed to specified financing to be obtained by the borrower at a later date. Without a subordination clause, a construction lender, desiring first position, would be unwilling to finance the improvements unless the first loan was paid.

61. (C) A partial reconveyance deed would reconvey the legal title to a specified lot or lots to the trustor in return for a partial payment on the trust note balance, thus releasing a specified lot or lots from under the blanket encumbrance.

62. (C) A subordination clause places a trust deed in a junior position. If a subordination clause is contained in a trust deed that has been recorded first, the beneficiary has agreed to "relinquish his priority" to existing or future liens on the property.

63. (C) A blanket mortgage is a single mortgage which covers more than one parcel of real estate. In this situation, since one property does not provide for sufficient collateral, a second property will be covered by one loan. An open-end mortgage allows for additional money to be advanced to the borrower without rewriting the mortgage.

64. (A) A subordination clause is an agreement by the lienholder to stay in a second or a junior position with regard to the priority of subsequent loans.

65. (A) An Offset Statement is customarily obtained from the property owner when existing mortgages or trust deeds are assigned to an investor. It sets forth the true condition of the mortgage lien and states whether the property owner has any claims that do not appear in the instrument being purchased by the investor. The offset statement is obtained in addition to the beneficiary statement from the lender.

66. (B) A qualified endorsement is one in which the holder adds the words "without recourse" to what would otherwise be a simple blank or special endorsement. This means that the endorser will not be liable for the amount, even if the maker refuses to pay.

67. (C) The trustor is the owner-borrower of a property "mortgaged by the use of a trust deed." As the property appreciates, the trustor's equity increases and he therefore benefits more than the other parties indicated.

68. (A) The characteristics listed describe those of an insurance company.

69. (C) FHA insurance is for the benefit of lenders, not borrowers. Choices (A), (B), and (D) are all advantages developed by the FHA plan.

70. (B) The Federal Reserve Board could create a tight money market by restricting the flow of money and credit. It could use one or a combination of any of the three methods following:

   1. Raise the reserve requirement of its member banks (not in any of the choices)

   2. Sell U.S. government bonds through its Federal Open Market Committee (eliminates choice (C))

   3. Raise the discount rate on short-term loans made to its member banks. (This eliminates choices (A) and (D) with (B) being correct).

71. (C) A down payment is not a requirement of a Veteran's Administration guaranteed loan (unless the certificate of reasonable value is less than the purchase price). However, the lender may require one. Conventional loans nearly always require some downpayment, and FHA and Cal-Vet loans do require down payments.

72. (A) If the short-term first loan is about to become due, the purchaser of the home may need to refinance the home in order to have money to pay off that loan.

73. (C) When a tight money situation exists and money is difficult to get for first trust deeds and mortgages, there is an increase in secondary financing.

74. (D) Since banks, savings and loan associations and mortgage bankers are more interested in primary loans, many junior loans are placed through individual lenders or private lenders. However, the institutions have expanded their markets in the area of junior loans with home equity loans and home equity lines of credit.

75. (B) Inflation will cause the borrower's equity to increase faster than it would from principal payments alone. Since inflation will not affect the interest rate on the mortgage, this is an advantage to the borrower but a definite disadvantage to the beneficiary (lender). The trustee is not affected in any measurable way.

76. (A) Fees for appraisals and credit reports are not included in the finance charge. Regulation Z lists among those charges included in the finance charge buyer's points, finder's fees, and premiums for mortgage guaranty or similar insurance.

77. (D) Lenders generally seek to minimize the number of substandard loans in their portfolios, thus reducing their risk of loss. A lender sometimes reduces the allowable loan to value ratio for a specific borrower to reduce the risk in making that loan, but the lender does not want to minimize the loan to value ratio.

78. (A) This question uses the word *mortgaged* in its generic sense; in that sense a mortgage is any device that puts property up as security for a loan. In that sense it is correct to say that in California we commonly use the trust deed as our form of mortgage. The equity in a mortgaged home belongs to the owner, or borrower. When a trust deed is used, the borrower is the trustor.

79. (A) Leverage results from the use of other people's money (OPM) to make a profit. When a mortgaged home appreciates in value, that increase belongs to the equity owner. The equity owner of a property encumbered with a trust deed lien is the trustor.

80. (A) Leverage is the use of debt financing of an investment to maximize the return per dollar of equity invested. In this example the equity invested is $75,000. The dollar increase in the value of the property is $30,000. $30,000 is 40% of the $75,000 equity investment.

81. (D) $420 interest x 4 quarters = $1,680 annual interest

$$\frac{\$1,680}{\$14,000} \quad = \quad .12 \quad = \quad \underline{12\%}$$

82. (C)   FHA mutual mortgage insurance insures the lender (mortgagee) against loss in the event a foreclosure sale fails to satisfy the debt obligation. The mortgage insurance premium (MIP) is paid by the borrower (mortgagor).

83. (B)   A land sales contract (land contract) is a security device sometimes used in place of the more commonly used note and trust deed when a seller extends credit. In the larger meaning of the word "mortgage"—any device that puts property up as security for a debt—a land contract, like a trust deed, is a form of mortgage. However, the land contract is not identical to the mortgage contract.

84. (B)   The interest rate for an FHA loan is negotiated by agreement between the borrower and the lender. FHA no longer sets limits as they once did in years past.

85. (B)   A notice of non-responsibility (for mechanics liens) would have no effect on the construction lender. A physical inspection of the property (Choice A) is very important to a construction lender to make certain that no work has started on the construction project before the construction loan trust deed is recorded. A subordination clause in the purchase money trust deed (Choice C) is required in order for the construction loan to have first priority. An ALTA title insurance policy (Choice D) is normally required by all institutional lenders.

86. (B)   Mortgages (including notes and trust deeds) are frequently sold and exchanged in the secondary money market. They are usually sold at a discount.

87. (C)   Collateral is marketable real or personal property that a borrower pledges as security for a loan. Thus, a mortgage loan is a loan collateralized by real property.

88. (B)   A low loan to value ratio indicates a high equity. A loan to value ration or $60,000 to $100,000 is lower than one of $80,000 to $100,000. In the first case, the owner has an equity of $40,000; in the second case, the equity is only $20,000.

89. (D)   Any lender of money makes a hard cash loan. A seller who sells property on credit does not make a hard money loan but only extends credit.

90. (B)   In real estate finance, the term "impounds" means reserves, which is a trust type account established by lenders for the accumulation of a borrower's funds to meet periodic payment of taxes and insurance as they become due.

91. (A)   The "price" of borrowed money is most commonly expressed as interest rates. These rates are set by the forces of supply and demand interacting in the open money market. The term "fluctuating money market rate" describes this "price" of borrowed money.

92. (C)   The loan to value ratio is the amount of the loan as a percentage of the appraised value. Example: An $80,000 loan on a property appraised at $100,000 would have a loan to value ratio of 80%.

93. (D)   The interest portion of a mortgage payment becomes the lender's money upon receipt. It is never a part of an impound account. The other payments mentioned are at times placed into impound accounts held by the lender for the benefit of the borrower.

94. (B) The lender under a deed of trust is the beneficiary. A lender may also be called a mortgagee, but the term beneficiary is more specific and thus a better answer.

95. (B) Under a straight note, interest is charged on the face amount of the loan for the full term of the loan. The expense of a straight note therefore is higher than in an installment loan that is paid off on a decreasing balance basis.

96. (D) Civil Code Section 2954.4 states: "No late charge may be imposed on any installment which is paid . . . within 10 days after due date."

97. (B) The demand sources of mortgage money are entities or activities that borrow money or cause money to be borrowed for mortgage loans. Sales financing (A) construction (C) and refinancing (D) all create a demand for mortgage money. Fannie Mae (FNMA) does not borrow mortgage money, but is a supply source.

98. (B) The federal Truth-in-Lending law requires a "Notice of Right to Rescind" only when security for the loan is the borrower's existing principal residence.

99. (D) Notes that are sold for less than the face amount or less than the unpaid balance are said to be sold at a discount.

100. (C) A trustee's foreclosure takes approximately 4 months and is referred to as foreclosure sale. A sheriff's sale would be a court foreclosure known as a judicial foreclosure and could take up to 4 years.

101. (B) FHA loans are insured by an agency of the US government and are a reduced risk to the lender compared with conventional loans. As a result, conventional loan interest rates are usually higher than similar FHA loan rates.

102. (B) Mortgage interest is paid to the lender as income to him and not held in an impound account. Choices (A), (C), and (D) are owed to someone other than the lender and might result in a default if not paid. To protect against such, the lender might ask that deposits for each of these be made into an impound account controlled by the lender to insure that the obligations be paid.

103. (D) No discount points are charged on a Cal-Vet loan.

104. (B) 18" crawl space is an "MPR," that is a Minimum Property Requirement under FHA requirements. There are exceptions, such as for houses on slab foundations.

105. (B) The law will not permit a deficiency judgment on any type of loan in which the seller is the beneficiary, nor will it permit an outside lender to obtain a deficiency judgment on a loan used to purchase an owner-occupied residential property of four units or less.

106. (C) The security for a mortgage loan is the value of the property. The lender will give consideration to many things, including the income of the borrower, in making a loan commitment decision. However, once the loan is made, in the event of default by the borrower, only the property value provides security for the loan.

107. (D) Of the choices given in this question, only "the amounts of the different monthly payments" would need to be disclosed in advertising.

108. (C) A "land sales contract" is a form of financing the sale of real property in which the buyer (vendee) is given possession of the property, but the legal title is held by the seller (vendor) until the full purchase price is paid. The buyer has only equitable title to the property, which is not the fee simple estate. While many property interests are capable of being inherited, only the fee estate is properly classified as an "estate of inheritance."

Exam 6 Answers - Valuation/Appraisal of Real Property

1. (A)   "Effective Gross Income" is:

    Gross income less allowance for (1) vacancies and (2) bad debts.

2. (C)   Choice (C) describes a condition that is perfectly usable and would not be considered substandard even though the wiring could not be approved for new construction.

3. (C)   The value per square foot of a lot times its depth is equal to its value per front foot. Written as a formula:

Value/sq. ft.	x	Depth	=	$\overline{)\text{Value / fr. ft.}}$
$4.40	x	200	=	**$880**/fr.ft.

4. (C)   The appraiser should assign a value to the "improvements in legal question" and indicate, One: his reason for belief that they are questionable, and Two: the potential loss on the total value conclusion should the questionable improvements lose their value to the property.

5. (A)   When an exterior wall is adequately insulated, the interior surface will be about the same temperature as the surface of interior walls because heat will not be seeping through the walls.

6. (B)   Economic obsolescence is a loss in value due to factors away from the subject property. The oversupply of properties lies outside of the subject property. Choices (A), (C), and (D) all reflect functional obsolescence.

7. (A)   Assessed value, choice (D), and cost, choice (C), are seldom accurate indicators of value. Square footage, choice (B), may sometimes be a consideration but if the property is not marketable and acceptable as in choice (A) the square footage would matter very little.

8. (B)   This figure can be divided into 4 rectangles.

(A)	12	x	6	=	72
(B)	12	x	15	=	180
(C)	8	x	31	=	248
(D)	22*	x	49**	=	1,078 Total
	=	**1,578**			

    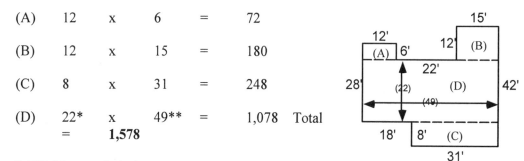

    1,530 (closest choice)

    *22' dimension is determined by subtracting the 6' in the area (A) dimension from 28' on the left side

    **49' dimension deduced from adding the dimensions across the top, that is 12' + 22' + 15'

9. (A) Fixed expenses continue whether the property in question is 100% leased or vacant, for instance: real estate taxes, insurance, and licenses.

   Variable expenses occur according to the extent the property is leased.

   Operating expenses are the combination of fixed and variable expenses.

10. (B) The outside dimension of a house is used to determine its square footage. The garage is not considered when determining square footage of a house and is measured separately because a garage can be replaced at a lower cost per square foot

11. (C) When interest rates increase, it indicates that investors are asking for a higher rate of return of their investments. This results in higher capitalization rates. If the "cap" rate increases and the income stays the same, the value of the property decreases.

12. (A) Amenities are the attractive or desirable features of a home or neighborhood. These may be physical attributes or perhaps the neighborhood's attitude toward schools, well kept lawns and so on. These may be tangible or intangible qualities measurable on the market.

13. (D) The appraiser considers both tangible and intangible aspects of real property: the land, improvements, any easement rights or burdens, other limitations or privileges applying to the "bundle of rights" an owner would receive with a given parcel.

14. (B) Depreciation can be from either inherent or extraneous causes.

15. (D) An appraiser of real property estimates the values of the land and the improvements thereon. However, the appraiser also estimates utility value and the value of all ownership rights (the bundle of rights). Utility includes the capacity to produce and affects judgment about the highest and best use of the land.

16. (C) The relationship of contract and economic rental levels is important because of the effect on the value of the fee estate. Contract rent below economic rent creates a leasehold estate at the expense of the value of the fee interest. When making a gross income estimate, the appraiser would secure copies of all existing leases for study and would consider all the data in choices (A) and (B).

17. (C) A kiosk is a small, light structure with one or more open sides often seen in shopping center malls as a photo shop, key shop, or newsstand.

18. (B) Under the new California Appraiser Licensing and Certification Law, an appraiser must be licensed or certified for a "federally related real estate appraisal activity." The term "appraisal" does not include an opinion given by a real estate licensee in the ordinary course of business, and such an opinion shall not be referred to as an "appraisal." A broker or salesperson may do a "competitive market analysis," for example, but may not term it an "appraisal."

19. (D) To determine effective gross income, make deductions from gross income for vacancies and uncollectible rents. Rent concessions are used in commercial buildings and shopping centers to attract tenants by reduction of rents for a period of time.

20. (A) Improved value is the combined value of land and building as distinguished from their separate values.

21. (D) "Rapidly changing economic conditions may limit the usefulness of the sales comparison approach." (AIREA)

22. (C) One house must have functional obsolescence. Since the properties are in the same location, the same age, and have been maintained the same, the difference in value cannot be attributed to economic obsolescence or wear and tear. As an example, one house may have only a single car garage or one bathroom or a less attractive floor plan.

23. (C) A strip commercial development is one in which a major arterial street is bordered by an almost continuous strip of retail stores.

24. (D) The gross multiplier method involves applying a market-established multiplier to the gross income. Vacant land does not usually produce income.

25. (A) Appraisal fees are set by agreement between the appraiser and the client.

26. (C) An increase in density and rapid turnover may occur from undesirable causes. The Principle of Conformity holds that maximum value is realized when a reasonable degree of homogeneity is present, in buildings, uses of property, and income levels of residents.

27. (B) According to *The Appraisal of Real Estate,* AIREA (Name now changed to The Appraisal Institute), "The square foot method is ideally suited to warehouses, loft buildings, store buildings, and structures of like character. The cubic foot method is normally applied to apartments and many times to office buildings (structures that have intricate interior finishes)."

28. (C) $5,000 x 12   = $60,000 annual gross income

$60,000	Gross income
−12,000	Expenses
$48,000	net income divided by .12 = $400,000

    (Total property value with total annual net income capitalized at 12% cap rate)

    $400,000 − $300,000 = $100,000 invested in land

    Note: In this simplified problem we use the same over-all cap rate for both land and building because we are given no information on which to include an "accrual for future depreciation" in the building cap rate.

29. (C) Future net income is capitalized in the income approach. It is difficult to be accurate in estimating any quantity in the future. This difficulty in being accurate about future net income results primarily from the difficulty in projecting future vacancy factors.

30. (C) A licensed or certified appraiser in California, or any other state, must adhere to the Uniform Standards of Professional Appraisal Practice at all times. A violation can result in loss of license. The URAR stands for Uniform Residential Appraisal Report.

31. (C)

Appraisal technique	desired result	
Land Residual	Land value	(L)
Building Residual	Building value	(B)
Property Residual	Property value	(L + B)

32. (C) A fee appraiser is one qualified by education, training, and experience who is hired to estimate the value of real and personal property based on experience, judgment, facts, and use of formal appraisal processes and is paid a fee for such services. A fee real estate appraiser must now be state licensed or state certified.

33. (C) Assessed value could be misleading to an appraiser in California because of the limitations placed on assessors by law (Prop. 13). Choices (A), (B), and (D) reflect essential data.

34. (B) An estimate of market value may be justified by market evidence, whereas a sale price may reflect caprice, unequal motivation or negotiating position, unusual terms, or other factors that caused price to deviate from value.

35. (D) The principle of substitution states that when several similar commodities, goods or services are available, the one with the lowest price attracts the greatest demand and widest distribution.

36. (A) Quality of income establishes the interest rate portion of the capitalization rate used in the appraisal of property and the greater the risk, the higher the rate.

37. (A) Among the choices presented, "Gross scheduled income" would yield "The maximum possible income . . .." "Scheduled income" represents the rent currently in effect on the property in question as if the property were fully occupied. If the property has space available, the "gross scheduled income" would be at the rent levels currently obtainable for the space in the local market.

38. (C) "Sales comparison" and "Income Capitalization" are two of the indirect methods employed by appraisers. Indirect means from the market. Direct methods are "Engineering" or "Breakdown" (a.k.a.: observed condition or cost to cure) and "Economic Age Life" (a.k.a.: Straight line method).

39. (D) $25,000 x .10 = $2,500 increase, which, without an increase in expenses, would also be an increase in net income.

$$\% \quad x \quad \text{PAID} \quad = \quad \overline{)\text{MADE}}$$

$$? \quad x \quad \$10{,}000 \quad = \quad \overline{)\$2{,}500}$$

$$\$10{,}000\overline{)\$2{,}500} \quad = \quad .25 \quad = \quad \underline{25\%}$$

40. (D) In the analysis of a commercial district the emphasis is on the quantity and quality of purchasing power available to the shopping area.

41. (D) The comparative analysis or market data approach to appraisal is a "quick method and easy to apply." The usual problem occurs where there are no comparable properties. The quantity survey and unit-cost-in-place methods are very detailed.

42. (C) The beginning or cover letter in a narrative form of appraisal sets forth the purpose of the appraisal and the final opinion of value. Everything that follows in this most comprehensive form of appraisal is the appraiser's data to support the appraiser's conclusion.

43. (B) In the quantity survey method, an estimate of the quantity and grade of each type of material, the labor hours required, the overhead, insurance, and contractor's profit must be considered. It is a very detailed and expensive appraisal to perform.

44. (A) GMM x   GMI   = $\overline{)\text{APPRAISAL}}$ (Sales Price)

As the formula indicates, if you didn't know the Gross Monthly Multiplier you would divide the Sales Price by the Gross Monthly Income.

45. (B) The Principle of Contribution is applied to a portion of the property (in this case the added swimming pool) and affirms that the value of an additional improvement is measured by its contribution to the net return of the combined enterprise.

46. (C) Sales prices of "comps" are adjusted to reflect what the comparable property might have sold for had it been more nearly identical to the subject property—or had "similar prominent characteristics to the subject property."

47. (B) An income producing investment that would maintain its value does so by providing an increased income when inflation makes money worth less. The property thus keeps its exchange value compared to other properties and so protects against inflation.

48. (B) The economic life is the period in which the building earns sufficient income to support itself. The building will still be standing even though its economic life may have expired.

49. (B) There are four basic procedures for the valuation of land: (1) Comparative (2) Abstraction (3) Development and (4) Land Residual. Equity is not a method.

50. (D) Depreciation can be from either inherent or extraneous factors.

51. (B) In using the comparison approach, an appraiser "adjusts the comparable properties to the subject property" in order to compensate for the differences.

52. (D) The appraiser is interested in today's cost (less depreciation, of course) and value. He or she is not concerned about the original cost or the cost of living index in 1910.

53. (B) Newness in itself would not be a stabilizing influence. Zoning regulations and private restrictions generally have as their primary function the protection and stabilization of property values. Availability of public transportation has always been a significant factor influencing property values in most residential areas.

54. (A) (1) $265,000 gross/qtr   x   4 qtrs   = $1,060,000   gross/yr

(2) $1,060,000 gross/yr   x   .32   =   − 339,200   expenses/yr

Total net annual income $ 720,800

55. (A) This is one expression of the principle of substitution.

56. (D) The former AIREA once stated in part: "No object, including a parcel of real estate, can have value unless it possesses in some degree the two factors of utility and scarcity." Land is the fundamental resource in all productivity ("Under All Is the Land") but is a limited resource. A parcel of real estate will not have value primarily because it (A) has high replacement cost; or (B) proximity to high rentals; or has (C) a prospect of speculative gain, even though these circumstances can influence value.

57. (C) The Restricted and Form types of appraisal reports are abbreviations or variations of the complete narrative form of report. The narrative appraisal report gives the appraiser the opportunity to support opinions and conclusions. Appraisal reports may vary in content and arrangement as long as they conform to USPAP. Those paragraphs mentioned in this question are generally included in the narrative report.

58. (B) A sole plate is a member, usually a 2 by 4, on which wall and partition studs rest.

59. (D) The Principal of Substitution states that when several similar commodities, goods, or services are available, the one with the lowest price attracts the greatest demand and widest distribution. The substitution of one property for another may be in terms of use, structural design, or earnings.

60. (D) The Principle of Substitution is applicable to all three traditional approaches to value: sales comparison (market data), income capitalization, and cost.

61. (A) Appraisers are only required to be licensed when performing "federally related transactions" such as loans made by a bank or S&L.

62. (B) Depth tables are used by appraisers in determining variations in value of property due to variations in depth.

63. (A) Before a building is constructed, assurance should be gained from an analysis of the market that the space can be rented at a price that will obtain a reasonable return on an investment. After the decision has been made to proceed with construction, all that can be done is hope that other parties will analyze the market and take space supply into consideration and refrain from glutting the market.

64. (C) $56,400 gross annual income x .15 = $8,460.00 annual net income divided by 12 months = $705.00.

65. (D) For appraisal purposes, mortgage payments and income tax are not allowable deductions to arrive at net operating income. Depreciation adjusts the cost basis but is not an expense for appraisal purposes. Wages paid for gardeners and maintenance personnel are deductible from gross income as operating expenses.

66. (A) The usefulness of the cost approach method of appraisal is limited when appraising an older property with many functional deficiencies because of the difficulty in determining all of the accrued depreciation. A "new structure" (B), or "for construction" (D), would probably have little, if any, functional deficiencies. "In an unusually active real estate market," (C), the comparison approach would be the most significant approach to use, but the cost approach could still be useful.

67. (B) The "purpose" of the appraisal determines the type of value being sought. It is not the same as "function" or "use". The function of the appraisal is the reason for which the appraisal is made or is intended to be used. It relates to the character of the decision to be based on the appraisal, for example, price at which to buy or sell, amount of mortgage to be made, etc. The appraiser under USPAP must state the intended use of users.

68. (A) Because of the action of the sun, the southwest corner is best. Therefore the northeast corner is the least desirable *corner of the street.*

69. (B) Capitalization of net income is unrelated to the cost approach to appraisal.

70. (A) "More buildings are torn down than fall down." This destruction of often physically sound improvements is caused by changes in the arts and by building obsolescence. Environmental, aesthetic and historical considerations are increasingly important in governmental view of highest and best use.

71. (A) When the business district of a city moves into a residential district, land values usually increase. If the land is under improved with a residence and is not realizing its highest and best use, its value is not as great as it should be. These extraneous changes result in economic obsolescence.

72. (A) Economic obsolescence is a loss in value due to factors outside of the subject property that adversely affect its value.

73. (B) Depreciation

Indirect Methods		Direct Methods	
(1)	Capitalized income	(1)	Straight line (Age-life)
(2)	Market data (Comparative)	(2)	Engineering
		(1)	Breakdown (cost to cure)

74. (D) The roof described is a hip roof.

75. (C) The process of capitalization is "dividing net income by a percentage rate of return to determine value." The capitalization rate is the relationship between value and net income, not net worth.

76. (C) For determining net income in the income approach to appraisal, mortgage interest is a personal expense of the owner, not an operating expense of the property. Choices A, B, and D are all "allowable" deductions in establishing net operating income for appraisal purposes.

77. (B) The use of a gross monthly multiplier indicates a subject property value of $96,000.

$$\frac{\$90,000}{600} = 150 \qquad 150 \ \times \ 640 = \underline{\$96,000}$$

78. (D) The principle of substitution holds that when two or more substantially similar properties are available, the one with the lower price receives the greatest demand.

79. (B)

$$R \quad \times \quad V \quad = \quad \overline{)I}$$

$$.09 \quad \times \quad \$800,000 \quad = \quad \overline{)?}$$

$$.09 \quad \times \quad \$800,000 \quad = \quad \overline{)\$72,000} \qquad \text{(net operating income)}$$

$$.12 \quad \times \quad ? \quad = \quad \overline{)\$72,000}$$

$$.12\overline{)\$72,000} \quad = \quad \underline{\$600,000}$$

80. (C) In the income approach (capitalization) an appraiser may be asked to project a series of possible developments on a site in order to establish the highest and best use of the land. In that sense the appraiser would be predicting values of certain hypothetical future developments. Generally, the value conclusion in an appraisal report can be made for any date in the past, but not for any date in the future. Capitalization is based on the principle of anticipation.

81. (B) A seller's market is characterized by an increase in demand and a decrease in supply. In these circumstances, sales prices tend to increase.

82. (C) 　　　Cap Rate　　　x　　　Value change　　=　　　Net Income Change

　　　.12　　　x　　　?　　　=　　　$4,800 per year

　　　$.12 \overline{)\,4,800}$ = $\underline{\$40,000}$ loss in value

83. (C) Once all of the elements of comparison between the comparable sales and subject property have been identified, they must be analyzed and adjustments made. Adjustments must be supported with data from the market. Techniques include the use of matched pairs, through the use of regression analysis and other complex mathematical techniques, percentage adjustments, or such devices as rating grids. Appraisers do not usually average data.

84. (D) Gross monthly $2,400　x　　12 months　　=　　$28,800/year

　　　Gross multiplierx　　Gross income　=　　Value estimate

　　　10.72　x　　$28,800=　　$308,736

　　　Closest　　　　　　$\underline{\$308,000}$

85. (C) Economic obsolescence is a loss in value due to factors away from or outside of the subject property. The Principle of Regression expresses the concept that the value of a superior property is adversely affected by its association with an inferior property of the same type. This placement of the $250,000 house would result in economic obsolescence.

86. (A) The Real Estate Reference Book, published by DRE, defines highest and best use as "that use which at the time of an appraisal is most likely to produce the greatest *net return* to the land and/or buildings over a given period of time."

87. (A) An appraiser making a site valuation would estimate the value of the lot at its highest and best use. A structure that prevents the highest and best use of the site is an underimprovement, with negative value. The cost of demolition of such a structure would be deducted from the value of the lot at its highest and best use, to establish present value.

88. (C) The sales comparison approach lends itself well to the appraisal of land, residences and other types of improvements that exhibit a high degree of similarity, and for which a ready market exists.

89. (D) Economic obsolescence is a loss in value due to factors outside of the subject property.

90. (C) An accrual for depreciation is a part of the income approach in appraisal. Appraisers describe remaining economic life as the period over which an investor would expect to recapture an investment in a property. An accrual for depreciation is a plan for recapture during this remaining economic life.

91. (A)   Replacement cost is defined as the cost of constructing an improvement with the "same utility," but with today's materials and costs. Reproduction cost is defined as the cost of constructing (reproducing a "replica") an improvement with the material used in the original construction.

92. (D)   The owner would apply the Principle of Contribution. He must be sure that the investment in the improvements will produce sufficient additional income to cover the expenditure. If the net income increases adequately, he should go ahead with the plan.

93. (B)   Varying depths of parcels are more common in commercial areas, especially older commercial areas. The depth table, is a table that evaluates depth as being more or less than the average lot, and would therefore be more significant in appraising commercial property.

94. (B)   In forecasting, the appraiser will use the past as a guide but must adjust this for changing conditions and make further adjustments based upon the appraiser's experience.

95. (A)   Assessed value, choice (D), and cost, choice (C), are seldom accurate indicators of value. Square footage, choice (B), may sometimes be a consideration but if the property is not marketable and available as in choice (A), the square footage would matter very little.

96. (C)   Functional obsolescence is inherent within the building and arises from poor or outdated architecture. Choices (A) and (B) are economic obsolescence. Choice (D) is physical deterioration.

97. (C)   "Foundation Plan" will show all the details of the subfloor, such as the size and dimension of concrete piers, footings, and other detailed construction measurements.

"Floor Plan" is a drawing made to scale showing floor dimensions, room sizes, placement of windows, doors, partitions, and so forth.

"Plot Plan" is a drawing made to scale which reveals lot dimensions, placement of improvements, walks and driveways and so forth.

"Elevation" is a sketch that shows the exteriors of a building, as it will appear when completed.

98. (A)   The Principle of Regression maintains that as properties of dissimilar value are placed in a neighborhood of better properties, the worth of the better homes is adversely affected and they tend to lose value.

99. (B)   The land residual technique of the income approach is used to determine the value of the land.

100. (C)   When interest rates increase, it indicates that investors are asking for a higher rate of return on their investment. This results in higher capitalization rates. If the capitalization rate increases and the income stays the same, the value of the property decreases.

101. (C)   Effective gross income is that income remaining after deducting vacancies and collection losses from gross income.

102. (B)   Economic obsolescence is affected by influences outside of the property. Air conditioning and heating problems occur on the property and are functional obsolescence.

103. (B)   The appraiser would subtract the value of the amenity from the sale price of the comparable property in order to get an indication of the value of the subject property.

104. (D) Submitting false information to a lender for the purpose of inducing the lender to make a loan is a felony. OREA could remove the appraiser's License also.

Exam 7 Answers - Real Estate Practice

1. (D) An offer is not a contract; it is an expression of willingness to enter into a contract. While the existence of agency is a question of fact and is not dependent on the existence of a contract, this question asks about an "agency contract." Choice (D) would not create an agency contract; the offer would have to be accepted in order for a "contract" to be created.

2. (B) A Fictitious Business Name Statement expires at the end of five (5) years from December 31st of the year in which it was filed in the Office of the County Clerk.

3. (D) With one exception, the principal has the power to terminate an agency, even if he does not have the right to do so under a contract. That one exceptions is "an agency coupled with an interest," as expressed in choice (D).

4. (D) The point at which an individual would be considered legally incapable of handling his own affairs because of mental incompetence, " . . . is when that has been judicially determined." In other words, a judge must make that determination. At that time, the judge appoints either a guardian or a conservator to handle the affairs of the person so incapacitated.

5. (D) An agent who is the "exclusive agent for the buyer" cannot also act as the seller's agent. If the buyer's agent also acts as the seller's agent, there is a dual agency, if disclosed, a divided agency, if not disclosed, and he cannot then be the "exclusive agent for the buyer." The buyer's agent can withhold negative information about his client, the buyer, as long as it is not a "material fact" which the seller might reasonably take into consideration in deciding to accept an offer.

6. (A) When applied to contracts, the word "executed" means "fully performed by both parties." (When the word "executed" is used in discussing deeds, it means, "signed.")

7. (B) The Agency Relationship in Residential Real Property Transactions Law (Civil Code Sections 2372-2381) became effective January 1, 1988. This disclosure law is so important to real estate licensees that the date of applicability is also important. Licensees should also be generally aware that the Mortgage Loan Disclosure Law, RESPA, and Truth in Lending are all laws that have been in effect for many years.

8. (D) A broker acting as an agent would not likely be able to sue his principal for specific performance because the broker is not a party to his principal's contract.

9. (C) Liquidity is the ability to convert assets into cash at a price close to its true value. Publicly traded stocks are a relatively liquid investment. Real estate is considered to be a long-term investment and is not highly liquid.

10. (B) A prudent seller, after consulting with the broker, obtains a structural pest control inspection report before putting the property on the market. The report can help in determining the pricing of the property.

11. (B) Broker Wilson acted incorrectly as he should present all offers.

12. (D) Choices (A), (B), and (C) are essential in the creation of a contract. Performance is the desired result and not an essential in the formation of a contract.

13. (D) A protection clause in a listing agreement binds the seller to the payment of a commission to the broker if the property is sold within a period of so many days after the expiration of the listing to a person with whom the broker negotiated during the listing period.

14. (D) A listing agreement, being a promise of payment given for a promise of a personal service, is a bilateral, executory, employment contract.

15. (C) A broker has a duty to disclose material facts; failure to disclose material facts to the parties involved could be considered negative fraud. As long as there is no illegal discrimination involved, there are many reasons why a broker may refuse to take a listing. For example, many brokers will refuse to take an unreasonably overpriced listing.

16. (C) When real property, such as the building housing the business, is also being sold to the same purchaser, the agent usually treats the sale of the business and the sale of the building as two separate and concurrent transactions, and the transfers may be completed through two concurrent and contingent escrows.

17. (C) Voidable means the contract is binding until some action is taken to rescind the contract.

18. (C) An affidavit is defined as a statement of facts sworn to or affirmed before an authorized official (usually a notary public).

19. (D) A licensee should disclose the licensee's agency relationship at the beginning of a transaction.

20. (D) Under the Exclusive Right to Sell listing, the owner promises to pay a commission even if he sells the property himself.

21. (B) An asset that can increase in "real value" builds the owner's equity and is a hedge against inflation (when money loses value).

22. (C) A protection clause in a listing agreement binds the seller to the payment of a commission to the broker if the property is sold within a period of so many days after the expiration of the listing to a person with whom the broker negotiated during the listing period.

23. (C) The broker does not have the authority to bind the principal to an offer as stated in choice (A). However, the broker may "obtain an offer" in order to "present it to the principal" for acceptance or rejection.

24. (C) An offeree rejects an offeror's offer. When the offeree rejects an offer it is terminated.

25. (A) In order for the offer to become a contract, the acceptance of the offer must be communicated from the offeree to the offeror. Once the broker has achieved a contract between a buyer and seller, the broker has *earned* a commission, even though there are usually contingencies that must be met before the broker can be *paid* the commission.

26. (D) A prudent investor would want some of his investments in a liquid position, that is, easily converted into cash in the event of need. Cash reserves would also be desirable as operating capital to help avoid the need to liquidate a profitable investment in the event of an emergency. Diversification assists in spreading the risk by not having "All your eggs in one basket."

27. (D)   Market Value $100,000

   –Liens   – 80,000
   =Equity $ 20,000

   "The difference between market value and outstanding liens," choice (A), would include "loans" in choice (C). Because a loan is a lien against the property, this makes both statements true. The $20,000 equity could be the result of a downpayment.

28. (A)   The party who had been adjudged incompetent thus lacked capacity to contract (one of the four essential elements of any contract). This apparent contract would be void, and all void contracts are unenforceable.

29. (B)   In this long list of many items, only choice (B) fails to include an item that would not likely be included in a listing. In choice (A) the "terms of the sale" goes beyond the listing to the deposit receipt. In choice (C) "sales cost" includes much more than commission alone and goes beyond the listing. In choice (D) the signatures of "both sellers" are not required for a bona fide listing on community real property, although good business practice would usually suggest it.

30. (A)   Crowley is obligated as per the terms of the contract independently negotiated with Rowe, and is not required to join Hansen as the parties are not jointly and severally liable.

31. (A)   When an agent acts "beyond the scope of authority," the agent is personally liable for any loss suffered by the principal as a result. Violation of the law of agency does not subject the agent to fine or imprisonment, and courts do not have jurisdiction over suspension or revocation of a license.

32. (D)   An offer may be withdrawn (revoked) by the offeror anytime prior to communication of the acceptance by the offeree regardless of the offeror's reason.

33. (A)   Consideration is not required of an agency relationship. The agency may be a gratuitous agency.

34. (C)   The principal is liable for the acts of his agent performed "within the scope of authority." The agent is liable for the agent's own acts performed "beyond the scope of authority."

35. (D)   Under normal circumstances, a commission is paid by check. However, as long as the principal and the broker agree, the commission may be paid in any of the forms suggested by the choices.

36. (B)   A contract, to be valid, must have an offer and acceptance. Neither recording nor acknowledgement is necessary for the contract or for the deed for the transfer of real property.

37. (C)   An attorney-in-fact is one who is authorized by another to perform certain acts for the other under a power of attorney. This power of attorney may be limited to a specific act(s) or may be general in scope.

38. (C)   An offeror cannot effectively revoke an offer after the acceptance has been communicated. Acceptance of an offer must be in the manner specified in the offer, but if no particular manner of acceptance is specified, then acceptance may be by any reasonable and usual mode. The courts have recognized that depositing an acceptance into the mail (posting) does constitute communication of acceptance. Choices A, B, and D all express a termination of an offer.

39. (D) The Real Estate Law (B&P Code Section 10176 [h]) requires that a broker who holds both a listing on and an option to buy the same property must, before he exercises the option to buy, "reveal in writing to the employer [owner/principal] the full amount of licensee's profit and obtain the written consent of the employer approving the amount of such profit."

40. (B) Mutual consent (offer and acceptance) is one of the four essential elements of a valid contract. The other three requirements are capacity of the parties, consideration, and lawful object.

41. (C) Neither a real estate sales contract nor even a deed is required to have a "legal description"—only an "adequate description." A description such as "My home in San Francisco" has been honored by a court when it could be shown that the grantor owned only one property in San Francisco. If the grantor had owned more than one parcel in that city, the court may not have been able to honor the deed.

42. (A) The broker is entitled to no commission. An exclusive agency listing is one which employs a broker as the sole agent for the seller of real property under the terms of which the broker is entitled to a commission if the property is sold through any other broker, but not if a sale is negotiated by the owner without the services of an agent.

43. (C) When the mutual consent to a contract is induced by fraud, duress, menace, or undue influence, the contract is voidable at the option of the wronged party. While such a contract is unenforceable against that wronged party, the contract is not totally unenforceable because it is enforceable against the other party. Therefore, Choice (C) is the best answer.

44. (B) Civil Code Section 1102, which requires the Real Transfer Disclosure Statement, applies to any sale of real property with up to four dwelling units. Transfers in foreclosure and in bankruptcy are specifically exempt.

45. (D) Agency is a matter of fact, not of contract. Therefore, a consideration is not necessary to make an authority, whether precedent (before the fact) or subsequent (after the fact), binding on the principal. The agent owes a fiduciary duty to his principal. Any person having capacity to contract may appoint an agent, and any person may be an agent, for any lawful object or purpose.

46. (D) An agency that accepts a deposit from a buyer, even though not authorized by the seller to do so, acts as an agent of the buyer as to the handling of that deposit. Since the seller would not be liable in the event of loss of the deposit, the buyer should be so informed.

47. (C) An agreement to sell (deposit receipt) would be unenforceable against the marital community if signed by one spouse only. It would be voidable for one year, not void.

48. (C) In an exchange, the broker is usually working for both parties and is most likely to receive a commission from both, if the broker gives them knowledge of the dual agency and gets their consent.

49. (B) The offer to purchase is expressly conditioned upon the buyer's obtaining a $65,000 loan payable according to a specific schedule. A contract based upon a condition will be enforceable only upon the happening of such condition. If the condition is not met, there is no contract nor are there any contractual duties. Choices (A) and (C) are alternatives for the buyers. Choice (B) is correct since it most nearly explains the "meaning of this clause."

50. (A) The deposit receipt states in line 1: "The obtaining of Buyer's financing is a contingency of this agreement." When a contingency in a contract fails, the entire contract fails. The offeror would have all of the deposit/downpayment returned.

51. (C)   If an offeror revokes his offer prior to communication of acceptance of the offer, the offer is terminated, and the offeror is entitled to return of his deposit. The deposit receipt states near the top of page 1: the deposit check is "to be held uncashed until acceptance of this offer . . ."

52. (B)   A trust deed lien is a specific lien. It is not a blanket lien unless it encumbers more than one parcel.

53. (C)   Paragraph 1. A. 2. is checked to state: "Financing contingency shall remain in effect until . . . 60 calendar days after acceptance of the offer."

54. (D)   From paragraph 1 of the deposit receipt:

A.	Deposit	$4,000
B.	Increased Deposit	$16,000
C.	Balance of Down Payment	$5,000
	Total downpayment	$25,000

55. (B)   One of the terms written in as a part of paragraph 1. I. says: "If there is a difference in the loan balance, seller will pay."

56. (B)   When buyer takes title subject to an existing lien, the buyer assumes no personal liability for the debt but merely takes the title knowing that the lien exists and must be paid. The buyer's only risk is his equity. If there is a possibility of a deficiency judgment upon foreclosure, only the seller could be held liable for such a judgment.

57. (A)   The $723 payment to amortize the loan includes principal and interest. Paragraph 1. E. says "including interest."

58. (D)   The Statute of Frauds requires that certain contracts be in writing to be enforceable in court; contracts that cannot be performed within one year as well as most contracts dealing with real property are included in this statute. Since choices (A), (B), and (C) concern themselves with business opportunities, which are personal property, these transactions fall outside the writing requirements of the statute.

59. (D)   The escrow is a dual agency and must be agreed upon by both parties. Neither has the right to choose without the other's consent. If there is no agreement, there will be no escrow.

60. (C)   Paragraph 4 is checked to state that the "Buyer *does* intend to occupy Property as Buyer's primary residence." *Personal residence*: yes. *Principal* residence: possibly.

61. (C)   It is entered in Paragraph 3: "Seller to pay 50% and Buyer to pay 50%" of escrow fees.

62. (D)   Paragraph 6. (a) states: "Title shall be transferred by grant deed,"

63. (D)   Paragraph 6 states, in part: "Title shall vest as designated in Buyer's escrow instructions." The seller is not usually concerned with the buyer's mode of taking title.

64. (D)   The seller's Real Estate Transfer Disclosure Statement must be completed by the seller.

65. (A)   California Civil Code Section 2079 provides that a real estate broker has a duty to the buyer of residential real property of one to four units to conduct a reasonably competent and diligent visual inspection of property offered for sale, and to disclose to the buyer all facts materially affecting the value or desirability of the property. This does not include areas that are normally and reasonably inaccessible to such an inspection, nor does it include the common areas of a condominium unit.

66. (A)   According to the liquidated damages clause: "Seller shall retain as liquidated damages the deposit actually paid, or an amount therefrom, not more than 3% of the purchase price and promptly return any excess to Buyer."

Downpayment	$30,000
Less 3% of $195,000	5,850
Amount to be returned	$24,150

67. (A)   There is no agreement for arbitration. Under these circumstances the buyer's only recourse to force a return of his deposit would be through the court.

68. (A)   In the Agency Confirmation Clause, it is checked that the "listing agent is the agent of both the Buyer and Seller."

69. (B)   The broker's commission is confirmed as 5% of the selling price.

.05   x $195,000   = $ 9,750

70. (B)   An offeror can revoke (terminate) an offer at any time prior to communication of acceptance of the offer. Under these circumstance the buyer could "terminate the offer and demand return of the deposit."

Exam 8 Answers - Tax Implications of Real Estate Ownership

1. (C) The capital gain exclusion for a married couple is $500,000 for a principal residence that they occupied for two or more years.

2. (D) A married couple is currently entitled to a maximum exclusion from capital gains of $500,000 as long as the property was their principal residence and they occupied it for over two years.

3. (C) Both of these agencies have the responsibility for assessment of real property in California as follows:

   (1) The County Assessor's Office, which establishes an assessment roll each year that reflects the full cash value of real property within their county.

   (2) Boards of Equalization, there are two kinds:

   One: the state Board, which among other duties, assesses public utilities (which cross county lines) and equalizes assessments among the counties.

   Two: the local Board of Equalization, which hears and adjusts complaints by owners within a county as to property assessments. This Board is the Board of Supervisors at authorized times—or may be a special Board of Tax Appeals in larger counties.

4. (B) To be eligible for a Section 1031 exchange, a property must be held for income or investment or be property held for productive use in trade or business. Choice (A) is incorrect, as boot would not be received in the trade for property of equal value with a smaller mortgage. Choice (C) is incorrect as the loss is not attributable at time of exchange. Choice (D) is incorrect as rental property can be exchanged for an office building.

5. (B) Among the choices given in this question, only intangible personal property is exempt from property taxes.

6. (A) NE of the NE of Section 9 $\quad = \quad$ 40 acres x $800/acre = $32,000

   S of the NE of Section 2 $\quad = \quad$ 80 acres x $500/acre = $40,000

   $40,000 $\quad -$ $32,000 $\quad =$ $8,000 boot

7. (C) The primary function of the County Assessor is to establish an assessment roll each year that reflects the full cash value of real property within the county. (Because the State Board of Equalization, among many other duties, limits its assessing to public utilities, which cross county lines, and equalizes those assessments among the counties, it is not the best of the four choices).

8. (A) In an exchange, if a party "pays no boot," the basis in the property acquired is the same as in the property traded away. Both parties keep the basis they started with if no boot is given by either side.

9. (C) "Boot" is something that is not of a like kind received in a tax-deferred exchange. It includes cash or equivalent, such as a note and trust deed, other personal property, and net debt relief (mortgage relief). It is unrelated to depreciation.

10. (D)   July 1

11. (D)   Under state law limited exemptions from local real property taxes for individuals who qualify are: (a) Senior citizens (and blind and disabled persons) who may defer their taxes (b) Veterans exemptions: $4,000 off assessed value (c) Homeowner's exemption: $7,000 off assessed value.

12. (A)   The "marginal tax rate" is different from the "effective tax rate," and is the rate that was applied to "the last dollar earned." Therefore, it could be said, as in this question, that it is the rate that would be applied to "the next dollar an investor would earn."

13. (C)   Choice (A)   Hyde's deferred gain is $85,000 not $75,000 ($155,000 Exchange Incorrect: Value less $70,000 Book Value)

      Choice (B) Incorrect: Hyde's gain is not "recognized" (taxable when received) because this is a tax "deferred" gain

      Choice (D) Incorrect: We know, Hyde has a "realized" gain

      Note: Since the question does not provide Foley's book value, we cannot determine his gain, if any. Since the other choices are patently incorrect, we may assume that Foley's basis was less than $160,000; therefore, a gain resulted. This is important because "boot" is taxable only to the extent of any realized gain.

14. (A)   While services received and the influence of Proposition 13 are factors, the most important element in property taxation is the property assessment. This can be appealed informally to the assessor and formally to the Local Board of Equalization. (Board of Supervisors sits as this appeals body at designated times each year.)

15. (A)   Every two years.

16. (C)   (1)   Newton's   Store

Dental Bldg. Building		Building
$225.000	Market Value	$198,000
−137,000	Mortgage	−125,000
$ 88,000	Equity	$73,000
	Cash	25,000

      (2)   Newton "Gets" $198,000 Property (Like Kind)
              + 12,000 Mortgage Relief   37,000
              + 25,000   Cash   Boot*
              $235,000   Total

      (3)   Less his basis
            in dental bldg.   −185,000
                                    50,000   realized (actual gain)

   *   (4)   Of which   37,000   is recognized (Taxable Now)*

      (5)   Leaving   13,000   Deferred gain

17. (D)   Original cost $300,000   To acquire property

Recaptured $110,000   by sheltering his income from tax. ("Took depreciation" or recapture of his investment)

Remaining book
value $190,000
Sold for   +300,000

Less Cost Basis $190,000
Equals Total $110,000   Long Term
                                      Capital Gain

Note: In this example, by coincidence the long-term capital gain is the same as the amount of the depreciation taken.

18. (D)   Property owners may contact the appropriate county assessor or Appeals Board Office for detailed information concerning property appraisals and classifications for protesting assessments. There are rules for both procedure and time limitations to be followed in regard to assessment appeals, and the applicant for an assessment appeal should be prepared to justify his appeal with supporting data as to sales, cost and income, as indicated.

19. (C)   The fiscal year commences on the first day of July and ends with the thirtieth of June following.

20. (A)   Assessments for bonds sold to finance the improvement of streets are made to each property in accordance with the benefits to be derived by the property owner.

21. (B)   Sales price $40,000(4 lots at the rate of $10,000 each)

Less Cost Basis   – 8,000   (4 acres at the rate of $2,000 per acre)
Long-term cap gain $32,000

22. (D)   Taxes become a lien on real property on March 1st prior to the beginning of the fiscal tax year (July 1 to July 1). Property taxes are liens on property, not personal obligations.

23. (A)   "Boot" is the $5,000 that Smith will receive and is taxable at the time of the exchange.

24. (C)   Smith can pro-rate the gain over the term of the installment contract.

25. (B)   The residence for deferring income tax on capital gain applies only to a person's one principal residence.

26. (A)   The tax-stamp sale starts the running of the 5 years within which a redemption may be made by the delinquent taxpayer. After 5 years, the property is deeded to the state. During the redemption period, a yearly installment plan of redemption may be used which includes payment of taxes and penalties.

27. (C)   Property taxes are assessed to provide revenue for payment of recurring costs of specific local improvements. Assessment bonds are on a parity with property taxes.

28. (C)   A residential property will always be reassessed when the property is sold. A property damaged or destroyed by fire can be restored to original condition without a reassessment.

29. (B) Market value changes can result in either a capital gain or capital loss upon the sale of a property. Mortgaging property (A) does not give rise to tax consequences. Liquidated damages (C) and discounts on short term notes (D) would affect ordinary income.

30. (A) The annual tax obligation depends on the assessed value, which is determined by the County Assessor's Office.

31. (B) Construction of a wooden fence would be a capital improvement and the costs would not be deducted in calculating annual net (taxable) income. Interest, depreciation, and manager's salary (an operating expense) are all allowable deductions for income tax purposes. (Note: Do not confuse the owner's taxable net income with net operating income for appraisal purposes.)

32. (C) "Boot" is defined as the taxable portion of an otherwise tax deferred exchange. It can be (1) cash or the equivalent of cash or (2) mortgage relief - either of which is taxable at the time of the exchange.

33. (C) Real property taxes and assessment liens prevail over private real property interests. (Among themselves, these governmental liens are held to be on a parity.)

34. (B) Under the 1911 Street Improvement Act, the city or county is permitted to order improvements and bill the owners for their share. The owners have 30 days in which to pay the bill, and any unpaid portion goes to bond.

35. (D) The REIT is a form of syndication. It can be organized as a corporation, but that is not essential as it can also be an unincorporated trust or association of investors, organized to take advantage of the federal Real Estate Investment Trust Act in the Internal Revenue Code.

36. (A) The assessment procedure is a means of financing improvements on the real property and actually increases its overall cost of acquisition.

37. (A) Allowable tax deductions on a principal residence include interest on acquisition indebtedness (up to $1 million), interest on home equity indebtedness (up to $100,000), and real property taxes. Maintenance costs and assessments for management of common areas in common interest developments are not tax-deductible expenses.

38. (C) A capital improvement is added to the cost basis of the property and is depreciated according to Internal Revenue Code schedules.

39. (C) Basis for income tax purposes is the cost of $380,000. Financing does not influence the cost basis.

40. (D) The realized gain is the total gain, which would include both the recognized gain and the deferred gain.

41. (B) Proposition 13, passed by the voters in 1978, established the assessed value of property as the "full cash value" either (1) as of the 1975 lien date or (2) the date on which property is purchased, is newly constructed, or changes ownership, increased by not more than 2% per year for an annual inflationary factor.

42. (A) Proposition 13 limits the annual property tax rate to 1% of assessed value plus an additional amount to pay for voter-approved bond indebtedness.

43. (A) All real estate transactions, including the sale of one's own home, must be reported to the IRS. The primary reporting responsibility falls to the person responsible for closing the transaction (e.g., the escrow company or title company, if there is one). If there is no person responsible for the closing, the responsibility falls, in order, to the primary mortgage lender, the seller's broker, or the buyer's broker.

44. (D) Every item mentioned can be an income tax advantage to real estate ownership.

45. (C) An owner who "takes depreciation" on income-producing property recaptures part of the investment out of annual income. That owner's book value (basis) is thus reduced by that same amount. The market value of the property is not affected by tax depreciation.

46. (A) Cost as it applies to real estate, means the amount expended (labor, material, and/or money) in acquiring or producing the commodity.

47. (A) Sales tax would be charged on trade fixtures and furniture, but not on intangible assets such as goodwill, or on the accounts receivable or stock-in-trade for resale.

48. (A) Ad valorem means "according to value." This is a method of taxation using the value of the thing taxed to determine the amount of tax.

49. (C)

(1) Marsh's Commercial   Apartment

Property		Building	
$ 175,000	Valued at	$187,000	
–147,000	Trust deed	–143,000	($4,000 lesser oblig.)
$ 28,000	Equity	44,000	
	Cash	$18,000	

(2) Marsh "Gets"

	$187,000	Property (like kind)
	4,000	Mort. Relief)
	+18,000	Cash) Boot $22,000
	$209,000	

(3) Less her basis in Commercial Property.

	–175,000	
	$34,000	Realized (actual) Gain

(4) Of which $22,000   is Recognized Gain and Taxable now

(5) Leaving $12,000 Deferred Gain

50. (D) Once declared in default, the clock starts for the five-year period. During that time, existing liens are unaffected. Upon sale, however they are extinguished.

51. (A) Prepaid rent is taxable in the year in which it is collected.

52. (D) Since the passage of Proposition 13 in 1978, real property is assessed at 100% of full cash value as of a certain date, increased by an inflationary factor of not more than 2% per year.

53. (D) Real estate taxes, interest on loans and the unreimbursed portion of casualty or theft losses are acceptable deductions on an owner occupied residence while the "cost of painting a bedroom" is not.

Exam 9 Answers – Brokerage

1. (C) Sidewalks in a condominium are nearly always common areas. There is no standard width. A tarmac is a paved airport runway or apron—paved with a combination of tar and gravel (tar + macadam).

2. (D) Choice   (D)   equals 4 square miles

   Choice   (A)   2 sections equals two square miles

   Choice   (B)   .10 (1/10th) x 36 sq. mi. = 3.6 Sq. mi.

   Choice   (C)   5,280' x 10,560' (2 miles) = 2 Sq. mi.

3. (C) Percentage of profit in real estate is based on cost, not selling price. Since he bought at 80% of the listed price, he sold for 1/4 more than he paid for it. (20 is 25% of 80).

   $$\% \quad\quad x \quad\quad PAID = \quad\overline{)MADE}$$

   $$?\% \quad\quad x \quad\quad 80\% \quad\quad = \quad\overline{)20\%}$$

   $$.80\overline{)\,.20} \quad = \quad .25 \quad = \quad \underline{25\%}$$

4. (C) If a buyer enters into a contract based on false or incorrect information given, the buyer has a basis for rescinding the contract.

5. (A) A trust account is set up as a means to separate trust funds from non-trust funds. A trust account protects principles' trust funds in situations in which legal action is taken against the broker or the broker dies or becomes incapacitated.

6. (C) Government Code Section 12955:

   "It shall be unlawful . . . for any person to make, print, or publish, any notice, statement, or advertisement, with respect to the sale or rental of any housing accommodation that indicates any preference, limitation, or discrimination based on race, color, religion, sex, marital status, national origin, or ancestry or any intention to make any such preference, limitation, or discrimination." Title VIII, Section 804 (Federal Fair Housing Act) is almost the identical wording.

7. (C) An agent can lawfully act for two principals in negotiation with each other provided that both principals have knowledge of and consent to the dual agency.

233

8. (B) (1)   Cost: (1.00 + Profit) x   Cost = $\overline{)\text{Selling Price}}$

Profit (50%) 1.50   x   Cost = $\overline{)\text{Selling Price}}$

(2)   Selling Price requires first determining:

(a)   How many lots were sold at $750 each?

32,670 sq. ft. ($\frac{3}{4}$ acre parcel x 43,560 sq. ft./acre)
21,780 sq. ft. ($\frac{2}{3}$ of the $\frac{3}{4}$ acre parcel)
54,450 sq. ft. Total in both parcels

W   x   L   = $\overline{)\text{Area}}$

110'   x   L   = $\overline{)54,450 \text{ sq. ft.}}$

$110'\overline{)54,450 \text{ sq. ft.}}$ = 495 front ft.

495 front feet ÷ 82.5 feet wide lots   = 6 lots total

(b)   Selling price: $750 each x 6 lots = $4,500 total

(3)   Cost of both parcels:

1.50   x   Cost   = $\overline{)\$4,500}$

$1.5\overline{)\$4,500}$ = $3,000 cost of both lots

(4)   Cost of $\frac{3}{4}$ acre = $3,000 – $1,400 cost of 2nd parcel = $\underline{\$1,600}$

9. (A)   The agent went beyond allowable "puffing" (putting things in their best light), in selling the property. While buyers do take risks, the agent made specific promises not substantiated. Buyer did not become aware of the misrepresentation until four years later, and the time for taking actions starts from this point. Civil liability and the possibility of disciplinary action by the Department of Real Estate exist in this situation.

10. (B)   The Subdivision Map Act is primarily a statewide enabling act giving local governments authority to control the physical characteristics of subdivisions within their jurisdictions, and outlining map-filing procedures on a statewide basis.

11. (D) This is the best choice because it is the most nearly complete. Any Consumer Reporting Agency (or user of information) that willfully fails to comply with any requirement of the California Civil Code 1785.31, with respect to any consumer, is civilly liable to that consumer in an amount equal to the sum of any

    (1) actual damages
    (2) punitive damages as the court may allow up to $5,000
    (3) cost of action (to enforce) together with reasonable attorney's fees as determined by the court

12. (B) A percolation test is a hydraulic engineer's test of soil to determine the ability of the ground to absorb and drain water. This information helps to determine the suitability of a site for certain kinds of development, and for the installation of septic tanks or injection wells for sewage treatment plants. A subdivider registering a subdivision with HUD must include a percolation report in the application.

13. (C) If the question had asked about a parcel 24 miles square, the precise answer would be 16. (Closest choice given is 17). Since a township is 6 miles square, the additional 4 miles in either direction would not permit an additional township to fit in (because a township is a shape as well as an area). Therefore, the correct answer remains 16 (Closest choice, <u>17</u>).

14. (B) Township lines run east and west, but township tiers are numbered north and south

    Range lines run north and south, but range columns are numbered east and west

15. (C) Choice (A) 5,280' (1 mile) x 10,560' (2 miles)   =   2 Sq. mi.

    Choice (B) .10 (1/10th) x 36 sq. mi. (Township) =   3.6 Sq. mi.

    Choice (C) Four square miles   =   <u>4 Sq. mi.</u>

    Choice (D) 1 mile x two miles   =   2 Sq. mi.

16. (D) The 50' width of the lot is reduced by the two 4' side yard setbacks giving a buildable width of 42'. The 150' depth is reduced by the 20' front yard setback and the 4' rear setback giving a buildable depth of 126'.

    42' x 126' = <u>5,292 sq. ft.</u>

17. (B) An "estate" in real property is a possessory interest. The tenants in apartment buildings have leasehold estates, regardless of the ownership of the buildings.

18. (D) The stem of this question defines a condominium unit, which could be used for residential, industrial or commercial purposes.

19. (A) A plot plan shows the layout of improvements on a property site (a plot). The plot plan usually includes location, dimensions, parking areas, landscaping and the like.

20. (C) $7,400 interest ($18,500   x   .08 = $1,480 x 5 yrs)

                    800 discount   ($20,000   x   .04)

                    400 penalty ($20,000   x   .02)

            $8,600

21. (D) The Department of Real Estate may take disciplinary action against an agent's license if the agent has been guilty of making any substantial misrepresentation.

22. (B) B&P Code Section 10131 (b) requires a broker's licensee of anyone who, for others and for compensation, "leases or rents" real property or a business opportunity.

23. (B) The Real Estate Law (B&P Code Section 10475) provides that no broker's or salesperson's license suspended under these circumstances can be reinstated until the Recovery Account has been repaid in full, plus interest at the prevailing legal rate.

24. (B) According to the Real Estate Law, the Mortgage Loan Disclosure Statement, Real Property Security Statement, and the Article 5 disclosure to a lender must be kept by the broker for three (3) years, effective 1998.

25. (C) (1.00 + Profit) x   Cost   = $\overline{)\text{Selling Price}}$

        (1.00 + .17)   x   ?   = $\overline{)\$76,000}$

        $1.17 \overline{)\$76,000}$ = 64,957

26. (D) In common interest developments such as a condominium project, the builder or seller is required to give to each prospective purchaser copies of the CC&Rs, the Articles of Incorporation, Bylaws, a current financial statement of the association, and a statement from the association describing any outstanding delinquent assessments.

27. (A) In Civil Code Section 1710.2, the legislature expressed the intent to reserve for itself regulation of disclosures about AIDS or about deaths occurring on the property. There are 3 rules. No cause of action arises against an owner or agent for failure to disclose to a transferee if the occurrence or manner of an occupant's death where the death has occurred more than 3 years earlier or if an occupant of that property was afflicted with, or died from, AIDS. This law does not immunize an owner or agent from liability for making an intentional misrepresentation in response to a direct inquiry.

28. (B) Use the Cost Rule:

        (100% + Profit %)   x   Cost   = $\overline{)\text{Selling Price}}$

                1.17   x   ?   = $\overline{)\$73,700}$

        $1.17 \overline{)\$73,700}$ = $62,992 (rounded)

236

29. (D) A township, which is six miles square, contains 36 square miles.

30. (A) After the first transaction:

% x PAID = $\overline{)\text{MADE}}$

? x $200,000 = $\overline{)\$20,000}$

$200,000 $\overline{)\$20,000}$ = .10 or 10% equity

After the second transaction:

% x PAID = $\overline{)\text{MADE}}$

? x $160,000 = $\overline{)\$20,000}$

$160,000 $\overline{)\$20,000}$ = .125 or 12.5% equity

The owner's equity in the encumbered parcels <u>increased</u> from 10% to 12.5%

31. (C) There is nothing in the Real Estate Law that prohibits an unlicensed individual from purchasing land at one price and later selling it for a higher price.

32. (C) W x L = $\overline{)\text{A}}$

? x 240' = $\overline{)43,560 \text{ sq.ft. (1 acre)}}$

240 $\overline{)43,560}$ = 181.5 total width

4 $\overline{)181.5}$ = <u>45.4</u> ft. per lot

33. (B) A fire insurance policy can be cancelled only after written notice has been given to the insured with a reasonable time for cancellation to take effect.

34. (C) "Theft" can be defined as (1) defrauding by misrepresentation (2) entering and removing part of the realty or (3) taking away part of the security for a mortgage with the intent to defraud the mortgagee. "Signing another person's name without his authorization" is forgery.

35. (A) <u>Acquired</u>   <u>Sold</u>

$72,000 Paid $144,000
-52,000 Mortgage   -52,000
$20,000 Down $92,000

Eliminate 000's: $20 Invested, $92 Received

* $92 divided by $20, $1 Invested,   <u>$ 4.60</u> *

237

36. (A) 1. 2,400 + 320 + 1,900 + 328 + 92 =
            5,040

      (comm) (penalty)   (discount)   (ins)   (escrow)   (s/costs)

      2. 40,000 – $32,000= 8,000

      (s/price)   (loan)   (equity)

      %   x   PAID   = $\overline{)\text{MADE}}$

      _?_   x   8,000   =   5,040

      $8,000\overline{)5,040}$ = .63 = 63%

37. (B) The District Attorney prosecutes violators of the real estate license law. Without a license one cannot receive compensation, a commission or fee for the performance of any of the acts defined as being within the purview of a licensed broker or salesperson. Since the person in the question is not licensed, the real estate commissioner would not have the authority to discipline this individual.

38. (C) The real estate law dictates that the broker must keep a copy for three years starting from the date of closing if such occurs. The date of the contract is used if the escrow does not close.

39. (D) Under RESPA, the lender must deliver to the borrower a Uniform Settlement Statement at or before settlement. If requested by the borrower the Uniform Settlement Statement may be "inspected" during the business day immediately preceding the date of settlement.

40. (C) The "company dollar" is the money earned by a real estate company and retained by the company after commissions have been paid. From the company dollar, operating expenses will have to be paid.

41. (B) Interpleader is a court proceeding by the stakeholder of property who claims no proprietary interest in it, for the purpose of deciding who among claimants is legally entitled to the property.

42. (C) Each of the tenants will be given 180 days written Notice of Intention to Convert prior to termination of tenancy.

43. (C)   First calculate the amount invested:

$1,400 (face value) – $210 (15% discount) = $1,190

Calculate the amount received and the amount of profit:

$122/month x 12 months = $1,464 total

$1,464 (received) – $1,190 (invested) = $274 profit

%	x	PAID	=	$\overline{)\text{MADE}}$
?	x	$1,190	=	$\overline{)\$274}$

$1,190 $\overline{)\$274}$ = .23 = <u>23%</u>

44. (C)   If the vacancies and management fees had been taken into account, the property would return less than 12%. Therefore, the broker made a false statement of fact or a "misrepresentation." (Misrepresentations may either be "fraudulent" or "negligent." Since the facts in the question are silent about any fraudulent intent, the act is presumed to be "negligent misrepresentation.") A "false promise" is a false statement about what the promisor (not the property) is going to do in the future.

45. (C)   An accidental dual agency has been formed by non-disclosure. This is also known as divided agency and is a specific violation of real estate law.

46. (C)   330'   (110 yds x 3' per yard)

    <u>x 660'</u>   (220 yds x 3' per yard)

217,800 sq. ft. ÷ 43,560 sq. ft./acre = <u>5 acres</u>

47. (D)   Fraud exists when these three factors are present: when a person misrepresents a material fact, while knowing it is not true, and the purchaser relies thereon in entering into the contract.

48. (D)   Only the Real Estate Commissioner has the legal authority to suspend or revoke a license.

49. (D)   Cooperative ownership of an apartment unit means that the owner has purchased shares in the corporation which holds title to the entire apartment building. With his stock in the corporation, the owner receives a proprietary lease entitling him to occupancy of a specific unit in the building. If other owners default on mortgage or tax payments, the other shareholders must cure the default or risk having the entire project sold for taxes or foreclosed. By special arrangement, the tax collector may issue a separate tax bill to each owner, but will not do so unless specifically requested.

50. (B)   The broker could be disciplined for not notifying the Commissioner of the violation and the salesperson could be disciplined for receiving commissions from someone other than the employing broker.

51. (C)   If a broker sells a property through a cooperating broker and, while the transaction is in escrow, learns the cooperating broker is selling a similar property to the same buyer at a higher price, the broker must inform his principal since he has a fiduciary duty to the seller even though the transaction is in escrow.

52. (D) Government Code Section 12987 provides that a person who has been discriminated against in the sale or rental of housing accommodations may be entitled to the sale or rental of the home if it is still available, or to the sale or rental of a like housing accommodation if one is available. Punitive damages of up to $1,000 may be awarded, as well as actual damages.

53. (A) The applicant may refuse to answer about race since the information is only requested and is optional on the typical real estate loan application. Both Federal and California law prohibit discrimination on the basis of marital status. Therefore, marital status cannot be considered by the lender to be a material fact. The borrower, then, may refuse to answer the question.

54. (D) The selling price, minus cost of selling, must equal the original cost.

    Use "Selling Price Rule"

%	x	PAID	=	$\overline{)\text{MADE}}$
(100% – Commission %)	x	Selling Price	=	$\overline{)\text{Net Amount}}$
(1.00 – .12)	x	?	=	$\overline{)\$63,360}$
.88	x	?	=	$\overline{)\$63,360}$

    $.88 \overline{)\$63,360} = 72,000$ Required selling price

    $72,000 - $63,360 = \underline{\$8,640}$ Required appreciation. This is an appreciation of 13.6%.

55. (D) Legally employees need to be covered by workman's compensation. As the law is not clear on the relationship between a broker and a salesperson, the broker would be prudent to cover their salespersons also.

56. (D) The housing and construction industry is governed by the Contractor's License Law, Local building Codes and the State Housing Act. Choices (A), (B), and (C) all include the Real Estate Law, which does not regulate the construction industry.

57. (C) (1) Cancelled: November 16, 20xx

        Began: March 1, 20xx
        Used: 8 months   leaving 27 months unused

    (2) $\dfrac{\$316.80 \text{ premium}}{36 \text{ months}} = $8.80/month$

    (3) $8.80/month x 27.5 months = $\underline{\$242.00}$

58. (A) The law specifies not less than one year for a bona fide club. This applies to such clubs as fraternal organizations as well as golf, swimming, yacht, and tennis clubs.

59. (C) The purpose of the Equal Credit Opportunity Act is " . . . to prohibit lenders from discriminating against credit applicants on the basis of race, color, religion, national origin, sex, marital status, and age (providing applicant has legal capacity)." Choice (C), taken out of context, is not a true statement, but viewed in context, is the best choice given.

60. (C) In both cases, there would be a violation of the Fair Housing Laws.

61. (C) <u>Total cost to buyer</u>

Purchasing price	$77,000	)	$79,310.00
Closing costs (3% x $77,000)	+ 2,310	)	

<u>Less proceeds to offset costs</u>

Loan (.80 x $75,000)	$60,000	)	−$61,200.00
Down payment	+ 1,200	)	

<u>To complete transaction</u> <u>$18,110.00</u>

62. (D) Many state, federal and local laws make it illegal for the owner of any housing accommodation to make or to cause to be made any written or oral inquiry concerning the race, color, religion, sex, marital status, national origin, or ancestry of any person seeking to purchase, rent, or lease any housing accommodation.

63. (C) A feasibility study for residential development must identify all economic factors which should be considered in developing detailed plans (specific data) for a proposed project. The specific data should be established after the feasibility study.

64. (D) Changes in the real estate market are currently being brought about by (A) growing land use regulation, (B) the growth of the philosophy of consumerism, and (C) extended legislative and judicial regulation of the real estate industry.

65. (B) The Rumford Act prohibits discrimination due to race, religion, color, sex, marital status, physical handicap, national origin, or ancestry in the sale, rental, lease, or financing of housing.

66. (D) The technique described as a means of obtaining listings is called "inducement to panic selling" or "blockbusting"—a certain violation of law. The word "peddling" is used as a slang expression for "selling"—thus "panic peddling."

67. (D) The cost of the home increased by a certain percentage because of the interest paid for the use of credit.

$90,000 – downpayment of $18,000 (1/5) = $72,000 loan

$606/month for 30 years = $218,160 total payments

$218,160 total – $72,000 principal = $146,160 interest

What % of the cost is the interest

$$? \text{x} \$90,000 = \overline{)\$146,160} $$

$$ \$90,000 \overline{)\$146,160} = 1.62 = \underline{162\%} $$

68. (B) (1)   Cancelled: Nov. 16, 20XX

           Began: March 1, 20XX
           Used: 8 mos.

    (2) $950.40   ÷   36 months   = $26.40 per month

    (3) $26.40   x   8.5 months   = $224.40 used portion

    (4) $950.40   – $224.40   = $726 unused portion

    Note: Insurance companies normally do not refund based on a proration as above. Return of premium to insured is "short-rated" which would amount to something less than the $726.00 unused portion.

69. (C)   <u>First, Determine Original Cost.</u>

     (1.00% + Profit %)   x   Cost   = $\overline{)\text{Selling Price}}$

         1.15   x   ?   = $\overline{)\$9,430}$

     $1.15\overline{)\$9,430}$ = $8,200 Cost

    <u>Determine Interest Loss on the $8,200.</u>

        (R x T)   x   P   = $\overline{)\text{I}}$

           .05   x $8,200   = $410   Interest Loss/Year

    <u>Total Expense:</u>

    Interest Loss: $410   x   4 yrs   = $1,640

    Taxes: $164   x   4 yrs   =   <u>656</u>
                                      $2,296   Total Expense

    <u>Gross Profit:</u>

        $9,430   – $8,200   = $1,230 Gross Profit
      (Selling Price)   (Cost)

    <u>Net Profit or Loss:</u>

        Total Expenses $2,296
        Gross Profit   <u>–1,230</u>
        Net Loss   <u>$1,066</u>

70. (C) $30,000 Net from foreclosure

     <u>– 6,000</u>   Due materialmen and mechanics*
     <u>$24,000</u>   Balance to lender

     *   Since material was delivered prior to recording of the deed, all lien claimants have priority over the trust deed.

71. (D) Acting for more than one party in a transaction without the knowledge and consent of all parties thereto is a violation of California Real Estate Law and the *Civil Code* and could therefore result in all the penalties recited.

72. (B) Restrictions prohibiting the use of property on the basis of race, color, sex, religion, ancestry or national origin are unenforceable because enforcement undertaken by the state would violate the 14th Amendment of the United States Constitution. Even if there is some area where they are not specifically prohibited, they are still "unenforceable."

73. (D) Neither of these promises by the broker would be a violation of law or regulations. Neither the seller nor buyer would be acting as an agent for another in this transaction, so no real estate license would be required of either. The courts have also ruled that disclosed payments by the broker to either the seller or buyer would not be a violation of the Real Estate Settlement Procedures Act (RESPA).

74. (D) Using an exclusive listing without a definite termination date is a violation of the real estate law.

75. (B) Area "A"   3960'   x   1980'   =   7,840,800 sq. ft.

Area "B"   3960'   x   1980' = $\dfrac{7,840,800 \text{ Sq. ft.}}{2}$ =   3,920,400 sq. ft.

Total square footage   11,761,200 sq. ft.

11,761,200 sq. ft. divided by 43,560 sq. ft./acre = 270 acres

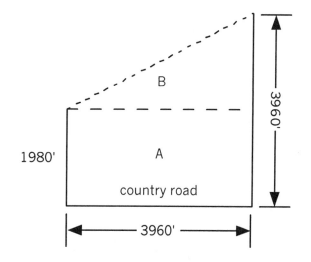

76. (B) Since trade fixtures are personal property, a bill of sale would be the proper instrument to use to convey the title. A chattel real, choice (A), describes a lease. A "deed," choice (C), conveys title to real property.

77. (D) "Blockbusting" and "panic selling" are words coined to describe the illegal conduct of the licensee's activities in this question.

78. (D) All offers must be submitted. By withholding the offer, the broker is withholding a material fact and could be disciplined by the Real Estate Commissioner. The broker has a fiduciary relationship with his client, in this case the seller who gave him the listing.

79. (B) It is improper (illegal) for a real estate licensee to keep from a prospective buyer a client's secret about a flaw in real property. Full disclosure of material facts about the property are required by law. Choice A would likely be considered "puffing." A real estate licensee is required to submit all offers, even oral offers, unless patently frivolous, until close of escrow.

80. (D) The Subdivided Lands Act applies to subdivisions of five or more parcels.

81. (A) 36 miles would be 6 townships wide; then 36 miles would be 6 townships deep. 6 x 6 = 36. The parcel would contain 36 townships.

82. (D) $111,561.30 + $1,210.50 = $112,771.80

$$\frac{(100\% - \text{Comm}\%) \quad \text{x} \quad \text{GSP}}{\text{NET (EEC) (Everything except com.)}} =$$

$$(1.00 - .06) \quad \text{x} \quad ? \quad = \quad) \overline{\$112,771.80}$$

$$.94 \quad \text{x} \quad ? \quad = \quad) \overline{\$112,771.80}$$

$$.94 \,) \overline{\$112,771.80} = \underline{\$119,970}$$

83. (C) $30,000/Lot x 3 Lots = $90,000 Selling price

$$\$36,000/\text{Lot} \quad \text{x} \quad 2 \text{ Lots} \quad = \quad \frac{72,000}{\$18,000} \quad \frac{\text{PAID}}{\text{MADE}}$$

$$\% \quad \text{x} \quad \text{PAID} \quad = \quad) \overline{\text{MADE}}$$

$$? \quad \text{x} \quad \$72,000 \quad = \quad) \overline{\$18,000}$$

$$72,000 \,) \overline{18,000} = .25 = \underline{25\%}$$

84. (C) Purchase Price $125,000 (Equity at purchase

Less Down Payment   −15,000*   * .12 cash down x $125,000)

Loan	$110,000
Selling Price	$139,750
Less Loan	−110,000
Equity	$ 29,750 (At time of sale)

85. (B) %   x   Paid   =   ) MADE $11,220

                              − 7,293

(?) x $11,220 =   ) $3,927 * $ 3,927 Discount "Made"*

$$\$11,220 \,) \overline{\$3,927} = .35 = \underline{35\%}$$

86. (B)   W   x   L   =   A

          30'   x   110   =   3,300

          (1)   395,340 sq. ft.   (2)   392,040 sq. ft.   =   9 acres
                −3,300 sq. ft.   43,560 sq. ft./acre   x $ 5,250
                392,040 sq. ft. $47,250

87. (A)   Period: Rate   x   Anl rent   =   Comm/yr   x   No. of years   =
                  Commission

          Year   1:   7%   x $30,000   = $2,100   x   1   = $2,100
          Next   4:   5%   x $30,000   = $1,500   x   4   = $6,000
          Next 14:   3%   x $30,000   = $900   x   14   = $12,600

          EOY 19   (End of Year 19) $20,700

88. (D)   The Consumer Credit Reporting Agencies Act (Civil Code Section 1785.1-35) requires that, upon request, a consumer credit reporting agency must provide to a consumer disclosures of the files about that consumer. The Code further specifies penalties of actual damages (Choice A), punitive damages up to $5,000 (Choice C), and reasonable attorney's fees (Choice B).

89. (A)   The developer has the responsibility to assure the installation of these facilities. After installation and dedication, they must be "maintained" by the city or county.

90. (B)   A broker's fiduciary obligation to the client requires obedience to all lawful instructions. It would be a violation of law for the seller or the seller's agent to withhold from a prospective buyer material facts about the property. For the broker to accept a listing under such terms would be to participate in a conspiracy to violate the law. To advise the owner to proceed alone or with someone else would be to advise the owner to violate the law.

91. (A)   Real Estate Commissioner's Regulation 1726 requires that every real estate broker have a written agreement with each employed salesperson and broker.

92. (A)   A conversion of an apartment building into five or more condominium units is a subdivision under both the Subdivision Map Act and the Subdivided Lands Act.

93. (B)   In 1968 the US Supreme Court, in the case of *Jones v. Mayer,* established an all-encompassing set of federal rules prohibiting unlawful discrimination in the sale or rental of property.

94. (A)   A section is one mile by one mile (one mile square) and contains one square mile.

95. (B)   %   x   PAID   = $\overline{)\text{MADE}}$

          (100% − Discount%)   x   Face Amt.   = $\overline{)\text{Amt. Received}}$

                  .965   x   ?   = $\overline{)\$69,580}$

          $.965\overline{)\$69,580}$ = 72,103.63 Closest $72,100

96. (D) 1. $7920 ÷ 240 = $33.00
           (total paid)   (mos)   (mo/pymt)

       2. $5,000 x 5% = 250 ÷ 12 = $20.83
          (loan)   (rate)   (int)   (mos)   (mo/int)

       3. $33.00 – $20.83 = $12.17 closest: <u>$12.18</u>
          (pymt)   (int)   (prin)

97. (B) The total number of square miles in a standard township is 36 square miles. Therefore, in of a standard township there are 18 square miles.

98. (B) The seller cannot rescind his contract with the buyer, but may institute civil action for damages sustained for the unfulfilled promise of the broker that induced him to enter the purchase contract.

99. (A) A "blind ad" is advertising by a licensee who does not disclose in the ad that the property is offered through an agent rather than by a principal. Choice (A) is not a strictly true statement, but it is the "best" answer given.

100. (C) The broker cannot use the Statute of Frauds as a defense in this situation. The Statute requires the listing contract be in writing to be enforceable in court but has nothing to do with misrepresentation.

101. (D) Maximum Costs: 5% or $390, whichever is greater $390

Maximum Comm: Junior TDs of 2 years or more $250
Total Costs and Commission $640

102. (B) The Subdivision Map Act applies to subdivisions of two or more parcels or units.

103. (C) A broker is responsible for supervision of employed salespersons. A failure to supervise salespersons that might contribute to the salesperson's violation of laws could lead to disciplinary action against the broker as well as against the salesperson. Only the Real Estate Commissioner can revoke a real estate license, never the court.

104. (D) In a 100% commission real estate office, an experienced salesperson pays the broker a flat desk fee or a desk fee plus a transaction fee and keeps all of the commission.

105. (C) Commissioner's Regulation 2799.1(3a) states: "Complete rules and procedures for any contest or drawing advertised in connection with the marketing of subdivision interests shall be included in the advertisement . . .."

106. (C) A "turnkey project" is defined as a construction project in which the builder delivers a completed facility, including all items necessary for occupancy. The occupant only "turns the key" and takes possession.

107 (C) A straight note is one in which the principal is repaid in one lump sum at maturity. Therefore, the interest is calculated on the entire original principal amount for the entire time of the loan.

.15 x $26,500 = $3,975 interest per year

$3,975 per year x 20 years = $79,500 total interest

108 (C) The broker must retain all documents at least 3 years, including the receipt for a final public report. (A few documents must be retained 4 years, including the disclosure statements from Articles 5, 6, and 7 of the Real Estate Law.)

109. (D) A Mortgage Loan Disclosure Statement must be presented, and the borrower's signature obtained, before the borrower becomes obligated.

Exam 10 Answers - Screening Exam A

1. (C)   Real property consists of (1) land (2) things affixed to the land (3) appurtenances and (4) that which is immovable by law. Two examples of appurtenances are: (1) Easements Appurtenant and (2) Stock in a mutual water company. According to the Civil Code, cultivated crops would be personal property if already sold, mortgaged, or growing on leased land (emblements).

2. (C)   The chief characteristic of a fee simple estate, also known as an estate of inheritance, is that it is of indefinite duration. The other choices are estates with limited duration.

3. (C)   The holder of a life estate may do anything with his interest except will it, unless the length of the estate is measured by the life of a third party.

4. (A)   This question illustrates the rare situation where a lease may be terminated by death. The lessor can lease the property only for the term of his life. Upon the lessor's death, he no longer has an interest in the property and the lessee's interest terminates.

5. (A)   The use of the power of eminent domain is often referred to as "condemnation." Building regulations, zoning laws and subdivision development regulations are all examples of police power.

6. (B)   Time, title, interest, and possession are the unities of a joint tenancy. The right of survivorship exists only under a joint tenancy.

7. (B)   The stockholders of a corporation and the limited partners in a partnership can lose no more than their initial investment. Under a general partnership agreement, however, each partner would be jointly and severally liable for all debts of the firm.

8. (D)   Eminent domain is the sovereign right of government to take property for public use. Compensation must be paid.

9. (D)   In order to create a joint tenancy, there must be equal interest. In community property, the interests are equal but without the right of survivorship. A joint tenancy may or may not involve a husband and wife.

10. (A)   Under a tenancy in common relationship, each tenant has the equal right of possession of the entire property and cannot be restricted to any specific portion of it.

11. (B)   Since a corporation does not die, there can never be a right of survivorship. Because of this, the law does not permit a corporation to hold title in joint tenancy.

12. (D)   A license is defined as a personal, revocable, non-assignable permission to enter upon the property of the owner.

13. (B)   A judgment is a general lien when the abstract of judgment is recorded.

14. (C)   A lien can be defined as a charge imposed upon specific property by which it is made security for the performance of an act, typically the payment of a debt.

15. (B) The dominant tenement may have the right to cross over three or four lots in one tract and not all of the servient tenements would be immediately adjacent (contiguous) to the dominant tenement.

16. (B) The owner of the servient tenement cannot revoke the easement. The owner of the dominant tenement, the parcel receiving the benefit, may terminate by giving a written release of the easement. Destruction of the servient tenement, by its very nature, would terminate the easement on such a parcel. An easement gained through prescription can be lost through nonuse for five years.

17. (C) Special assessments are for non-recurring costs of local improvements. Property taxes are assessed to provide revenue for the payment of recurring costs of local government. Special Assessments take priority along with property taxes, neither taking priority over the other.

18. (C) California sales tax applies to most tangible personal property. The tax is based on the sales price and not the value of the goods (ad valorem).

19. (C) In a tax-deferred exchange in which no boot is paid, the basis of the acquired property is established by transferring the old cost basis to the newly acquired property. Book value on the second property would be $220,000 because no boot was paid.

20. (A) Ad valorem means "according to value." This is a method of taxation using the value of the thing taxed to determine the amount of tax.

21. (D) Homesteads will not protect the owner from property taxes and would have no effect on them.

22. (A) Unadjusted basis (cost basis) is the original cost of the property. The "adjusted basis" is primarily the resultant figure on the taxpayer's books after adding capital improvements and subtracting depreciation.

23. (C) For income tax purposes, property taxes and mortgage interest on a personal residence are deductible from ordinary income. Depreciation, upkeep, and wear and tear are not allowable deductions on a personal residence.

24. (C) Marsh "Gets"

$187,000	Property (like kind)	
+ 4,000	Mortgage Relief (Boot)	
+ 18,000	Cash (Boot)	
$209,000		

Less basis in Commercial Bldg −175,000

Gives her	$ 34,000	Realized (Actual) Gain
Of which	$ 22,000	= Recognized Gain (Taxable Now – Boot)
Leaving	$12,000	Deferred Gain

25. (A)

| % | x | PAID | = |)‾MADE |

.0115   x $120,000   =   ?

.0115   x $120,000   = $1,380 annual tax

12)$1,380   = $<u>115</u> monthly tax bill

26. (B) The taxes have been paid to July 1, 1998, which is three months short of the close of escrow, September 30, 1998. The seller is obligated to pay the buyer for the taxes for the months of July, August, and September.

   (1) C.O.E.: September 30, 1998

   (2) <u>D.I. : July 1, 1998</u>*   *Date of Item: Taxes paid to July 1998

   (3) Short of C.O.E.   3 Mos. Therefore Seller Owes 3 Months

27. (A) NE of NE of section 9 = 40 acres x $800 = $32,000

   S of NE of section 2 = 80 acres x $600 = $48,000

   48,000 – 32,000 = $<u>16,000 boot ans.</u>

28. (C) Since the land cannot be depreciated, the land value must be subtracted from the cost of acquisition to establish the depreciable amount. The amounts of the down payment and the loan do not affect the depreciable amount.

29. (B) To avoid the main artery along which the bus runs and to avoid the lights, noise, and congestion of the shopping center, the prudent buyer will look to the center of the tract. The surrounding homes create a buffer from these other influences. A key lot tends to be less valuable than lots that are otherwise comparable.

30. (C)

GMM   x   GMI   =   )‾APPRAISAL

?   x $775   =   )‾$139,500

<u>180</u>   x $775   =   )‾$139,500

180   x $950   =   <u>$171,000</u> Appraised Value

31. (A) Industrial land is valued in terms of dollars per square foot or per acre.

32. (D) "Application of this principle is found in each of the three approaches to value which are the basic methodology of the appraisal process . . .." AIREA on appraisal.

33. (A) Before making an appraisal, an appraiser must define the problem to see what is to be done and how it is to be accomplished.

34. (D) The comparative-unit method represents a relatively uncomplicated approach to a cost estimate and is widely used.

35. (B) The land residual technique of the income approach is used to determine the value of land.

36. (B) Conduit is used in the electrical trade.

37. (B) The appraiser will endeavor to determine if the additional investment in the improvement will yield a higher net return, that is, will it "contribute" to a greater yield.

38. (C) When interest rates increase, it indicates that investors are asking for a higher rate of return on their investment. This results in higher cap rates. If the cap rate increases and the income stays the same, the value of the property decreases.

39. (B) The gross multiplier method is based upon the rental value and sale price of comparable properties. A comparison is made between these properties and the subject property; land is never appraised separately using this method.

40. (D) For appraisal purposes, mortgage payments and income tax are not allowable expenses. Depreciation adjusts the cost basis but is not an expense. Wages paid for gardeners and maintenance personnel are deductible from gross income as operating expenses.

41. (D) The appraiser is interested in today's cost (less depreciation, of course) and value and is not concerned about the original cost or the cost of living index in 1910.

42. (A) The net income is capitalized into value by the income approach, the approach used on investment property.

43. (C) Effective gross income is that income remaining after deducting an allowance for vacancies and collection losses from gross income.

44. (C) Functional and economic obsolescence factors are a much greater cause of depreciation than age or other factors of deterioration.

45. (A) Improved value is the combined value of land and building as distinguished from their separate values.

46. (C) A feasibility study for residential development must identify all economic factors which should be considered in developing detailed plans (specific data) for a proposed project. The specific data should be established after the feasibility study.

47. (A) The best definition of market value is the highest price a property would likely bring in a sale in the open market. Price is an indication of value.

48. (D) Cash flow refers to the money the investor has at the end of the year after deducting all out-of-pocket expenses from gross income. Do not confuse with net spendable, which is computed by deducting income tax from cash flow.

49. (C) In mathematics, one variable quantity is a function of another when the value of one depends on and varies with the other. The "productivity" of real estate is the income it produces. Income and value will vary directly and proportionately. Thus, each is a function of the other.

50. (A) For a dwelling to have utility, it must have the power to give satisfaction or arouse desire for possession. The functional utility of a property is the sum of its (1) attractiveness (e.g. architecture) and (2) its usefulness or utility. Therefore, the functional utility in a dwelling is dependent upon the desires of its occupants.

51. (C) Backfill is used in construction to replace excavated earth into a hole or against a structure.

52. (D) The statement is completely reversed. The trust deed is the "security" for the promissory note and incidental to the debt. The other three statements are true.

53. (D) If a deed of trust (or mortgage) is executed during the act of and for the purpose of purchasing property for which it is the security, then it is a "purchase money" deed of trust (or mortgage) regardless of whether the beneficiary (lender) is the seller or a third party.

54. (D) The trustor is the one who receives the money or the extension of credit. The trustor signs the note as a promise to repay and gives the lender security by signing the trust deed conveying the legal title to the trustee.

55. (D) The owner of the property (trustor) conveys the bare legal title to the trustee with the provision that in the event of default the trustee can sell the property.

56. (D) The trustee holds the legal title in trust. The one who conveys the title must sign the instrument.

57. (B) Their right of reinstatement permits them to make up the delinquent payments plus any penalties during the 3-month notification of default. Redemption refers to recovery of property after it has been sold.

58. (B) The period in which a mechanic's lien may be filed will vary from 30 to 90 days. Depending on the circumstances, the lender will not release the final payment until the lien period has expired.

59. (A) The 1911 Street Improvement Act authorizes the local government to order improvements and pass the expense on to the landowner. This authority cannot be used for the original purchase of the land for a subdivision.

60. (B) A loan commitment given before a buyer is obtained and subject to approval of buyer by lender is termed a conditional commitment.

61. (C) Of the four listed, the Federal Savings and Loan Association is the only one operating in the primary loan market. Today, more residential loans are made by commercial banks than S&Ls.

62. (A) The difference between the market value and the loan is the owner's equity. If this gap is large the owner has a higher equity interest.

63. (A) These are the characteristics of a commercial bank's lending policy.

64. (B) Since 1965, insurance companies have steadily withdrawn from mortgage lending on individual residences. Mr. Smith would have a better chance of receiving his loan from one of the other three lenders.

65. (B) Mortgage interest is paid to the lender as income to the lender and is not held in an impound account. Choices (A), (C), and (D) are owed to some one other than the lender and might result in a default if not paid. To protect against that risk the lender might ask that deposits for each of these be made into an impound account controlled by the lender to insure that such obligations be paid.

66. (D) A take-out loan is the long-term financing that replaces the interim construction loan. It "takes" the construction lender "out" of the financing picture.

67. (A) An assumption fee is the lender's charge for changing over and processing new records for a new owner who is assuming an existing loan.

68. (C) If the law permits a deficiency judgment, it does not make any difference if the basis for the judgment was a conventional loan or a government insured loan.

69. (D) To curb inflation, the Federal Reserve Board would raise the reserve requirements for its member banks and enter into the bond market in a selling capacity.

70. (C) FHA loans can be readily assumed without increasing the interest rate or additional points. From a practical standpoint, only a Cal-Vet may assume a Cal-Vet loan. Insurance companies have high qualifications for assumption.

71. (A) The Annual Percentage Rate represents the relationship of the total finance charge to the total amount financed. The "total finance charge" includes the total of all costs paid directly or indirectly by the borrower. However, there are certain costs that are exempt including, but not limited to, appraisal fees and credit reporting fees.

72. (A) Individuals constitute the largest percentage of savings and loan depositors.

73. (A) Coverage through RESPA is applicable only if financing is with federally related mortgages. This includes FHA, VA, or other government assisted loans and loans made by institutions with federally insured deposits.

74. (D) No discount points are charged on a Cal-Vet loan.

75. (C) This is one way of defining "amortization."

76. (B) Choices (A), (C) and (D) would have an effect, but a conventional lender would be most concerned with the degree of risk involved in the loan.

77. (D) The mortgage contract is the security for the debt but not a "negotiable instrument" as defined by law. Notes (A), checks (B), and drafts (C), providing they have the required elements, can be negotiable.

78. (C) The law construes that everyone is given constructive notice when a document affecting title to real property is recorded where it can be seen by anyone. Recording gives constructive "notice to the world." Actual notice is expressed information of fact experienced by the person to whom given.

79. (A) The standard policy of title insurance insures against:

(1) Matters of record

(2) Forgery and fraud

(3) Lack of capacity

(4) Improper delivery

Choice (B) requires a special endorsement. Choice (C); is incorrect because no policy will insure against "Items that the insured knew were faulty."

253

80. (D)   Title insurance companies evolved from abstract companies that first issued "abstracts of title." This abstract was basically the opinion of the attorney who searched the records. The next process in time was the issuance of a "certificate of title" which indicated the records of title, except for those noted. Later years found the abstract companies issuing only a "guarantee of title," but this was insufficient since the guarantee was only as good as the company backing it. The Insurance Commissioner eventually regulated the industry and the best protection is now afforded by means of a title insurance policy that insures against both "off-record" and "on-record" risks.

81. (C)   A deed must be acknowledged to be recorded. The fact that it has been recorded indicates that the grantor signed it, acknowledged it and let it out of his hands; therefore, a presumption of delivery is made, albeit a rebuttable presumption.

82. (A)   The Probate Code does not have a prearranged commission schedule. Commissions are set at the discretion of the court. The representative of the estate may, with the court's approval, give a broker an exclusive listing, not to exceed 90 days; an offer must be at least 90% of the court's appraisal. The court may then approve the sale and set the commission.

83. (D)   If a fee owner leases the property, he has created a leasehold estate for the tenant; under this situation, two estates exist in the same property. Title can pass by operation of law.

84. (A)   The landlord is not obliged to repair excessive wear and tear caused by the tenant. He is obliged to keep the home in habitable condition.

85. (D)   Civil Code Section 1935 enables joint tenancies to be created by (1) simple will or transfer, (2) transfer from sole owner to himself or herself and others, (3) transfer from tenants in common or joint tenants to themselves or to themselves and others, (4) transfer from husband and wife (holding title as community property or otherwise) to themselves or to themselves and others, and (5) transfer to executors of an estate or trust.

86. (C)   When preceded by a 3-day notice, the unlawful detainer is the proper procedure designed by law by which the lessor can have the tenant evicted.

87. (C)   The Civil Code so defines this form of ownership as a condominium.

88. (D)   The bearing walls, central heating system, and elevator are parts of the common area.

89. (B)   Many counties in California use a description in the tax bill other than a legal description—that is, an "Assessor's Parcel Number."

90. (D)   Under RESPA, the lender must deliver to the borrower a Uniform Settlement Statement at or before settlement. If requested by the borrower the Uniform Settlement Statement may be "inspected" during the business day immediately preceding the date of settlement.

91. (A)   Under the Real Estate Settlement Procedures Act, the lender is not permitted to charge for the preparation of either the Uniform Settlement Statement or for the Truth in Lending Statement.

92. (D)   In order for a real estate broker to be exempt from escrow licensing by the Corporations Commissioner, he or she must have acted for one of the parties in the escrow transaction.

93. (C)   An executory contract is one that is to be performed, as distinct from an executed contract that has been fully performed.

94. (A) The Statute of Frauds requires that a listing for the sale of real property, or for the negotiation of a lease for more than a year, must be in writing to be enforceable for the payment of a commission.

95. (D) A broker who holds an option to purchase real property is a principal. He is not representing a seller but is dealing on his own behalf, a fact that must be disclosed to a purchaser.

96. (D) An agent cannot act for two principals in negotiations with each other unless both have knowledge of and consent to the dual agency. The agent could be denied commission from either and the undisclosed divided agency is a ground for rescission by either principal. The broker's license could be revoked or suspended by the Department of Real Estate.

97. (A) Death of the offeror, prior to the communication of the acceptance, revokes the offer.

98. (D) Under the law of contracts, for an offer to create a binding contract it must be accepted on time and be unqualified according to the terms. If an offer is not accepted and the acceptance communicated prior to the expiration of the acceptance period, the offer is terminated. Since the offer then no longer exists, it cannot be accepted.

99. (C) The broker cannot use the Statute of Frauds as a defense in this situation. The Statute requires that the listing contract be in writing to be enforceable in court but has nothing to do with misrepresentation.

100. (B) An owner who reserves the right to sell the property himself has signed an Exclusive Agency Listing. This means that if any other person sells the property the listing broker is entitled to a commission.

101. (D) The Statute of Limitations requires any legal action to commence within four years on any written contract.

102. (C) In exchange for the seller's promise to pay a commission, the broker promises to use diligence. This mutual exchange of promises makes it a bilateral contract. A unilateral contract requires a promise from only one party and performance from the other.

103. (A) The four essential elements of a simple contract are consideration, competent parties, a lawful object and mutual assent. The Statute of Frauds requires that only certain contracts must be in writing to be enforceable in court, not all.

104. (B) The broker, through the acts of his salesperson, acted in excess of authority. By accepting a check when not authorized, the salesperson created an agency between the buyer and the broker, but only with regard to the deposit.

105. (D) Since the broker is not a party to the contract, the broker cannot request an action for specific performance.

106. (C) The purchase price that may be paid by a transferee or received by a transferor for an on-sale general license shall not exceed $6,000 unless a period of 5 years has passed since the issuance of the original license, at which time there is no restriction as to the purchase price.

107. (C) Advertising. Advertising of any service for which a license issued under provision of the Real Estate Law is required, shall at least set forth the name of a salesperson, as an agent.

108. (C) A trust deed is used in California to put a lien on (hypothecate) real property. A security agreement is used to hypothecate personal property.

255

109. (B)   One acre   =   43,560 sq. ft.

4,067 sq. yd.   =   36,603 sq. ft. (9 sq. ft./sq. yd.)

and one sq. rod =   272.25 sq. ft. (16.5 ft. x 16.5 ft.)

110. (A)   The deed would be valid. Persons under 18 who are married are emancipated minors and have the legal capacity to deal in real property.

111. (C)   To become a binding purchase contract, an offer must be accepted and the acceptance communicated to the offeror.

112. (A)   The Real Estate Law permits a broker to hold the check when he has been ordered to do so by a principal. Since he was not authorized by the seller to accept a personal check, his acceptance of such a check makes him the agent of the buyer for the amount of the check.

113   (C)   A broker has a duty to disclose material facts; failure to disclose material facts to the parties involved could be considered negative fraud.

114. (B)   The Uniform Vendor and Purchaser Risk Act provides that if possession has not been transferred, the risk of loss is the seller's. However, if possession has been transferred, the risk of loss is on the purchaser.

115. (B)   From a financing standpoint, the Snyders are extending credit to the Binghams. A beneficiary does the same to a trustor.

116. (C)   Choices (A), (B), and (D) must be in writing according to the Statute of Frauds. However, an agreement between two partners to purchase or sell an apartment building need not be in writing.

117. (D)   Choice (D) is correct. (B) and (C) are eliminated by the fact that no deed can be given because vendee does not have legal title. A vendee may assign his rights but not his obligations.

118. (C)   Real Estate Law requires most documents to be kept for a minimum of three years.

119. (C)   Civil Code Section 2985.6 gives a buyer of residential property (up to 4 units) the right to prepay all or any part of a land contract at any time after 12 months following the sale. The inclusion of such a void prepayment prohibition, however, does not affect the validity of the remainder of the contract.

120. (C)   According to the Statute of Limitations, action for performance of a written contract for a commission must be brought within 4 years of earning the commission.

121. (A)   When Broker Katz told the prospective buyer that the owner would sell for less than the listing price, when the broker had not been specifically instructed to disclose that confidential information, the broker violated his fiduciary obligation to his principal.

122. (D)   Choices (A), (B), and (C) all describe exclusive listing agreements which must have a final and definite termination date; not open listings.

123. (C)   The essence of an option is that an offeror grants to an optionee an option to purchase (or to renew a lease, etc.) a certain property under certain terms for a specified time. If the document did not state these terms, the terms would not exist. Statements (A), (B), and (D) are not required.

124. (B) An optionee acquires a contractual right but acquires no legal interest in the property until after the optionee exercises the option.

125. (C) When the mutual consent to a contract is induced by fraud, duress, menace, or undue influence, the contract is voidable at the option of the wronged party. While such a contract is unenforceable against that wronged party, the contract is not totally unenforceable because it is enforceable against the other party. Therefore, Choice (C) is the best answer.

126. (C) A lessor may not discriminate based on marital status, as would be the case in requiring a single tenant to have a co-signor.

127. (C) (1)

$15,000/Lot	x	3 Lots =	$45,000	Selling price
$18,000/Lot	x	2 Lots =	36,000	Paid
			$ 9,000	Made

(2)

%	x	PAID	=	)MADE
?	x	$36,000	=	)$9,000
25%	x	$36,000	=	)$9,000

128. (C) Under the terms of choice (C), the broker as an agent of the seller must comply with the seller's instruction. The instruction not to show the property applies to all prospective buyers, regardless of race.

129. (C) This is the law's basic purpose: to provide all persons in the United States with fair housing opportunities.

130. (A) The Rumford Act prohibits discrimination due to race, religion, color, sex, marital status, physical handicap, national origin, or ancestry in the sale, rental lease, or financing of housing.

131. (D) Generally, conflicts of law are decided with the health, safety, and general welfare of the people as the highest standard.

132. (D) The housing and construction industry is governed by the Contractor's License Law, Local Building Codes and the State Housing Act.

133. (C) Percentage of profit in real estate is based on cost, not selling price. Since he bought at 80% of the listed price, when he sold, he sold for more than he paid for it. (20 is 25% of 80). Use our % x Paid = Made rule.

%	x	PAID	=	)MADE
?%	x	80%	=	)20%
.25	x	80	=	20

257

134. (C)   <u>Period:</u> Rate   x   Anl rent   =   Comm/yr.   x   No. years   =
                   Commission

       Year 1: 7%   x $15,000= $1,050 x   1   = $ 1,050

       Next 4: 5%   x $15,000= $ 750 x   4   = $ 3,000

       <u>Next 14:</u>   3%   x $15,000= $ 450 x   14   =   <u>$ 6,300</u>

       <u>EOY 19</u> (End of Year 19)   <u>$10,350</u>

135. (C) $550.00 P&I   – $43.85 P   = $506.15 I/1st month

            $506.15 I   x   12 mos = $6,073.80 I/1 year

            (R x T)   x   P   = $\overline{)I}$

            ?   x $56,500= $\overline{)\$6,073.80}$

       56,500 $\overline{)6,073.80}$ = .1075 = <u>10.75%</u>

136. (A)   Since the broker has a fiduciary relationship with both Brown and Green, this failure to get consent from *both* parties creates an undisclosed dual agency, or divided agency, and denies the broker's right to collect from either party.

137. (C)   (R x T) x   P   =   I

            .085   x $1,968 = $167.28x   3 yrs.   = $501.84

       12 mos $\overline{)\$167.28}$ = $13.94 x   10 mos.= $139.40

            $13.94 x   2/3 mos.   = $9.29

       Closest: <u>$650</u> $650.53

138. (B)   %   x   PAID   = $\overline{)MADE}$

            (100% – discount %)   x   Face Amount   = $\overline{)Amount\ Received}$

            (1.00 – .035)   x   ?   = $\overline{)\$69,580}$

       .965 $\overline{)\$69,580}$ = $72,103.63   (Closest choice: <u>$72,100</u>)

139. (A) (1) <u>Determine Listing Price</u>

$350/Acre   x   20 Acres* $7,000

*S of the NW of the NE of Sec. 11

<u>20</u>   40   160   640

(2) <u>Determine Buyer's Payment</u>

$6,100 offer + $610 commission (10% x $6,100)$6710

(3) <u>Determine difference</u>

$7,000 (List Price) less $6,710 (Accepted Price) <u>$290</u>

140. (C) Step 1: Establish selling price: $ 9,300Cost plus

+ <u>3,100</u>   (^{n} of $9,300)

$12,400Selling price

Step 2: Determine net selling price: $12,400Selling price

<u>minus 1,860</u>   (15% of $12,400) bad debt

$10,540Net selling price

Step 3: Establish profit: $10,540Net selling price

<u>minus 9,300</u>   Cost of goods sold

<u>$ 1,240</u>Profit

141. (B) A Fictitious Business Name Statement expires at the end of five (5) years from December 31st of the year in which it was filed in the Office of the County Clerk.

142. (C) Under Article 7, the maximum commission and fee is:

$4,000 2nd Trust Deed

<u>x .15</u> (15% of the principal of a loan of 3 years or more)

600   Maximum commission

<u>+ 390</u> Maximum fees (5% or $390 – whichever is greater)

<u>$ 990</u> Maximum commission and fees

143. (D) Signed copies of the agreement must be retained for a reasonable period of time from the date of termination of the agreement.

144. (D) The Real Estate Settlement Procedures Act (RESPA) forbids kickbacks, referral fees or any other unearned fees. Referral fees between real estate brokers and agents are permissible but not between real estate agents and non-licensees.

145. (D) One acre $=$ 43,560 square feet

$$240\overline{)\$43,560 \text{ sq. ft.}} = 181.5'$$

$$4\overline{)181.5'} = \underline{45.4'}$$

146. (A) The agent went beyond allowable "puffing" (putting things in their best light) in selling the property. While buyers do take risks, the agent made specific promises not substantiated. The buyer did not become aware of the misrepresentation until four years later, and the time for taking actions starts from this point. Civil liability and the possibility of disciplinary action by the Department of Real Estate exist in this situation.

147. (A) The Board will issue the Certificate of Clearance if the seller of a business has paid his sales tax in full.

148. (C) In real estate law there is an express prohibition against implying any yield or return on a promissory note different from the interest rate in the note itself unless the advertisement sets forth both the actual rate and the difference between the outstanding balance of the note and the price at which it is being offered for sale, that is, the discount.

149. (C) The $100 collected by the broker is an "advance fee" because it is used in a special brochure published by Otis, distinguished from advertising in some regular publication such as a newspaper. By law, in order to avoid possible misuse or errors, such advance fees must be treated as trust funds and handled as shown in choice (C).

150. (A) (1) To find cost: $(1.00 + \text{Profit} \times \text{Cost}) \quad = \quad \overline{)\text{Selling Price}}$

$1.50 \times \text{Cost} \quad = \quad \overline{)\text{Selling Price}}$

(2) To find selling price requires first determining,

(a) How many lots were sold at $750 each?

32,670 sq. ft. (¾ acre parcel)

<u>21,780</u> sq. ft. (2/3 of the ¾ acre parcel)

54,450 sq. ft. Total in both parcels

W x L = $\overline{)\text{Area}}$

? x 110' = $\overline{)54,450\,\text{sq. ft.}}$

495 front feet ÷ 82.5 feet wide lots = 6 lots total

(b) Selling price: $750 each x 6 lots = $4,500 total

(3) Cost of both parcels

$1.50 \quad \text{x} \quad \text{Cost} \quad = \quad \overline{)\$4,500}$

$1.5\overline{)\$4,500} = $3,000 cost of both

(4) Cost of ¾ acre = $3,000 − $1,400 cost of ½ acre = <u>$1,600</u>

Exam 11 Answers - Screening Exam B

1. (B) Requiring higher deposits from single males would be unlawful discrimination on the basis of sex and marital status. Limiting advertising to referrals from present tenants would not be in violation of any anti-discrimination law. Not all of the tenants were of any one racial group, and there is no indication that their friends would all be of any one race, color, creed, etc.

2. (B) Accretion is the gradual build-up of land as the result of the action of water.

    Avulsion (opposite) is the sudden tearing away of land by the violent action of a watercourse.
    Erosion is gradual wearing away of land by current, wind or tide.
    Dereliction is land left uncovered by the receding of water from its former bed. Process also called reliction.

3. (B) Article 5 of the Real Estate Law stipulates: Unless a lender has given written authorization to the broker, the broker may not disburse the loan funds until after recording the trust deed securing the note evidencing the loan. If the lender has given the broker authority to release funds prior to recordation, the securing trust deed must be recorded, or delivered to the obligee with a written recommendation for immediate recordation, within ten days, following the disbursement of loan funds.

4. (C) A percentage lease is a lease on property, the rental for which is determined by the amount of business done by the lessee. This is usually a percentage of the gross income plus a provision for a minimum rental payment.

5. (D) Neither a land contract, grant deed nor ALTA policy of title insurance requires a listing of the buildings or improvements. A legal description is all that is required.

6. (B) Tenancy is the mode of holding. The estate may be held in joint tenancy, tenancy in common, etc.

7. (D) When personal property (movable) becomes affixed to land it becomes real property, for example, fence posts when installed. Personal property may be conveyed, using a Bill of Sale, or hypothecated, that is, used as security for a loan.

8. (A) When overbuilding results in oversupply, the amount of space may exceed the demand, producing a general increase in vacancies.

9. (D) Real property consists of that which is immovable by law.

10. (C) To transfer fee simple title, encumbered or unencumbered, the grantor must sign the deed. If this is done in violation of a due on sale clause, the beneficiary (lender) may call the loan, but cannot prevent the transfer.

11. (D) Since the life estate is based upon the life of "X" it is not terminated by the death of "B." "B's" interest would descend to his heirs who would retain the life estate until the death of "X."

12. (B) A lease is a less-than-freehold estate that is not real property, merely an interest in real property.

13. (D) When the tenant has breached the contract by not paying rent, the landlord must institute an unlawful detainer action in court. Part of this procedure is to give the tenant a three-day written notice but the action has to go through court.

14. (D) Any party holding possession of real property is a tenant. Under an assignment of the remaining balance of the lease, the assignee receives possession and becomes the tenant, not the sublessee.

15. (C)

(R x T)	x	P	=	)I
(R x T)	x	$56,500	=	)$6,073.80 *
10.75%	x	$56,500	=	)$6,073.80

```
*    $550.00    P & I/Mo.
  -    43.85    P
     $506.15    I/Mo.
  x      12    Mos.
     $6073.8   I/Yr.
```

16. (C)

(R x T)	x	P	=	)I
(?%/Yr.)	x	$8,000	=	)$880 *
11%/Yr	x	$8,000	=	)$880

```
*      $220    I/90 days
  x       4    Quarters
       $880    I/Yr.
```

17. (C) Recording a deed gives constructive notice to the world of the contents of the deed. The recording laws were enacted to protect innocent third parties. In this instance, the grantee did not record the deed; therefore, he or she cannot expect the courts to protect the title against third parties or subsequent recorded interests that have no knowledge of the document. The deed itself is valid between the grantor and the grantee, but invalid as against an innocent purchaser without notice.

18. (A) The grantor is the owner of whatever rights are to be conveyed, whether by grant deed or quitclaim deed.

19. (B) There are five (5) essentials for acquiring title by adverse possession: (1) Open and notorious occupation (residence not required), (2) Continuous possession for 5 consecutive years, (3) Held under claim of right or color of title, (4) Payment of the taxes for 5 consecutive years, and (5) Hostile to true owner, that is, without any degree of permission. A confrontation with the owner is not a requirement.

20. (C) Since the buyer went with the broker to the escrow company and the buyer made out the check there and handed it directly to the escrow, the check did not pass through the broker's hands and is not a trust fund. The broker is not required to make any record of this.

21. (C) Upon the death of one joint tenant, the interest passes to the survivor free and clear of claims by the creditors. Since the brother's creditors did not institute court action to sell the property and satisfy their lien prior to his death, they have no right to the title now held in severalty by the sister.

22. (C) All joint tenants must have equal interests in the property.

23. (B) Since a general partner can be held personally liable for the partnership debts, the partner wants to make every effort to help manage the business. He or she has the advantage of using the other partners' assets in developing the business.

24. (A) Jones created an easement by reservation in the deed at the time title was conveyed to Smith. Since this easement was created by a deed, it is not lost through nonuse. Only an easement acquired by prescription is lost by nonuse.

25. (C) No title insurance is available to protect the owner against adverse zoning restrictions.

26. (B) Recording gives constructive notice "to the world," and anyone dealing with the property has constructive notice even though the public records have not been inspected.

27. (B) A policy of title insurance is a contract to indemnify against loss through defects in the title, or against liens or encumbrances that may affect the title at the time the policy is issued.

28. (C) A conditional/installment sales contract, commonly called a land contract, transfers equitable title to the buyer, but the seller keeps the legal title until the contract has been fulfilled.

29. (A) Public utility companies and similar public and semipublic bodies may exercise the power of eminent domain.

30. (D)

$50,000   Purchase price
30,000   Loan
$20,000   Equity

$$500\overline{)20,000} = 40 \times .55 = \underline{\$22.00}$$

31. (B) Choice (B) lists all specific liens. A judgment lien would be a general lien, as would inheritance taxes.

32. (D) Taxes become a lien on real property on March 1st prior to the beginning of the fiscal tax year (from July 1 to June 30). Property taxes are not a personal liability.

33. (A) The trustor is the borrower, the one who has the right to the possession of the property during any redemption period that may exist in judicial foreclosure.

34. (B) Their right of reinstatement permits them to make up the delinquent payments plus any penalties during the 3-month notification of default. Redemption refers to recovery of property after it has been sold.

35. (D) The law states that a minimum of 3 months must elapse after the recording of the Notice of Default before the publication phase of the foreclosure proceedings can begin.

36. (C)

%	x	PAID	–	)MADE
?	x	$1,200*	=	)$372 **
31%	x	$1,200	=	)$372

*Paid: $1,500 x .80 (1.00 – .20 disc.) = $1,200 PAID

**Made: (1) $131 x 12 Mos. = $1,572 P I/Yr. }

LESS PRINCIPAL = –1,500 } = $ 72 Int.

(2) $1,500 Note

–1,200 Purchase Price = + 300 Disc.

TOTAL MADE $372 MADE

37. (A) Questions that deal with discrimination should be answered with a colorblind attitude and without bias. Any choice that hints at discrimination is probably the wrong choice. Choice (B) is incorrect because although the house the minority prospect wants is in a minority neighborhood, this does not mean he wants the house because of its proximity to other minorities. The only choice that is not discriminatory is choice (A).

38. (D) The Real Estate Law prohibits any solicitation based upon the entry into a neighborhood of a person of another race, color, sex, religion, ancestry, physical status, marital status, or national origin. The slang expression for this practice is "blockbusting."

39. (D) Discrimination is illegal, unlawful, and against public policy.

40. (D) Only the Real Estate Commissioner has the legal authority to suspend or revoke a license.

41. (D) The Unruh Act covers the civil rights of persons in business establishments. By renting only to members of the Caucasian race, the broker is in violation of this act and is liable for actual damages plus $250. The broker also would be subject to suspension or revocation of their real estate license.

42. (B) A subordination clause benefits the trustor (borrower) by making it easier to obtain additional financing using the title of the same property as security. The lender of a prior loan that includes such a clause agrees to relinquish the priority of the first trust deed to specified financing to be obtained by the borrower at a later date. Without a subordination clause, a construction lender, desiring first position, would be unwilling to finance the improvements unless the first loan was paid.

43. (D)

W	x	L	=	)A
1,780'	x	1,780'	=	?
1,780'	x	1,780'	=3,168,400 sq. ft.	

43,560) 3,168,400 = 72.7 = approx. 73 acres

44. (C) A subordination clause places a trust deed in a junior position. If a subordination clause is contained in a trust deed that has been recorded first, the beneficiary has agreed to relinquish his priority to existing or future liens on the property.

45. (D) Choices (A), (B), and (C) are all legitimate reasons for the release schedule to be out of proportion in favor of the beneficiary.

46. (A) The 1911 Street Improvement Act authorizes the local government to order improvements and pass the expense on to the landowner. This authority cannot be used for the original purchase of the raw land.

47. (B) The dominant tenement may have the right to cross over three or four lots in one tract and not all of the servient tenements would be contiguous to the dominant tenement.

48. (B) A deed conveying the fee title to an indefinite parcel of land would be void because of uncertainty of description; but a deed to an unlocated easement is valid because the exact location could be determined later. However, it may not be enforceable.

49. (C) An easement is an encumbrance, but not a lien or a restriction.

50. (C) (1) Cancelled: Nov. 16, 20XX

        Began: Mar. 1, 20XX

        Used: 8 months leaving 27 months unused

    (2) $\frac{\$316.80 \text{ premium}}{36 \text{ Mos.}} = \$8.80/\text{Mo.}$

    (3) $8.80/month x 27.5 months = $242.00

51. (C) In most cases, laws (including zoning ordinances) cannot be enacted which are retroactive. In ridding an area of nonconforming uses of the land, the courts and zoning authorities, in order to satisfy the policy of gradual and eventual elimination of such nonconforming uses, employ the methods of (A) Prohibition of rebuilding, (B) Prohibition of expansion, and (D), Allowing a reasonable time (amortization period) within which the abuses may be eliminated.

52. (D) The R-3 designation generally means residential property of 3 units or more.

53. (C) The final balances on the seller's and buyer's closing statements are seldom the same, but may be the same.

54. (D) The first three choices are all grounds for discipline of a licensee. Under the provisions of Business and Professions Code Section 10131.6, licensees may "sell or offer to sell, buy or offer to buy, solicit prospective purchasers of, obtain listings of, or negotiate the purchase, sale or exchange of any mobilehome if it has been registered." There are no size limitations.

55. (D) The land description in a survey should contain all three items listed in choices (A), (B), and (C).

56. (B) The property is held by the husband and wife. She may file a homestead exemption of $75,000. The property would not be sold because the $19,000 loan and the $75,000 exemption exceed the $33,000 market value of the property.

57. (A) (1) Determine Listing Price

$350/Acre   x   20 Acres* $7,000

> *
>
> S ½ of NW ¼ of the NE ¼ of Section 11
>
>   20   40   160
>   640

      (2) Determine Buyer's Payment

$6,100 offer + $610 Commission $6,710

(10% x $6,100 Offer)

      (3) Determine difference

$7,000 (List Price) Less $6,710 (Accepted Price) <u>$290</u>

58. (B) Condominiums are able to utilize a smaller space for more units and therefore will undoubtedly become more popular due to the increase in land values.

59. (D) The bearing walls, central heating system, and elevator are part of the common area.

60. (A) The assessor issues separate tax bills to each owner of a condominium. The bill includes an assessment for the unit in which the owner has fee title and a prorated assessment to correspond to the owner's interest in the common area.

61. (C)

(Rate x Time)	x	Principal	=	Interest
.085	x	$1,968	=	?
.085	x	$1,968	=	$167.28 (one year)
3 yrs: $167.28/yr	x	3 years	=	$501.84
10 mos: $167.28 / 12 mos	= $13.94/mo x 10 mos		=	+139.40
20 days: $13.94/mo / 30 days	= .46/day x 20 days		=	9.29

Total interest for the period   <u>$650.53</u>

62. (C) The word novation comes from the Latin words meaning to make new.

63. (D) All three notices listed in choices (A), (B), and (C) have important effect on the time of filing and the validity of a mechanic's lien.

64. (C) A bilateral agreement is one in which promises are exchanged. An executory contract is related to performance and something remaining to be done by one or both parties. The agreement between broker and salesperson is an example of a bilateral executory contract.

65. (D) The original purchase and subsequent sale are both valid transactions. There is nothing illegal about either transaction.

267

66. (A) The word executed has two meanings. One meaning refers to a contract that has been signed. The other one, though not mentioned in the choices, refers to a contract that has been fully performed.

67. (C) A grantee of a deed or the beneficiary of a will is required only to be alive to have capacity to hold title. Therefore, the person judicially declared incompetent can receive title to both real and personal property.

68. (D) A broker who holds an option to purchase real property is a principal. He or she is not representing a seller but is dealing on his or her own behalf, a fact that must be disclosed to a purchaser.

69. (C) Under Article 7, the maximum commission and fee is:

$4,000 2nd Trust Deed

x .15 15% of the principal of a loan of 3 years or more)

600 Maximum commission

x 390 Maximum fees (5% or $390 — whichever is greater)

$990 Maximum commission and fees

70. (B) Ratification is the adoption or approval of an act performed on behalf of a person without previous authorization.

71. (A) Mortgage interest payments, prepayment penalties and real estate taxes are all deductible expenses. Choice (B) broker's commission and late charges; choice (C) capital improvements; and choice (D) premium payments on a fire insurance policy, are not deductible. From mortgage payments only the interest is deductible, not the entire payment.

72. (B) If the owner reserves the right to sell the property, an exclusive agency listing has been signed. This means that if any other person sells the property the listing broker is entitled to a commission.

73. (D) Since a principal is responsible for all acts of the agent, Able could be sued by Smith. Since Able informed broker Baker of the defect, however, he or she could recover any loss from the broker.

74. (D) The probate court usually must approve the sale as well as the amount of the commission.

75. (D) Under the law of contracts, an offer creating a binding contract must be accepted on time and be unqualified according to the terms. Any change in the terms creates a counter-offer and voids the original offer.

76. (C) Any form of deposit may be taken by the broker provided it is properly described on the deposit receipt so the seller will be made aware when the offer is presented.

77. (C) At common law, an estate at will is terminable at the will or unilateral decision of either party. By statute, California has modified the abrupt conclusion of such estates and requires advance 30-day notice of termination by each party. If this question had referred to common law, the answer would have been choice (D).

78. (B) If you make an offer on a property and the seller accepts the offer and communicates the acceptance to you before you can revoke it, it is a binding contract. Until the contract is binding, death of either party will cancel the offer.

79. (C) Conversion is to change from one use to another as in the case of misappropriating funds entrusted to a licensee. Commingling is mixing funds of the agent with those of the client, and failure to make full disclosure can be referred to as negative fraud.

80. (D) Any person or employee doing business under any law of this state, or any other state relating to banks, trust companies, savings and loan associations, industrial loan companies, pension trusts, credit unions or insurance companies are not required to have a license.

81. (B) According to the Real Estate Law, the Mortgage Loan Disclosure Statement (and Real Property Security Statement) must be kept by the broker for 3 years.

82. (A) Both canals and streets are man made and would be considered artificial monuments. Trees and rocks, although man can move them, normally are considered natural marking points.

83. (C)

(R x T)	x	P	=	)̄ I
.08	x	?	=	)̄ $720 (12 mos x $60/mo)
.08	x	$9,000	=	)̄ $720

84. (B) Compound interest is interest paid on the original principal and also on the accrued and unpaid interest that has accumulated. Simple interest is interest that is paid on the unpaid principal balance only.

85. (C) These are the characteristics of insurance companies.

86. (A) Conventional interest rates rise in a tight money market. Usually the buyer under VA can pay no more than a 1% origination fee. Discount points are now negotiable.

87. (A) When one party has fulfilled his or her part of the obligation, it is considered a tender.

88. (C) The Department of Veterans Affairs is the state department that handles Cal-Vet loans. Since the state is handling the transaction no discount points are charged.

89. (D) Under a VA loan, the veteran is required to pay cash for any excess of the purchase price over the appraisal (Certificate of Reasonable Value). No down payment is normally required unless the price exceeds the appraisal.

90. (C) Vacancy factors will vary from time to time but can be estimated with accuracy.

91. (C)

Period:	Rate	x	Anl rent	=	Comm/Yr	x	No of yrs	=	Comm
Year 1	7%	x	$15,000	=	$1,050	x	1	=	$ 1,050
Next 4	5%	x	$15,000	=	$ 750	x	4	=	$ 3,000
Next 14	3%	x	$15,000	=	$ 450	x	14	=	$ 6,300
EOY 19	...		(End of Year 19)..						$10,350

92. (D) The seller was not liable on the trust deed note and would not be liable for the default of the trustor. He or she further assured against liability by stating that the sale was "without recourse." (This means that the buyer could not look to the seller of the note for satisfaction of the buyer's default.) The buyer of the note is entitled to foreclose on the face value of the note for $25,000, not the $23,500 he paid for it.

93. (B) FHA appraisals are ordered from FHA by the lender who has agreed to make the loan, not by the buyer. This appraisal is actually a commitment by FHA to insure a loan in a certain amount if made by the ordering lender.

94. (B) One of the features of an FHA loan is the mortgage insurance. This protects the lender against possible loss and reduces the risk to the lender.

95. (D) FHA will not permit secondary financing on the initial purchase of the home. Since the buyer does not have enough cash to use FHA financing, it will be impossible to secure FHA financing and the broker should refuse to accept this offer.

96. (C) Federal Reserve System Regulation Z, also known as Truth-in-Lending, requires that advertising shall state financing charge expressed as an annual percentage rate.

97. (B) When the discount rate increases, interest rates increase, making money more costly and harder to get

98. (C) The most complete and accurate statement for "adjusted basis" is: "acquisition cost plus capital improvements minus depreciation."

99. (B) Inflation, tight money, and demand for funds are all factors that directly influence interest rates. Unemployment has the least effect of the choices presented.

100. (B) An asset that can increase in real value builds the owner's equity and is a hedge against inflation (when money loses value).

101. (B) Inflation will cause the trustor's equity to increase faster than it would from principal payments alone. Since inflation will not affect the interest rate on the note, this is an advantage to the trustor but a definite disadvantage to the beneficiary. The trustee is not affected in any measurable way.

102. (D) Under RESPA, a broker cannot charge a fee for any services performed in connection with the dissemination of information required under this law. This would include the Truth-in-Lending statement and the uniform disclosure/settlement statement.

103. (D) A summation is the final step by the appraiser in any appraisal and is the act of bringing together conclusions in a short concise statement. The terms sales, comparative, and comparable are used in the sales comparison approach.

104. (D) Under RESPA, the lender must furnish a copy of a special information booklet prescribed by HUD together with a good faith estimate of closing costs to every person from whom the lender receives a written application for federally related mortgage loans. The lender shall supply the good faith estimates by delivering or placing them in the mail not later than three business days after the application is received.

105. (B) RESPA requires the lender to furnish the borrower the following two items by delivering them or placing them in the mail not later than 3 business days after the application of the borrower is received: (1) a special information booklet prepared or approved by HUD which explains settlement costs; and (2) a good faith estimate of the loan costs.

106. (B)

%	x	Paid	=	$\overline{)\,\text{Made}}$
.05	x	?	=	$\overline{)\,\$900\ (12\ \text{mos}\ x\ \$75}$
.05	x	$\underline{\$18.000}$	=	$\overline{)\,\$900}$

107. (D) When a buyer files application for a loan, the lender is required by RESPA to provide a good faith estimate of the cost of settlement services. The buyer has a chance to shop around for settlement services to insure that he has obtained good value for the money.

108. (D) Spot zoning, conditional use permit, and variance are all remedies to the described situation. Either allows a change in the local zoning ordinance that permits a particular use not consistent with the area's zoning classification. Either remedy may be granted from the local zoning Board of Appeals for a small area provided:

(1) Undue hardship can be shown, and (2) the use permitted must still be consistent with the general plan of the area.

109. (D) The unique feature of VA loans is that they generally require no down payment; conventional loans nearly always require a significant down payment.

110. (D)

(1.00	–	Comm)	x	GSP	=	$\overline{)\,\text{NET (EEC)}}$
(1.00	–	.04)	x		=	$\overline{)\,\$37,600}$ *
		.96	x	$\underline{\$39.167}$	=	$\overline{)\,\$37,600}$

```
    *  $37,000
    +     600
       $37,600   (EEC)
```

111. (D) Acting for more than one party in a transaction without the knowledge and consent of all parties thereto is a violation of California Real Estate Law and could therefore result in all the penalties recited.

112. (C) The lien and attachment laws are created by the legislative bodies of the state. A state enabling act gives legislative powers to local governing authorities, such as city councils and county board of supervisors, to enact local ordinances.

113. (C) The Fiscal Year commences on the first day of July and ends with the thirtieth of June following.

114. (D) Cost basis is the same as tax basis or book value. The addition of a capital improvement would increase cost basis.

115. (B) A tax-free exchange is accomplished by transferring the old cost basis to the newly acquired property. Since the taxpayer paid no boot, his book value on the second property would remain $220,000.

116. (C) Choices (A), (B), and (D) are all accepted methods of providing for depreciation. Obsolescence is not a method, but a type of depreciation.

117. (B) Investors usually find the limited partnership to be the best means of forming a syndicate. A corporation is subject to double taxation and the investment trust requires at least 100 members.

271

118. (D) A prudent investor would want some investments in a liquid position, that is, easily converted into cash in the event of need. Cash reserves would also be desirable as operating capital to help avoid the need to liquidate a profitable investment in the event of an emergency. Diversification assists in spreading the risk by not having all your eggs in one basket. Any one investor might be most concerned with any one of these.

119. (B) The law exempts a real estate broker from the license requirement while performing acts in the course of a real estate transaction in which the broker is performing an act for which a real estate license is required. The broker may not hold escrows for other brokers or for individuals acting without a broker.

120. (B) In order for a real estate broker to be exempt from licensing by the Corporations Commissioner, he or she must have acted for one of the parties in the escrow transaction.

121. (C) The term "recurring costs" describes the expenses that the buyer can expect year after year. These include property taxes, fire insurance and interest.

122. (D) When the escrow closing date has not been set, it then falls to a reasonable time that may be 5 days, 90 days or one year. The type of transaction would dictate the limit when there is no agreement. Escrow instructions normally include a "default" time limit.

123. (C)

%	x	Paid	=	$\overline{)\text{Made}}$
.45	x	.06	=	.027
.027	x		=	$8,100

$.027\overline{)\$8,100}$ = $\underline{\$300,000}$

124. (A) Taxes become a lien on January 1, 1998 preceding the fiscal tax year.

125. (D) Homesteads will not protect the owners from property taxes and would have the least effect on them.

126. (C) Annually, the Tax Collector publishes a notice of sale of real property on which taxes are delinquent. This is not a sale but a declaration of default denoting the beginning of a five-year redemption period. This declaration of default must be made on or before June 30th, usually the last business day of the month.

127. (C) The primary function of the County Assessor is to establish an assessment roll each year that reflects the full cash value of real property within the county. Since the State Board of Equalization limits its assessing to public utilities (which cross county lines) and equalizing those assessments among counties, it is not the best of the four choices.

128. (B) The second installment becomes due February 1st and becomes delinquent April 10th.

129. (D) "Deciduous" is the term used to identify the type of tree that sheds its leaves annually. The other three choices refer to types of soil, or soil condition.

130. (A) Orientation is the placing or positioning of a structure on the lot with regard to exposure to the sun, prevailing winds, privacy, and protection from noise.

131. (A) Soil pipe is a pipe carrying waste out from the house to the main sewer line.

132. (A)   Unearned increment is an increase in value of real estate due to no effort on the part of the owner often due to increase in population. Amenities may or may not be due to the owner's effort.

133. (B)   There are four basic procedures for the valuation of land:

Comparative, abstraction, development and land residual.

Economic is not a method.

134. (B)

R	x	V	=	)I
.12	x	?V	=	)$30,000
.12	x	$300,000	=	)$30,000

135. (C)   There are four essential elements or characteristics of value. They are utility, scarcity, demand and transferability. Cost represents a measure of past expenditures but does not create value.

136. (A)   The buyer and seller agree on a price, and the contract is signed. This would indicate the market value of property on that date. Values taken at any later date would defeat the willing seller-willing buyer concept.

137. (B)   The economic life is the period in which the building earns sufficient income to support itself. The building will still be standing even though its economic life may have expired.

138. (D)   All three techniques are used in the appraisal of income-property.

139. (D)   "Voidable" indicates the contract is binding on both parties until some action is taken by the wronged party to unilaterally rescind the contract.

140. (B)   The property will decrease in value by more than the amount of the taxes based on the reduced annual net income (Assume a $500 tax increase, and a 10% capitalization rate; loss of value would be $5,000).

141. (D)   The cost approach tends to set the upper limit of value.

142. (D)   The appraiser is interested in today's cost (less depreciation, of course) and is not concerned about the original cost or the cost of living index in 1910.

143. (A)   The three methods listed in the question are all ways to arrive at an estimate of value in the cost approach.

144. (B)   The cost to replace a like property usually sets the upper limit of value.

145. (D)   Bearing walls support the weight of a part of a structure in addition to its own weight.

146. (B)   Conduit is used in the electrical trade.

147. (D)   The ridge board is placed at the peak of the roof.

148. (A)   The appraiser should preserve a professional confidential relationship with his or her client and should report the conclusions and valuation concerning the property only to the client. Although Brown owns the property, Brown is not entitled to information paid for by Jones.

273

Lenders do have an obligation by law to provide a copy of the appraisal to a borrower under specific circumstances.

149. (C) Depreciation is the difference between the reproduction cost new of the improvements and their present value measured at the same date. The older the building, the more difficult it is to estimate reproduction cost and depreciation accurately.

150. (C) An increase in density and rapid turnover may occur from undesirable causes. The Principle of Conformity holds that maximum value is realized when a reasonable degree of homogeneity is present, in buildings, uses of property, and income levels of residents.

Pullout Exam Answer Sheet

Exam Name: _____

Date: _____

Score: _____

Number Correct: _____

divided by

Number in Exam: _____

Percentage Correct: _____

	A B C D		A B C D		A B C D		A B C D		A B C D		A B C D
1	○ ○ ○ ○	26	○ ○ ○ ○	51	○ ○ ○ ○	76	○ ○ ○ ○	101	○ ○ ○ ○	126	○ ○ ○ ○
2	○ ○ ○ ○	27	○ ○ ○ ○	52	○ ○ ○ ○	77	○ ○ ○ ○	102	○ ○ ○ ○	127	○ ○ ○ ○
3	○ ○ ○ ○	28	○ ○ ○ ○	53	○ ○ ○ ○	78	○ ○ ○ ○	103	○ ○ ○ ○	128	○ ○ ○ ○
4	○ ○ ○ ○	29	○ ○ ○ ○	54	○ ○ ○ ○	79	○ ○ ○ ○	104	○ ○ ○ ○	129	○ ○ ○ ○
5	○ ○ ○ ○	30	○ ○ ○ ○	55	○ ○ ○ ○	80	○ ○ ○ ○	105	○ ○ ○ ○	130	○ ○ ○ ○
6	○ ○ ○ ○	31	○ ○ ○ ○	56	○ ○ ○ ○	81	○ ○ ○ ○	106	○ ○ ○ ○	131	○ ○ ○ ○
7	○ ○ ○ ○	32	○ ○ ○ ○	57	○ ○ ○ ○	82	○ ○ ○ ○	107	○ ○ ○ ○	132	○ ○ ○ ○
8	○ ○ ○ ○	33	○ ○ ○ ○	58	○ ○ ○ ○	83	○ ○ ○ ○	108	○ ○ ○ ○	133	○ ○ ○ ○
9	○ ○ ○ ○	34	○ ○ ○ ○	59	○ ○ ○ ○	84	○ ○ ○ ○	109	○ ○ ○ ○	134	○ ○ ○ ○
10	○ ○ ○ ○	35	○ ○ ○ ○	60	○ ○ ○ ○	85	○ ○ ○ ○	110	○ ○ ○ ○	135	○ ○ ○ ○
11	○ ○ ○ ○	36	○ ○ ○ ○	61	○ ○ ○ ○	86	○ ○ ○ ○	111	○ ○ ○ ○	136	○ ○ ○ ○
12	○ ○ ○ ○	37	○ ○ ○ ○	62	○ ○ ○ ○	87	○ ○ ○ ○	112	○ ○ ○ ○	137	○ ○ ○ ○
13	○ ○ ○ ○	38	○ ○ ○ ○	63	○ ○ ○ ○	88	○ ○ ○ ○	113	○ ○ ○ ○	138	○ ○ ○ ○
14	○ ○ ○ ○	39	○ ○ ○ ○	64	○ ○ ○ ○	89	○ ○ ○ ○	114	○ ○ ○ ○	139	○ ○ ○ ○
15	○ ○ ○ ○	40	○ ○ ○ ○	65	○ ○ ○ ○	90	○ ○ ○ ○	115	○ ○ ○ ○	140	○ ○ ○ ○
16	○ ○ ○ ○	41	○ ○ ○ ○	66	○ ○ ○ ○	91	○ ○ ○ ○	116	○ ○ ○ ○	141	○ ○ ○ ○
17	○ ○ ○ ○	42	○ ○ ○ ○	67	○ ○ ○ ○	92	○ ○ ○ ○	117	○ ○ ○ ○	142	○ ○ ○ ○
18	○ ○ ○ ○	43	○ ○ ○ ○	68	○ ○ ○ ○	93	○ ○ ○ ○	118	○ ○ ○ ○	143	○ ○ ○ ○
19	○ ○ ○ ○	44	○ ○ ○ ○	69	○ ○ ○ ○	94	○ ○ ○ ○	119	○ ○ ○ ○	144	○ ○ ○ ○
20	○ ○ ○ ○	45	○ ○ ○ ○	70	○ ○ ○ ○	95	○ ○ ○ ○	120	○ ○ ○ ○	145	○ ○ ○ ○
21	○ ○ ○ ○	46	○ ○ ○ ○	71	○ ○ ○ ○	96	○ ○ ○ ○	121	○ ○ ○ ○	146	○ ○ ○ ○
22	○ ○ ○ ○	47	○ ○ ○ ○	72	○ ○ ○ ○	97	○ ○ ○ ○	122	○ ○ ○ ○	147	○ ○ ○ ○
23	○ ○ ○ ○	48	○ ○ ○ ○	73	○ ○ ○ ○	98	○ ○ ○ ○	123	○ ○ ○ ○	148	○ ○ ○ ○
24	○ ○ ○ ○	49	○ ○ ○ ○	74	○ ○ ○ ○	99	○ ○ ○ ○	124	○ ○ ○ ○	149	○ ○ ○ ○
25	○ ○ ○ ○	50	○ ○ ○ ○	75	○ ○ ○ ○	100	○ ○ ○ ○	125	○ ○ ○ ○	150	○ ○ ○ ○

Pullout Exam Answer Sheet

Exam Name: _____

Date: _____

Score: _____

Number Correct: _____
divided by
Number in Exam: _____

Percentage Correct: _____

	A B C D		A B C D		A B C D		A B C D		A B C D		A B C D
1	○○○○	26	○○○○	51	○○○○	76	○○○○	101	○○○○	126	○○○○
2	○○○○	27	○○○○	52	○○○○	77	○○○○	102	○○○○	127	○○○○
3	○○○○	28	○○○○	53	○○○○	78	○○○○	103	○○○○	128	○○○○
4	○○○○	29	○○○○	54	○○○○	79	○○○○	104	○○○○	129	○○○○
5	○○○○	30	○○○○	55	○○○○	80	○○○○	105	○○○○	130	○○○○
6	○○○○	31	○○○○	56	○○○○	81	○○○○	106	○○○○	131	○○○○
7	○○○○	32	○○○○	57	○○○○	82	○○○○	107	○○○○	132	○○○○
8	○○○○	33	○○○○	58	○○○○	83	○○○○	108	○○○○	133	○○○○
9	○○○○	34	○○○○	59	○○○○	84	○○○○	109	○○○○	134	○○○○
10	○○○○	35	○○○○	60	○○○○	85	○○○○	110	○○○○	135	○○○○
11	○○○○	36	○○○○	61	○○○○	86	○○○○	111	○○○○	136	○○○○
12	○○○○	37	○○○○	62	○○○○	87	○○○○	112	○○○○	137	○○○○
13	○○○○	38	○○○○	63	○○○○	88	○○○○	113	○○○○	138	○○○○
14	○○○○	39	○○○○	64	○○○○	89	○○○○	114	○○○○	139	○○○○
15	○○○○	40	○○○○	65	○○○○	90	○○○○	115	○○○○	140	○○○○
16	○○○○	41	○○○○	66	○○○○	91	○○○○	116	○○○○	141	○○○○
17	○○○○	42	○○○○	67	○○○○	92	○○○○	117	○○○○	142	○○○○
18	○○○○	43	○○○○	68	○○○○	93	○○○○	118	○○○○	143	○○○○
19	○○○○	44	○○○○	69	○○○○	94	○○○○	119	○○○○	144	○○○○
20	○○○○	45	○○○○	70	○○○○	95	○○○○	120	○○○○	145	○○○○
21	○○○○	46	○○○○	71	○○○○	96	○○○○	121	○○○○	146	○○○○
22	○○○○	47	○○○○	72	○○○○	97	○○○○	122	○○○○	147	○○○○
23	○○○○	48	○○○○	73	○○○○	98	○○○○	123	○○○○	148	○○○○
24	○○○○	49	○○○○	74	○○○○	99	○○○○	124	○○○○	149	○○○○
25	○○○○	50	○○○○	75	○○○○	100	○○○○	125	○○○○	150	○○○○

Pullout Exam Answer Sheet

Exam Name: _____

Date: _____

Score: _____

Number Correct: _____

divided by

Number in Exam: _____

Percentage Correct: _____

	A B C D		A B C D		A B C D		A B C D		A B C D		A B C D
1	○ ○ ○ ○	26	○ ○ ○ ○	51	○ ○ ○ ○	76	○ ○ ○ ○	101	○ ○ ○ ○	126	○ ○ ○ ○
2	○ ○ ○ ○	27	○ ○ ○ ○	52	○ ○ ○ ○	77	○ ○ ○ ○	102	○ ○ ○ ○	127	○ ○ ○ ○
3	○ ○ ○ ○	28	○ ○ ○ ○	53	○ ○ ○ ○	78	○ ○ ○ ○	103	○ ○ ○ ○	128	○ ○ ○ ○
4	○ ○ ○ ○	29	○ ○ ○ ○	54	○ ○ ○ ○	79	○ ○ ○ ○	104	○ ○ ○ ○	129	○ ○ ○ ○
5	○ ○ ○ ○	30	○ ○ ○ ○	55	○ ○ ○ ○	80	○ ○ ○ ○	105	○ ○ ○ ○	130	○ ○ ○ ○
6	○ ○ ○ ○	31	○ ○ ○ ○	56	○ ○ ○ ○	81	○ ○ ○ ○	106	○ ○ ○ ○	131	○ ○ ○ ○
7	○ ○ ○ ○	32	○ ○ ○ ○	57	○ ○ ○ ○	82	○ ○ ○ ○	107	○ ○ ○ ○	132	○ ○ ○ ○
8	○ ○ ○ ○	33	○ ○ ○ ○	58	○ ○ ○ ○	83	○ ○ ○ ○	108	○ ○ ○ ○	133	○ ○ ○ ○
9	○ ○ ○ ○	34	○ ○ ○ ○	59	○ ○ ○ ○	84	○ ○ ○ ○	109	○ ○ ○ ○	134	○ ○ ○ ○
10	○ ○ ○ ○	35	○ ○ ○ ○	60	○ ○ ○ ○	85	○ ○ ○ ○	110	○ ○ ○ ○	135	○ ○ ○ ○
11	○ ○ ○ ○	36	○ ○ ○ ○	61	○ ○ ○ ○	86	○ ○ ○ ○	111	○ ○ ○ ○	136	○ ○ ○ ○
12	○ ○ ○ ○	37	○ ○ ○ ○	62	○ ○ ○ ○	87	○ ○ ○ ○	112	○ ○ ○ ○	137	○ ○ ○ ○
13	○ ○ ○ ○	38	○ ○ ○ ○	63	○ ○ ○ ○	88	○ ○ ○ ○	113	○ ○ ○ ○	138	○ ○ ○ ○
14	○ ○ ○ ○	39	○ ○ ○ ○	64	○ ○ ○ ○	89	○ ○ ○ ○	114	○ ○ ○ ○	139	○ ○ ○ ○
15	○ ○ ○ ○	40	○ ○ ○ ○	65	○ ○ ○ ○	90	○ ○ ○ ○	115	○ ○ ○ ○	140	○ ○ ○ ○
16	○ ○ ○ ○	41	○ ○ ○ ○	66	○ ○ ○ ○	91	○ ○ ○ ○	116	○ ○ ○ ○	141	○ ○ ○ ○
17	○ ○ ○ ○	42	○ ○ ○ ○	67	○ ○ ○ ○	92	○ ○ ○ ○	117	○ ○ ○ ○	142	○ ○ ○ ○
18	○ ○ ○ ○	43	○ ○ ○ ○	68	○ ○ ○ ○	93	○ ○ ○ ○	118	○ ○ ○ ○	143	○ ○ ○ ○
19	○ ○ ○ ○	44	○ ○ ○ ○	69	○ ○ ○ ○	94	○ ○ ○ ○	119	○ ○ ○ ○	144	○ ○ ○ ○
20	○ ○ ○ ○	45	○ ○ ○ ○	70	○ ○ ○ ○	95	○ ○ ○ ○	120	○ ○ ○ ○	145	○ ○ ○ ○
21	○ ○ ○ ○	46	○ ○ ○ ○	71	○ ○ ○ ○	96	○ ○ ○ ○	121	○ ○ ○ ○	146	○ ○ ○ ○
22	○ ○ ○ ○	47	○ ○ ○ ○	72	○ ○ ○ ○	97	○ ○ ○ ○	122	○ ○ ○ ○	147	○ ○ ○ ○
23	○ ○ ○ ○	48	○ ○ ○ ○	73	○ ○ ○ ○	98	○ ○ ○ ○	123	○ ○ ○ ○	148	○ ○ ○ ○
24	○ ○ ○ ○	49	○ ○ ○ ○	74	○ ○ ○ ○	99	○ ○ ○ ○	124	○ ○ ○ ○	149	○ ○ ○ ○
25	○ ○ ○ ○	50	○ ○ ○ ○	75	○ ○ ○ ○	100	○ ○ ○ ○	125	○ ○ ○ ○	150	○ ○ ○ ○

Pullout Exam Answer Sheet

Exam Name: _____   Number Correct: _____
                                        divided by
Date: _____   Number in Exam: _____

Score: _____   Percentage Correct: _____

	A B C D		A B C D		A B C D		A B C D		A B C D		A B C D
1	○ ○ ○ ○	26	○ ○ ○ ○	51	○ ○ ○ ○	76	○ ○ ○ ○	101	○ ○ ○ ○	126	○ ○ ○ ○
2	○ ○ ○ ○	27	○ ○ ○ ○	52	○ ○ ○ ○	77	○ ○ ○ ○	102	○ ○ ○ ○	127	○ ○ ○ ○
3	○ ○ ○ ○	28	○ ○ ○ ○	53	○ ○ ○ ○	78	○ ○ ○ ○	103	○ ○ ○ ○	128	○ ○ ○ ○
4	○ ○ ○ ○	29	○ ○ ○ ○	54	○ ○ ○ ○	79	○ ○ ○ ○	104	○ ○ ○ ○	129	○ ○ ○ ○
5	○ ○ ○ ○	30	○ ○ ○ ○	55	○ ○ ○ ○	80	○ ○ ○ ○	105	○ ○ ○ ○	130	○ ○ ○ ○
6	○ ○ ○ ○	31	○ ○ ○ ○	56	○ ○ ○ ○	81	○ ○ ○ ○	106	○ ○ ○ ○	131	○ ○ ○ ○
7	○ ○ ○ ○	32	○ ○ ○ ○	57	○ ○ ○ ○	82	○ ○ ○ ○	107	○ ○ ○ ○	132	○ ○ ○ ○
8	○ ○ ○ ○	33	○ ○ ○ ○	58	○ ○ ○ ○	83	○ ○ ○ ○	108	○ ○ ○ ○	133	○ ○ ○ ○
9	○ ○ ○ ○	34	○ ○ ○ ○	59	○ ○ ○ ○	84	○ ○ ○ ○	109	○ ○ ○ ○	134	○ ○ ○ ○
10	○ ○ ○ ○	35	○ ○ ○ ○	60	○ ○ ○ ○	85	○ ○ ○ ○	110	○ ○ ○ ○	135	○ ○ ○ ○
11	○ ○ ○ ○	36	○ ○ ○ ○	61	○ ○ ○ ○	86	○ ○ ○ ○	111	○ ○ ○ ○	136	○ ○ ○ ○
12	○ ○ ○ ○	37	○ ○ ○ ○	62	○ ○ ○ ○	87	○ ○ ○ ○	112	○ ○ ○ ○	137	○ ○ ○ ○
13	○ ○ ○ ○	38	○ ○ ○ ○	63	○ ○ ○ ○	88	○ ○ ○ ○	113	○ ○ ○ ○	138	○ ○ ○ ○
14	○ ○ ○ ○	39	○ ○ ○ ○	64	○ ○ ○ ○	89	○ ○ ○ ○	114	○ ○ ○ ○	139	○ ○ ○ ○
15	○ ○ ○ ○	40	○ ○ ○ ○	65	○ ○ ○ ○	90	○ ○ ○ ○	115	○ ○ ○ ○	140	○ ○ ○ ○
16	○ ○ ○ ○	41	○ ○ ○ ○	66	○ ○ ○ ○	91	○ ○ ○ ○	116	○ ○ ○ ○	141	○ ○ ○ ○
17	○ ○ ○ ○	42	○ ○ ○ ○	67	○ ○ ○ ○	92	○ ○ ○ ○	117	○ ○ ○ ○	142	○ ○ ○ ○
18	○ ○ ○ ○	43	○ ○ ○ ○	68	○ ○ ○ ○	93	○ ○ ○ ○	118	○ ○ ○ ○	143	○ ○ ○ ○
19	○ ○ ○ ○	44	○ ○ ○ ○	69	○ ○ ○ ○	94	○ ○ ○ ○	119	○ ○ ○ ○	144	○ ○ ○ ○
20	○ ○ ○ ○	45	○ ○ ○ ○	70	○ ○ ○ ○	95	○ ○ ○ ○	120	○ ○ ○ ○	145	○ ○ ○ ○
21	○ ○ ○ ○	46	○ ○ ○ ○	71	○ ○ ○ ○	96	○ ○ ○ ○	121	○ ○ ○ ○	146	○ ○ ○ ○
22	○ ○ ○ ○	47	○ ○ ○ ○	72	○ ○ ○ ○	97	○ ○ ○ ○	122	○ ○ ○ ○	147	○ ○ ○ ○
23	○ ○ ○ ○	48	○ ○ ○ ○	73	○ ○ ○ ○	98	○ ○ ○ ○	123	○ ○ ○ ○	148	○ ○ ○ ○
24	○ ○ ○ ○	49	○ ○ ○ ○	74	○ ○ ○ ○	99	○ ○ ○ ○	124	○ ○ ○ ○	149	○ ○ ○ ○
25	○ ○ ○ ○	50	○ ○ ○ ○	75	○ ○ ○ ○	100	○ ○ ○ ○	125	○ ○ ○ ○	150	○ ○ ○ ○

Pullout Exam Answer Sheet

Exam Name: _____

Date: _____

Score: _____

Number Correct: _____

divided by

Number in Exam: _____

Percentage Correct: _____

	A B C D		A B C D		A B C D		A B C D		A B C D		A B C D
1	○ ○ ○ ○	26	○ ○ ○ ○	51	○ ○ ○ ○	76	○ ○ ○ ○	101	○ ○ ○ ○	126	○ ○ ○ ○
2	○ ○ ○ ○	27	○ ○ ○ ○	52	○ ○ ○ ○	77	○ ○ ○ ○	102	○ ○ ○ ○	127	○ ○ ○ ○
3	○ ○ ○ ○	28	○ ○ ○ ○	53	○ ○ ○ ○	78	○ ○ ○ ○	103	○ ○ ○ ○	128	○ ○ ○ ○
4	○ ○ ○ ○	29	○ ○ ○ ○	54	○ ○ ○ ○	79	○ ○ ○ ○	104	○ ○ ○ ○	129	○ ○ ○ ○
5	○ ○ ○ ○	30	○ ○ ○ ○	55	○ ○ ○ ○	80	○ ○ ○ ○	105	○ ○ ○ ○	130	○ ○ ○ ○
6	○ ○ ○ ○	31	○ ○ ○ ○	56	○ ○ ○ ○	81	○ ○ ○ ○	106	○ ○ ○ ○	131	○ ○ ○ ○
7	○ ○ ○ ○	32	○ ○ ○ ○	57	○ ○ ○ ○	82	○ ○ ○ ○	107	○ ○ ○ ○	132	○ ○ ○ ○
8	○ ○ ○ ○	33	○ ○ ○ ○	58	○ ○ ○ ○	83	○ ○ ○ ○	108	○ ○ ○ ○	133	○ ○ ○ ○
9	○ ○ ○ ○	34	○ ○ ○ ○	59	○ ○ ○ ○	84	○ ○ ○ ○	109	○ ○ ○ ○	134	○ ○ ○ ○
10	○ ○ ○ ○	35	○ ○ ○ ○	60	○ ○ ○ ○	85	○ ○ ○ ○	110	○ ○ ○ ○	135	○ ○ ○ ○
11	○ ○ ○ ○	36	○ ○ ○ ○	61	○ ○ ○ ○	86	○ ○ ○ ○	111	○ ○ ○ ○	136	○ ○ ○ ○
12	○ ○ ○ ○	37	○ ○ ○ ○	62	○ ○ ○ ○	87	○ ○ ○ ○	112	○ ○ ○ ○	137	○ ○ ○ ○
13	○ ○ ○ ○	38	○ ○ ○ ○	63	○ ○ ○ ○	88	○ ○ ○ ○	113	○ ○ ○ ○	138	○ ○ ○ ○
14	○ ○ ○ ○	39	○ ○ ○ ○	64	○ ○ ○ ○	89	○ ○ ○ ○	114	○ ○ ○ ○	139	○ ○ ○ ○
15	○ ○ ○ ○	40	○ ○ ○ ○	65	○ ○ ○ ○	90	○ ○ ○ ○	115	○ ○ ○ ○	140	○ ○ ○ ○
16	○ ○ ○ ○	41	○ ○ ○ ○	66	○ ○ ○ ○	91	○ ○ ○ ○	116	○ ○ ○ ○	141	○ ○ ○ ○
17	○ ○ ○ ○	42	○ ○ ○ ○	67	○ ○ ○ ○	92	○ ○ ○ ○	117	○ ○ ○ ○	142	○ ○ ○ ○
18	○ ○ ○ ○	43	○ ○ ○ ○	68	○ ○ ○ ○	93	○ ○ ○ ○	118	○ ○ ○ ○	143	○ ○ ○ ○
19	○ ○ ○ ○	44	○ ○ ○ ○	69	○ ○ ○ ○	94	○ ○ ○ ○	119	○ ○ ○ ○	144	○ ○ ○ ○
20	○ ○ ○ ○	45	○ ○ ○ ○	70	○ ○ ○ ○	95	○ ○ ○ ○	120	○ ○ ○ ○	145	○ ○ ○ ○
21	○ ○ ○ ○	46	○ ○ ○ ○	71	○ ○ ○ ○	96	○ ○ ○ ○	121	○ ○ ○ ○	146	○ ○ ○ ○
22	○ ○ ○ ○	47	○ ○ ○ ○	72	○ ○ ○ ○	97	○ ○ ○ ○	122	○ ○ ○ ○	147	○ ○ ○ ○
23	○ ○ ○ ○	48	○ ○ ○ ○	73	○ ○ ○ ○	98	○ ○ ○ ○	123	○ ○ ○ ○	148	○ ○ ○ ○
24	○ ○ ○ ○	49	○ ○ ○ ○	74	○ ○ ○ ○	99	○ ○ ○ ○	124	○ ○ ○ ○	149	○ ○ ○ ○
25	○ ○ ○ ○	50	○ ○ ○ ○	75	○ ○ ○ ○	100	○ ○ ○ ○	125	○ ○ ○ ○	150	○ ○ ○ ○

Pullout Exam Answer Sheet

Exam Name: _____

Date: _____

Score: _____

Number Correct: _____

divided by

Number in Exam: _____

Percentage Correct: _____

	A B C D		A B C D		A B C D		A B C D		A B C D		A B C D
1	○ ○ ○ ○	26	○ ○ ○ ○	51	○ ○ ○ ○	76	○ ○ ○ ○	101	○ ○ ○ ○	126	○ ○ ○ ○
2	○ ○ ○ ○	27	○ ○ ○ ○	52	○ ○ ○ ○	77	○ ○ ○ ○	102	○ ○ ○ ○	127	○ ○ ○ ○
3	○ ○ ○ ○	28	○ ○ ○ ○	53	○ ○ ○ ○	78	○ ○ ○ ○	103	○ ○ ○ ○	128	○ ○ ○ ○
4	○ ○ ○ ○	29	○ ○ ○ ○	54	○ ○ ○ ○	79	○ ○ ○ ○	104	○ ○ ○ ○	129	○ ○ ○ ○
5	○ ○ ○ ○	30	○ ○ ○ ○	55	○ ○ ○ ○	80	○ ○ ○ ○	105	○ ○ ○ ○	130	○ ○ ○ ○
6	○ ○ ○ ○	31	○ ○ ○ ○	56	○ ○ ○ ○	81	○ ○ ○ ○	106	○ ○ ○ ○	131	○ ○ ○ ○
7	○ ○ ○ ○	32	○ ○ ○ ○	57	○ ○ ○ ○	82	○ ○ ○ ○	107	○ ○ ○ ○	132	○ ○ ○ ○
8	○ ○ ○ ○	33	○ ○ ○ ○	58	○ ○ ○ ○	83	○ ○ ○ ○	108	○ ○ ○ ○	133	○ ○ ○ ○
9	○ ○ ○ ○	34	○ ○ ○ ○	59	○ ○ ○ ○	84	○ ○ ○ ○	109	○ ○ ○ ○	134	○ ○ ○ ○
10	○ ○ ○ ○	35	○ ○ ○ ○	60	○ ○ ○ ○	85	○ ○ ○ ○	110	○ ○ ○ ○	135	○ ○ ○ ○
11	○ ○ ○ ○	36	○ ○ ○ ○	61	○ ○ ○ ○	86	○ ○ ○ ○	111	○ ○ ○ ○	136	○ ○ ○ ○
12	○ ○ ○ ○	37	○ ○ ○ ○	62	○ ○ ○ ○	87	○ ○ ○ ○	112	○ ○ ○ ○	137	○ ○ ○ ○
13	○ ○ ○ ○	38	○ ○ ○ ○	63	○ ○ ○ ○	88	○ ○ ○ ○	113	○ ○ ○ ○	138	○ ○ ○ ○
14	○ ○ ○ ○	39	○ ○ ○ ○	64	○ ○ ○ ○	89	○ ○ ○ ○	114	○ ○ ○ ○	139	○ ○ ○ ○
15	○ ○ ○ ○	40	○ ○ ○ ○	65	○ ○ ○ ○	90	○ ○ ○ ○	115	○ ○ ○ ○	140	○ ○ ○ ○
16	○ ○ ○ ○	41	○ ○ ○ ○	66	○ ○ ○ ○	91	○ ○ ○ ○	116	○ ○ ○ ○	141	○ ○ ○ ○
17	○ ○ ○ ○	42	○ ○ ○ ○	67	○ ○ ○ ○	92	○ ○ ○ ○	117	○ ○ ○ ○	142	○ ○ ○ ○
18	○ ○ ○ ○	43	○ ○ ○ ○	68	○ ○ ○ ○	93	○ ○ ○ ○	118	○ ○ ○ ○	143	○ ○ ○ ○
19	○ ○ ○ ○	44	○ ○ ○ ○	69	○ ○ ○ ○	94	○ ○ ○ ○	119	○ ○ ○ ○	144	○ ○ ○ ○
20	○ ○ ○ ○	45	○ ○ ○ ○	70	○ ○ ○ ○	95	○ ○ ○ ○	120	○ ○ ○ ○	145	○ ○ ○ ○
21	○ ○ ○ ○	46	○ ○ ○ ○	71	○ ○ ○ ○	96	○ ○ ○ ○	121	○ ○ ○ ○	146	○ ○ ○ ○
22	○ ○ ○ ○	47	○ ○ ○ ○	72	○ ○ ○ ○	97	○ ○ ○ ○	122	○ ○ ○ ○	147	○ ○ ○ ○
23	○ ○ ○ ○	48	○ ○ ○ ○	73	○ ○ ○ ○	98	○ ○ ○ ○	123	○ ○ ○ ○	148	○ ○ ○ ○
24	○ ○ ○ ○	49	○ ○ ○ ○	74	○ ○ ○ ○	99	○ ○ ○ ○	124	○ ○ ○ ○	149	○ ○ ○ ○
25	○ ○ ○ ○	50	○ ○ ○ ○	75	○ ○ ○ ○	100	○ ○ ○ ○	125	○ ○ ○ ○	150	○ ○ ○ ○

Pullout Exam Answer Sheet

Exam Name: _____

Date: _____

Score: _____

Number Correct: _____

divided by

Number in Exam: _____

Percentage Correct: _____

	A B C D		A B C D		A B C D		A B C D		A B C D		A B C D
1	○ ○ ○ ○	26	○ ○ ○ ○	51	○ ○ ○ ○	76	○ ○ ○ ○	101	○ ○ ○ ○	126	○ ○ ○ ○
2	○ ○ ○ ○	27	○ ○ ○ ○	52	○ ○ ○ ○	77	○ ○ ○ ○	102	○ ○ ○ ○	127	○ ○ ○ ○
3	○ ○ ○ ○	28	○ ○ ○ ○	53	○ ○ ○ ○	78	○ ○ ○ ○	103	○ ○ ○ ○	128	○ ○ ○ ○
4	○ ○ ○ ○	29	○ ○ ○ ○	54	○ ○ ○ ○	79	○ ○ ○ ○	104	○ ○ ○ ○	129	○ ○ ○ ○
5	○ ○ ○ ○	30	○ ○ ○ ○	55	○ ○ ○ ○	80	○ ○ ○ ○	105	○ ○ ○ ○	130	○ ○ ○ ○
6	○ ○ ○ ○	31	○ ○ ○ ○	56	○ ○ ○ ○	81	○ ○ ○ ○	106	○ ○ ○ ○	131	○ ○ ○ ○
7	○ ○ ○ ○	32	○ ○ ○ ○	57	○ ○ ○ ○	82	○ ○ ○ ○	107	○ ○ ○ ○	132	○ ○ ○ ○
8	○ ○ ○ ○	33	○ ○ ○ ○	58	○ ○ ○ ○	83	○ ○ ○ ○	108	○ ○ ○ ○	133	○ ○ ○ ○
9	○ ○ ○ ○	34	○ ○ ○ ○	59	○ ○ ○ ○	84	○ ○ ○ ○	109	○ ○ ○ ○	134	○ ○ ○ ○
10	○ ○ ○ ○	35	○ ○ ○ ○	60	○ ○ ○ ○	85	○ ○ ○ ○	110	○ ○ ○ ○	135	○ ○ ○ ○
11	○ ○ ○ ○	36	○ ○ ○ ○	61	○ ○ ○ ○	86	○ ○ ○ ○	111	○ ○ ○ ○	136	○ ○ ○ ○
12	○ ○ ○ ○	37	○ ○ ○ ○	62	○ ○ ○ ○	87	○ ○ ○ ○	112	○ ○ ○ ○	137	○ ○ ○ ○
13	○ ○ ○ ○	38	○ ○ ○ ○	63	○ ○ ○ ○	88	○ ○ ○ ○	113	○ ○ ○ ○	138	○ ○ ○ ○
14	○ ○ ○ ○	39	○ ○ ○ ○	64	○ ○ ○ ○	89	○ ○ ○ ○	114	○ ○ ○ ○	139	○ ○ ○ ○
15	○ ○ ○ ○	40	○ ○ ○ ○	65	○ ○ ○ ○	90	○ ○ ○ ○	115	○ ○ ○ ○	140	○ ○ ○ ○
16	○ ○ ○ ○	41	○ ○ ○ ○	66	○ ○ ○ ○	91	○ ○ ○ ○	116	○ ○ ○ ○	141	○ ○ ○ ○
17	○ ○ ○ ○	42	○ ○ ○ ○	67	○ ○ ○ ○	92	○ ○ ○ ○	117	○ ○ ○ ○	142	○ ○ ○ ○
18	○ ○ ○ ○	43	○ ○ ○ ○	68	○ ○ ○ ○	93	○ ○ ○ ○	118	○ ○ ○ ○	143	○ ○ ○ ○
19	○ ○ ○ ○	44	○ ○ ○ ○	69	○ ○ ○ ○	94	○ ○ ○ ○	119	○ ○ ○ ○	144	○ ○ ○ ○
20	○ ○ ○ ○	45	○ ○ ○ ○	70	○ ○ ○ ○	95	○ ○ ○ ○	120	○ ○ ○ ○	145	○ ○ ○ ○
21	○ ○ ○ ○	46	○ ○ ○ ○	71	○ ○ ○ ○	96	○ ○ ○ ○	121	○ ○ ○ ○	146	○ ○ ○ ○
22	○ ○ ○ ○	47	○ ○ ○ ○	72	○ ○ ○ ○	97	○ ○ ○ ○	122	○ ○ ○ ○	147	○ ○ ○ ○
23	○ ○ ○ ○	48	○ ○ ○ ○	73	○ ○ ○ ○	98	○ ○ ○ ○	123	○ ○ ○ ○	148	○ ○ ○ ○
24	○ ○ ○ ○	49	○ ○ ○ ○	74	○ ○ ○ ○	99	○ ○ ○ ○	124	○ ○ ○ ○	149	○ ○ ○ ○
25	○ ○ ○ ○	50	○ ○ ○ ○	75	○ ○ ○ ○	100	○ ○ ○ ○	125	○ ○ ○ ○	150	○ ○ ○ ○

Pullout Exam Answer Sheet

Exam Name: _____

Date: _____

Score: _____

Number Correct: _____
divided by
Number in Exam: _____

Percentage Correct: _____

	A B C D		A B C D		A B C D		A B C D		A B C D		A B C D
1	○ ○ ○ ○	26	○ ○ ○ ○	51	○ ○ ○ ○	76	○ ○ ○ ○	101	○ ○ ○ ○	126	○ ○ ○ ○
2	○ ○ ○ ○	27	○ ○ ○ ○	52	○ ○ ○ ○	77	○ ○ ○ ○	102	○ ○ ○ ○	127	○ ○ ○ ○
3	○ ○ ○ ○	28	○ ○ ○ ○	53	○ ○ ○ ○	78	○ ○ ○ ○	103	○ ○ ○ ○	128	○ ○ ○ ○
4	○ ○ ○ ○	29	○ ○ ○ ○	54	○ ○ ○ ○	79	○ ○ ○ ○	104	○ ○ ○ ○	129	○ ○ ○ ○
5	○ ○ ○ ○	30	○ ○ ○ ○	55	○ ○ ○ ○	80	○ ○ ○ ○	105	○ ○ ○ ○	130	○ ○ ○ ○
6	○ ○ ○ ○	31	○ ○ ○ ○	56	○ ○ ○ ○	81	○ ○ ○ ○	106	○ ○ ○ ○	131	○ ○ ○ ○
7	○ ○ ○ ○	32	○ ○ ○ ○	57	○ ○ ○ ○	82	○ ○ ○ ○	107	○ ○ ○ ○	132	○ ○ ○ ○
8	○ ○ ○ ○	33	○ ○ ○ ○	58	○ ○ ○ ○	83	○ ○ ○ ○	108	○ ○ ○ ○	133	○ ○ ○ ○
9	○ ○ ○ ○	34	○ ○ ○ ○	59	○ ○ ○ ○	84	○ ○ ○ ○	109	○ ○ ○ ○	134	○ ○ ○ ○
10	○ ○ ○ ○	35	○ ○ ○ ○	60	○ ○ ○ ○	85	○ ○ ○ ○	110	○ ○ ○ ○	135	○ ○ ○ ○
11	○ ○ ○ ○	36	○ ○ ○ ○	61	○ ○ ○ ○	86	○ ○ ○ ○	111	○ ○ ○ ○	136	○ ○ ○ ○
12	○ ○ ○ ○	37	○ ○ ○ ○	62	○ ○ ○ ○	87	○ ○ ○ ○	112	○ ○ ○ ○	137	○ ○ ○ ○
13	○ ○ ○ ○	38	○ ○ ○ ○	63	○ ○ ○ ○	88	○ ○ ○ ○	113	○ ○ ○ ○	138	○ ○ ○ ○
14	○ ○ ○ ○	39	○ ○ ○ ○	64	○ ○ ○ ○	89	○ ○ ○ ○	114	○ ○ ○ ○	139	○ ○ ○ ○
15	○ ○ ○ ○	40	○ ○ ○ ○	65	○ ○ ○ ○	90	○ ○ ○ ○	115	○ ○ ○ ○	140	○ ○ ○ ○
16	○ ○ ○ ○	41	○ ○ ○ ○	66	○ ○ ○ ○	91	○ ○ ○ ○	116	○ ○ ○ ○	141	○ ○ ○ ○
17	○ ○ ○ ○	42	○ ○ ○ ○	67	○ ○ ○ ○	92	○ ○ ○ ○	117	○ ○ ○ ○	142	○ ○ ○ ○
18	○ ○ ○ ○	43	○ ○ ○ ○	68	○ ○ ○ ○	93	○ ○ ○ ○	118	○ ○ ○ ○	143	○ ○ ○ ○
19	○ ○ ○ ○	44	○ ○ ○ ○	69	○ ○ ○ ○	94	○ ○ ○ ○	119	○ ○ ○ ○	144	○ ○ ○ ○
20	○ ○ ○ ○	45	○ ○ ○ ○	70	○ ○ ○ ○	95	○ ○ ○ ○	120	○ ○ ○ ○	145	○ ○ ○ ○
21	○ ○ ○ ○	46	○ ○ ○ ○	71	○ ○ ○ ○	96	○ ○ ○ ○	121	○ ○ ○ ○	146	○ ○ ○ ○
22	○ ○ ○ ○	47	○ ○ ○ ○	72	○ ○ ○ ○	97	○ ○ ○ ○	122	○ ○ ○ ○	147	○ ○ ○ ○
23	○ ○ ○ ○	48	○ ○ ○ ○	73	○ ○ ○ ○	98	○ ○ ○ ○	123	○ ○ ○ ○	148	○ ○ ○ ○
24	○ ○ ○ ○	49	○ ○ ○ ○	74	○ ○ ○ ○	99	○ ○ ○ ○	124	○ ○ ○ ○	149	○ ○ ○ ○
25	○ ○ ○ ○	50	○ ○ ○ ○	75	○ ○ ○ ○	100	○ ○ ○ ○	125	○ ○ ○ ○	150	○ ○ ○ ○

Pullout Exam Answer Sheet

Exam Name: _____

Date: _____

Score: _____

Number Correct: _____

divided by

Number in Exam: _____

Percentage Correct: _____

	A B C D		A B C D		A B C D		A B C D		A B C D		A B C D
1	○ ○ ○ ○	26	○ ○ ○ ○	51	○ ○ ○ ○	76	○ ○ ○ ○	101	○ ○ ○ ○	126	○ ○ ○ ○
2	○ ○ ○ ○	27	○ ○ ○ ○	52	○ ○ ○ ○	77	○ ○ ○ ○	102	○ ○ ○ ○	127	○ ○ ○ ○
3	○ ○ ○ ○	28	○ ○ ○ ○	53	○ ○ ○ ○	78	○ ○ ○ ○	103	○ ○ ○ ○	128	○ ○ ○ ○
4	○ ○ ○ ○	29	○ ○ ○ ○	54	○ ○ ○ ○	79	○ ○ ○ ○	104	○ ○ ○ ○	129	○ ○ ○ ○
5	○ ○ ○ ○	30	○ ○ ○ ○	55	○ ○ ○ ○	80	○ ○ ○ ○	105	○ ○ ○ ○	130	○ ○ ○ ○
6	○ ○ ○ ○	31	○ ○ ○ ○	56	○ ○ ○ ○	81	○ ○ ○ ○	106	○ ○ ○ ○	131	○ ○ ○ ○
7	○ ○ ○ ○	32	○ ○ ○ ○	57	○ ○ ○ ○	82	○ ○ ○ ○	107	○ ○ ○ ○	132	○ ○ ○ ○
8	○ ○ ○ ○	33	○ ○ ○ ○	58	○ ○ ○ ○	83	○ ○ ○ ○	108	○ ○ ○ ○	133	○ ○ ○ ○
9	○ ○ ○ ○	34	○ ○ ○ ○	59	○ ○ ○ ○	84	○ ○ ○ ○	109	○ ○ ○ ○	134	○ ○ ○ ○
10	○ ○ ○ ○	35	○ ○ ○ ○	60	○ ○ ○ ○	85	○ ○ ○ ○	110	○ ○ ○ ○	135	○ ○ ○ ○
11	○ ○ ○ ○	36	○ ○ ○ ○	61	○ ○ ○ ○	86	○ ○ ○ ○	111	○ ○ ○ ○	136	○ ○ ○ ○
12	○ ○ ○ ○	37	○ ○ ○ ○	62	○ ○ ○ ○	87	○ ○ ○ ○	112	○ ○ ○ ○	137	○ ○ ○ ○
13	○ ○ ○ ○	38	○ ○ ○ ○	63	○ ○ ○ ○	88	○ ○ ○ ○	113	○ ○ ○ ○	138	○ ○ ○ ○
14	○ ○ ○ ○	39	○ ○ ○ ○	64	○ ○ ○ ○	89	○ ○ ○ ○	114	○ ○ ○ ○	139	○ ○ ○ ○
15	○ ○ ○ ○	40	○ ○ ○ ○	65	○ ○ ○ ○	90	○ ○ ○ ○	115	○ ○ ○ ○	140	○ ○ ○ ○
16	○ ○ ○ ○	41	○ ○ ○ ○	66	○ ○ ○ ○	91	○ ○ ○ ○	116	○ ○ ○ ○	141	○ ○ ○ ○
17	○ ○ ○ ○	42	○ ○ ○ ○	67	○ ○ ○ ○	92	○ ○ ○ ○	117	○ ○ ○ ○	142	○ ○ ○ ○
18	○ ○ ○ ○	43	○ ○ ○ ○	68	○ ○ ○ ○	93	○ ○ ○ ○	118	○ ○ ○ ○	143	○ ○ ○ ○
19	○ ○ ○ ○	44	○ ○ ○ ○	69	○ ○ ○ ○	94	○ ○ ○ ○	119	○ ○ ○ ○	144	○ ○ ○ ○
20	○ ○ ○ ○	45	○ ○ ○ ○	70	○ ○ ○ ○	95	○ ○ ○ ○	120	○ ○ ○ ○	145	○ ○ ○ ○
21	○ ○ ○ ○	46	○ ○ ○ ○	71	○ ○ ○ ○	96	○ ○ ○ ○	121	○ ○ ○ ○	146	○ ○ ○ ○
22	○ ○ ○ ○	47	○ ○ ○ ○	72	○ ○ ○ ○	97	○ ○ ○ ○	122	○ ○ ○ ○	147	○ ○ ○ ○
23	○ ○ ○ ○	48	○ ○ ○ ○	73	○ ○ ○ ○	98	○ ○ ○ ○	123	○ ○ ○ ○	148	○ ○ ○ ○
24	○ ○ ○ ○	49	○ ○ ○ ○	74	○ ○ ○ ○	99	○ ○ ○ ○	124	○ ○ ○ ○	149	○ ○ ○ ○
25	○ ○ ○ ○	50	○ ○ ○ ○	75	○ ○ ○ ○	100	○ ○ ○ ○	125	○ ○ ○ ○	150	○ ○ ○ ○

Pullout Exam Answer Sheet

Exam Name: _____

Date: _____

Score: _____

Number Correct: _____

divided by

Number in Exam: _____

Percentage Correct: _____

	A B C D		A B C D		A B C D		A B C D		A B C D		A B C D
1	○ ○ ○ ○	26	○ ○ ○ ○	51	○ ○ ○ ○	76	○ ○ ○ ○	101	○ ○ ○ ○	126	○ ○ ○ ○
2	○ ○ ○ ○	27	○ ○ ○ ○	52	○ ○ ○ ○	77	○ ○ ○ ○	102	○ ○ ○ ○	127	○ ○ ○ ○
3	○ ○ ○ ○	28	○ ○ ○ ○	53	○ ○ ○ ○	78	○ ○ ○ ○	103	○ ○ ○ ○	128	○ ○ ○ ○
4	○ ○ ○ ○	29	○ ○ ○ ○	54	○ ○ ○ ○	79	○ ○ ○ ○	104	○ ○ ○ ○	129	○ ○ ○ ○
5	○ ○ ○ ○	30	○ ○ ○ ○	55	○ ○ ○ ○	80	○ ○ ○ ○	105	○ ○ ○ ○	130	○ ○ ○ ○
6	○ ○ ○ ○	31	○ ○ ○ ○	56	○ ○ ○ ○	81	○ ○ ○ ○	106	○ ○ ○ ○	131	○ ○ ○ ○
7	○ ○ ○ ○	32	○ ○ ○ ○	57	○ ○ ○ ○	82	○ ○ ○ ○	107	○ ○ ○ ○	132	○ ○ ○ ○
8	○ ○ ○ ○	33	○ ○ ○ ○	58	○ ○ ○ ○	83	○ ○ ○ ○	108	○ ○ ○ ○	133	○ ○ ○ ○
9	○ ○ ○ ○	34	○ ○ ○ ○	59	○ ○ ○ ○	84	○ ○ ○ ○	109	○ ○ ○ ○	134	○ ○ ○ ○
10	○ ○ ○ ○	35	○ ○ ○ ○	60	○ ○ ○ ○	85	○ ○ ○ ○	110	○ ○ ○ ○	135	○ ○ ○ ○
11	○ ○ ○ ○	36	○ ○ ○ ○	61	○ ○ ○ ○	86	○ ○ ○ ○	111	○ ○ ○ ○	136	○ ○ ○ ○
12	○ ○ ○ ○	37	○ ○ ○ ○	62	○ ○ ○ ○	87	○ ○ ○ ○	112	○ ○ ○ ○	137	○ ○ ○ ○
13	○ ○ ○ ○	38	○ ○ ○ ○	63	○ ○ ○ ○	88	○ ○ ○ ○	113	○ ○ ○ ○	138	○ ○ ○ ○
14	○ ○ ○ ○	39	○ ○ ○ ○	64	○ ○ ○ ○	89	○ ○ ○ ○	114	○ ○ ○ ○	139	○ ○ ○ ○
15	○ ○ ○ ○	40	○ ○ ○ ○	65	○ ○ ○ ○	90	○ ○ ○ ○	115	○ ○ ○ ○	140	○ ○ ○ ○
16	○ ○ ○ ○	41	○ ○ ○ ○	66	○ ○ ○ ○	91	○ ○ ○ ○	116	○ ○ ○ ○	141	○ ○ ○ ○
17	○ ○ ○ ○	42	○ ○ ○ ○	67	○ ○ ○ ○	92	○ ○ ○ ○	117	○ ○ ○ ○	142	○ ○ ○ ○
18	○ ○ ○ ○	43	○ ○ ○ ○	68	○ ○ ○ ○	93	○ ○ ○ ○	118	○ ○ ○ ○	143	○ ○ ○ ○
19	○ ○ ○ ○	44	○ ○ ○ ○	69	○ ○ ○ ○	94	○ ○ ○ ○	119	○ ○ ○ ○	144	○ ○ ○ ○
20	○ ○ ○ ○	45	○ ○ ○ ○	70	○ ○ ○ ○	95	○ ○ ○ ○	120	○ ○ ○ ○	145	○ ○ ○ ○
21	○ ○ ○ ○	46	○ ○ ○ ○	71	○ ○ ○ ○	96	○ ○ ○ ○	121	○ ○ ○ ○	146	○ ○ ○ ○
22	○ ○ ○ ○	47	○ ○ ○ ○	72	○ ○ ○ ○	97	○ ○ ○ ○	122	○ ○ ○ ○	147	○ ○ ○ ○
23	○ ○ ○ ○	48	○ ○ ○ ○	73	○ ○ ○ ○	98	○ ○ ○ ○	123	○ ○ ○ ○	148	○ ○ ○ ○
24	○ ○ ○ ○	49	○ ○ ○ ○	74	○ ○ ○ ○	99	○ ○ ○ ○	124	○ ○ ○ ○	149	○ ○ ○ ○
25	○ ○ ○ ○	50	○ ○ ○ ○	75	○ ○ ○ ○	100	○ ○ ○ ○	125	○ ○ ○ ○	150	○ ○ ○ ○

Pullout Exam Answer Sheet

Exam Name: _____ Number Correct: _____
divided by
Date: _____ Number in Exam: _____

Score: _____ Percentage Correct: _____

	A B C D		A B C D		A B C D		A B C D		A B C D		A B C D
1	○ ○ ○ ○	26	○ ○ ○ ○	51	○ ○ ○ ○	76	○ ○ ○ ○	101	○ ○ ○ ○	126	○ ○ ○ ○
2	○ ○ ○ ○	27	○ ○ ○ ○	52	○ ○ ○ ○	77	○ ○ ○ ○	102	○ ○ ○ ○	127	○ ○ ○ ○
3	○ ○ ○ ○	28	○ ○ ○ ○	53	○ ○ ○ ○	78	○ ○ ○ ○	103	○ ○ ○ ○	128	○ ○ ○ ○
4	○ ○ ○ ○	29	○ ○ ○ ○	54	○ ○ ○ ○	79	○ ○ ○ ○	104	○ ○ ○ ○	129	○ ○ ○ ○
5	○ ○ ○ ○	30	○ ○ ○ ○	55	○ ○ ○ ○	80	○ ○ ○ ○	105	○ ○ ○ ○	130	○ ○ ○ ○
6	○ ○ ○ ○	31	○ ○ ○ ○	56	○ ○ ○ ○	81	○ ○ ○ ○	106	○ ○ ○ ○	131	○ ○ ○ ○
7	○ ○ ○ ○	32	○ ○ ○ ○	57	○ ○ ○ ○	82	○ ○ ○ ○	107	○ ○ ○ ○	132	○ ○ ○ ○
8	○ ○ ○ ○	33	○ ○ ○ ○	58	○ ○ ○ ○	83	○ ○ ○ ○	108	○ ○ ○ ○	133	○ ○ ○ ○
9	○ ○ ○ ○	34	○ ○ ○ ○	59	○ ○ ○ ○	84	○ ○ ○ ○	109	○ ○ ○ ○	134	○ ○ ○ ○
10	○ ○ ○ ○	35	○ ○ ○ ○	60	○ ○ ○ ○	85	○ ○ ○ ○	110	○ ○ ○ ○	135	○ ○ ○ ○
11	○ ○ ○ ○	36	○ ○ ○ ○	61	○ ○ ○ ○	86	○ ○ ○ ○	111	○ ○ ○ ○	136	○ ○ ○ ○
12	○ ○ ○ ○	37	○ ○ ○ ○	62	○ ○ ○ ○	87	○ ○ ○ ○	112	○ ○ ○ ○	137	○ ○ ○ ○
13	○ ○ ○ ○	38	○ ○ ○ ○	63	○ ○ ○ ○	88	○ ○ ○ ○	113	○ ○ ○ ○	138	○ ○ ○ ○
14	○ ○ ○ ○	39	○ ○ ○ ○	64	○ ○ ○ ○	89	○ ○ ○ ○	114	○ ○ ○ ○	139	○ ○ ○ ○
15	○ ○ ○ ○	40	○ ○ ○ ○	65	○ ○ ○ ○	90	○ ○ ○ ○	115	○ ○ ○ ○	140	○ ○ ○ ○
16	○ ○ ○ ○	41	○ ○ ○ ○	66	○ ○ ○ ○	91	○ ○ ○ ○	116	○ ○ ○ ○	141	○ ○ ○ ○
17	○ ○ ○ ○	42	○ ○ ○ ○	67	○ ○ ○ ○	92	○ ○ ○ ○	117	○ ○ ○ ○	142	○ ○ ○ ○
18	○ ○ ○ ○	43	○ ○ ○ ○	68	○ ○ ○ ○	93	○ ○ ○ ○	118	○ ○ ○ ○	143	○ ○ ○ ○
19	○ ○ ○ ○	44	○ ○ ○ ○	69	○ ○ ○ ○	94	○ ○ ○ ○	119	○ ○ ○ ○	144	○ ○ ○ ○
20	○ ○ ○ ○	45	○ ○ ○ ○	70	○ ○ ○ ○	95	○ ○ ○ ○	120	○ ○ ○ ○	145	○ ○ ○ ○
21	○ ○ ○ ○	46	○ ○ ○ ○	71	○ ○ ○ ○	96	○ ○ ○ ○	121	○ ○ ○ ○	146	○ ○ ○ ○
22	○ ○ ○ ○	47	○ ○ ○ ○	72	○ ○ ○ ○	97	○ ○ ○ ○	122	○ ○ ○ ○	147	○ ○ ○ ○
23	○ ○ ○ ○	48	○ ○ ○ ○	73	○ ○ ○ ○	98	○ ○ ○ ○	123	○ ○ ○ ○	148	○ ○ ○ ○
24	○ ○ ○ ○	49	○ ○ ○ ○	74	○ ○ ○ ○	99	○ ○ ○ ○	124	○ ○ ○ ○	149	○ ○ ○ ○
25	○ ○ ○ ○	50	○ ○ ○ ○	75	○ ○ ○ ○	100	○ ○ ○ ○	125	○ ○ ○ ○	150	○ ○ ○ ○

Pullout Exam Answer Sheet

Exam Name: _____

Date: _____

Score: _____

Number Correct: _____

divided by

Number in Exam: _____

Percentage Correct: _____

	A B C D		A B C D		A B C D		A B C D		A B C D		A B C D
1	O O O O	26	O O O O	51	O O O O	76	O O O O	101	O O O O	126	O O O O
2	O O O O	27	O O O O	52	O O O O	77	O O O O	102	O O O O	127	O O O O
3	O O O O	28	O O O O	53	O O O O	78	O O O O	103	O O O O	128	O O O O
4	O O O O	29	O O O O	54	O O O O	79	O O O O	104	O O O O	129	O O O O
5	O O O O	30	O O O O	55	O O O O	80	O O O O	105	O O O O	130	O O O O
6	O O O O	31	O O O O	56	O O O O	81	O O O O	106	O O O O	131	O O O O
7	O O O O	32	O O O O	57	O O O O	82	O O O O	107	O O O O	132	O O O O
8	O O O O	33	O O O O	58	O O O O	83	O O O O	108	O O O O	133	O O O O
9	O O O O	34	O O O O	59	O O O O	84	O O O O	109	O O O O	134	O O O O
10	O O O O	35	O O O O	60	O O O O	85	O O O O	110	O O O O	135	O O O O
11	O O O O	36	O O O O	61	O O O O	86	O O O O	111	O O O O	136	O O O O
12	O O O O	37	O O O O	62	O O O O	87	O O O O	112	O O O O	137	O O O O
13	O O O O	38	O O O O	63	O O O O	88	O O O O	113	O O O O	138	O O O O
14	O O O O	39	O O O O	64	O O O O	89	O O O O	114	O O O O	139	O O O O
15	O O O O	40	O O O O	65	O O O O	90	O O O O	115	O O O O	140	O O O O
16	O O O O	41	O O O O	66	O O O O	91	O O O O	116	O O O O	141	O O O O
17	O O O O	42	O O O O	67	O O O O	92	O O O O	117	O O O O	142	O O O O
18	O O O O	43	O O O O	68	O O O O	93	O O O O	118	O O O O	143	O O O O
19	O O O O	44	O O O O	69	O O O O	94	O O O O	119	O O O O	144	O O O O
20	O O O O	45	O O O O	70	O O O O	95	O O O O	120	O O O O	145	O O O O
21	O O O O	46	O O O O	71	O O O O	96	O O O O	121	O O O O	146	O O O O
22	O O O O	47	O O O O	72	O O O O	97	O O O O	122	O O O O	147	O O O O
23	O O O O	48	O O O O	73	O O O O	98	O O O O	123	O O O O	148	O O O O
24	O O O O	49	O O O O	74	O O O O	99	O O O O	124	O O O O	149	O O O O
25	O O O O	50	O O O O	75	O O O O	100	O O O O	125	O O O O	150	O O O O